RENDER
UNTO
CAESAR

RENDER
UNTO
CAESAR

THE STRUGGLE OVER CHRIST AND

CULTURE IN THE NEW TESTAMENT

JOHN DOMINIC
CROSSAN

HarperOne

An Imprint of HarperCollinsPublishers

HarperCollins books may be purchased for educational, business, or sales promotional use. For information, please email the Special Markets Department at SPsales@harpercollins.com.

FIRST EDITION

Illustrations courtesy of Classical Numismatic Group, www.cngcoins.com

Designed by SBI Book Arts, LLC

Library of Congress Cataloging-in-Publication Data is available upon request.

ISBN 978-0-06-296493-9

22 23 24 25 26   LSC   10 9 8 7 6 5 4 3 2 1

For

our friends

Linda and David Houseal

CONTENTS

PART THREE

CULTURE CONFRONTED AND CRITICIZED

RENDER
UNTO
CAESAR

TRIUMPH TOO SOON, TRAGEDY TOO FAST

Between the great wars of conquest and the rise of the Caesars [80s–30s BCE] . . . [is] an era full of historical echoes that will sound eerily familiar to the modern reader . . . rising economic inequality, dislocation of traditional ways of life, increasing political polarization, the breakdown of unspoken rules of political conduct, the privatization of the military, rampant corruption, endemic social and ethnic prejudice, battles over access to citizenship and voting rights, ongoing military quagmires, the introduction of violence as a political tool, and a set of elites so obsessed with their own privileges that they refused to reform the system in time to save it.[1]

—Mike Duncan, *The Storm Before the Storm*

WHAT IS OFTEN MISSED WHEN STUDYING THE LIFE AND ministry of Jesus is his movement's location within the larger drama of the Roman Empire at the time—something people during Jesus's time could never forget. From the 80s to the 30s BCE, Rome, having become an empire, lost its republic. Throughout those successive decades, through political venom and armed violence, Rome self-slaughtered its way relentlessly toward dictatorial autocracy. It achieved it under Augustus, who, as inscribed on monuments, was officially designated "Conqueror"—IMP (*imperator* in Latin, *autokrator* in Greek).

Around 40 BCE, the Roman poet Virgil, mistaking lull for peace, proclaimed the return to Rome of earth's Golden Age as "the great line of the centuries begins anew" with a messianic vision of unlabored fertility and feral pacifism (*Eclogue* 4.5). Not so for another contemporary Roman poet-theologian, as Horace (65–8 BCE) flatly contradicted Virgil's vision. Yes, he said, the latest round in the Roman Republic's lurch toward dictatorship was over—with Julius Caesar and Pompey Magnus dead by assassination. But the next round was already well underway between their sons Octavian Caesar and Sextus Pompey. And, after that, what? Another round in a permanent on-again, off-again civil war?

In rebuttal to Virgil's rhapsodic hymn, Horace launched an indictment, as savage as it was accurate, against the murderous polarization of Roman republican power. He asked, "Does some blind frenzy drive us on, or some stronger power, or guilt (*culpa*)?" and wondered whether "a bitter fate pursues the Romans" since their fratricidal origins in Romulus's killing of Remus, "a curse upon posterity" (*Epode* 7.13-20). Against such inaugural damnation, what eventual salvation could there be?

Since nobody can conquer all-powerful Rome, Horace wondered, as "already a second generation is being ground to pieces by civil war," if "this selfsame city we ourselves shall ruin, we, an impious generation, of stock accurst." His bitterly sarcastic solution was to abandon Rome to the wild beasts and sail westward to some never-never utopia (*Epode* 16.9-22). The Golden Age was not here in Rome, but far from Rome!

That was rhetorical hyperbole, to be sure, but the challenge was clear as Rome's senatorial Republic stumbled toward dictatorial autocracy. No external power could overcome the Roman Republic, said Horace, but Rome could still destroy itself internally. Also, he asked, was such internal destruction already symbolized in or even caused by Rome's foundational murder, the fratricide of Remus by Romulus?

The challenge of maintaining a democratic republic is not limited to past centuries. You may recall John Adams's reply to John Taylor on December 17, 1814: "Democracy never lasts long. It soon wastes, exhausts and murders itself. There never was a democracy yet that did not commit suicide." You may also recall that earlier, in a letter of presidential farewell to his "fellow citizens," published on September 19, 1796, George Washington warned that a republic's death is often an *assisted* suicide: "The disorders and miseries . . . seek security and repose in the absolute power of an individual . . . [who] turns this disposition to . . . his own elevation, on the ruins of public liberty."

Horace wondered if the Roman Republic was cursed by the inaugural fratricide of Remus by Rome/ulus. The American Republic too has had an inaugural fratricide, decades after those two warning letters, in an absolutely hot civil war that continued and still continues as a relatively cold civil war. Republics fall—possibly—by fratricidal curses, but they fall—certainly—by fratricidal politics.

Furthermore, within a far fuller matrix, we humans are an evolutionary anomaly, a *social* species with *individual* wills. (Our genetic woe is not original sin but original state.) As such, we survive on a tightrope suspended over the chasmic extremes of anarchic individualism and autocratic communalism. When we are wise, therefore, we always walk slowly, carefully, and with relentless concentration.

———

On Wednesday to Friday, May 3–5, 2006, the Japan Bible Society held an International Bible Forum with the theme, "From the Original Text to Modern Translations: How to Convey the Bible to Modern Society?" My wife, Sarah, and I spent those days in Tokyo as I gave two lectures during that symposium. Afterward, we took the Shinkansen bullet train from Tokyo for two days in Kyoto and then, on Monday, May 8, took another one from there to Hiroshima.

Before leaving home, I had finished *God and Empire: Jesus Against Rome, Then and Now* and took a first draft of its prologue with me to Japan. I deliberately wanted to work on it to and from Hiroshima, to let that tragedy interact with it, and, yes, to name *that* city as the place of *that* prologue.

I mentioned in it that, from the 1990s onward, writers had asserted—as either triumph or tragedy—that America was now "Nova Roma," the "New Roman Empire," "Rome on the Potomac." I noted that such claims started before our Civil War and that, since our fratricidal slaughter paralleled Rome's, America's Roman destiny was confirmed. At the end of that prologue, my final question was: "Is Bible-fed Christian violence supporting or even instigating our imperial violence as the New Roman Empire?"[2]

It is now fifteen years later as I write another prologue to another finished book. But now the Rome/America parallel has turned all too soon from triumph to tragedy. We no longer live in the certainty of imperial success abroad, but in the uncertainty of imperial decline at home. America is still—as the above epigraph/epitaph suggests—like Rome, but less like that *republic* on the ascent to internationally violent glory than on the descent to nationally violent ignominy. Any Rome/America parallel must now focus on that mutual moment when foreign violence rebounds as—increasing—domestic violence, when republicanism slouches toward dictatorship, and when our poisoned chalice returns to our own lips.

In this book, I move to deeper questions than those parallels—whether of ascendant imperialism or descendant republicanism—between ancient Rome and modern America. I turn from any parallel between "the things of Rome" and "the things of America" to Jesus's famous contrast between "the things of Caesar" and "the things of God" (Matt. 22:21; Mark 12:17; Luke 20:25). But what still and ever holds from that to this book is whether escalatory violence is a human inevitability and nonviolent resistance against it is but a human fantasy.

Furthermore, the Greek transcription of Jesus's challenge is *ta tou Theou*, or "the [things] of God," and *ta Kaisaros*, or "the [things] of Caesar." In English, "things" is a perfectly good insertion, but so would be, for example, "affairs" or "matters" or "demands." Compare, for example, the Greek of Mark 8:33, which speaks of "the [things] of God" and "the [things] of humans."

In this book, as you know already from its subtitle, "things" is taken to mean "culture" in its fullest sense as one's religiopolitical and socioeconomic world. Indeed, within the Bible's covenantal theology and Rome's imperial theology, the "cultural things" of God or Caesar could just as accurately be transcribed as the "rule things" of God or Caesar. "The [things] of" is a deliberately open phrase that begs specification and application—so think of it as "culture," but understand it as "rule."

That dichotomy generates these constitutive questions. What is meant by the culture ("things") of God as distinct from the culture ("things") of Caesar? Is the culture of God to be equated with, distinguished from, or opposed to the culture of Caesar? Where is each of those cultures set in relation to violent domination or nonviolent resistance? What about acculturation from the culture of God to the culture of Caesar or the reverse? How did early Christians reconcile practically what Jesus has separated theoretically? How do Christians do so today?

Specifically, what answers on acculturation between the cultures of God and Caesar are present in the New Testament in response to Jesus's challenge? Where precisely do we go to find them most fully? Obviously, the worlds of God and Caesar are incarnated and come face-to-face when Jesus confronts Pilate at the former's arrest and crucifixion.

But, as for book-length rather than chapter-length texts, the first two major sources for consideration are Revelation and Luke-Acts. Then, since those represent polar opposites, is there any third option available in the New Testament?

———

First, I begin this book with an Overture on that famous scene in which Jesus, shown a tribute coin with its Greek "inscription" GOD AUGUSTUS CAESAR, denies that equation and asserts the separation of those two framing titles into "the things of God" and "the things of Caesar." Jesus, you will notice, separates *God* and *Caesar*, not Christ and Caesar, or religion and politics, let alone church and state. Granted that *theoretical* separation, the book's constitutive question is: How are God and Caesar to be reconciled on the *practical* level?

Next, since Jesus's apodictic comment established the problem of God *versus* Caesar—always a contentious one throughout American history—how do we contemporary Christians live in a single world with both God *and* Caesar? The obvious first step is to turn to the New Testament for an answer to that dichotomy, but in doing so we soon discover a reason the issue is so controversial.

In the New Testament itself, the issue is already fully contested by a past religiopolitical polarization as extreme as the present one in which we ourselves are standing. Furthermore, one New Testament response certainly equates "the things of God" and "the things of Caesar" and does so on the level of transcendental violence.

One side of the New Testament's religiopolitical polarization on God and Caesar is in the book of Revelation. There, contemporary culture is *rejected and demonized* (which is explored in Part One of this book). The writer reasons that Rome slaughtered Christians in the immediate past and so, in just vengeance, Christ will return in the imminent future to slaughter Romans. Living Christians are not invited to join that program. But why not? Why not go the route of *The Chronicles of Narnia* or the *Left Behind* series, both of which end with humans deeply involved in the apocalyptic battles, or even thereby justify January 6, with blood outside and prayer inside the United States Capitol?

Another side of the New Testament's religiopolitical polarization on God and Caesar is in the two-volume book of Luke-Acts. Here contemporary culture is *accepted and canonized* (Part Two of this book). The author imagines the future of Christianity not as Jewish, but as Roman, and celebrates the Holy Spirit's transfer of headquarters from Jerusalem to Rome. As the first step toward what would occur under Constantine, this author alone got the future right—for better or for worse.

What if contemporary Christians—especially but not exclusively American Christians—accept demonization of other cultures based on Revelation's false claim that Rome regularly slaughtered Christians and, at the same time, accept canonization of "our" culture based on the claim of Luke-Acts that Rome regularly exculpated Christians? What if alternative biblical facts, fake good news, and religiopolitical lies from *then* inspire such mendacity anew *now*?

Granted those temptations from the New Testament's rather absolute dichotomy between culture demonized and culture canonized, where else can Christians turn to ponder Jesus's response on God and culture? The obvious answer is to see if and how Jesus reconciled his own asserted separation between God and Caesar elsewhere or throughout his own life. But having just seen the New Testament create—in the name of the same Jesus—two such discordant responses to that question of reconciling God and Caesar (Part One and Part Two), it seemed to me unwise to excavate a third option in that same Jesus's name from that same small library.

My solution was to begin with a historical experiment conducted completely outside the New Testament and ask what we could know about God and Caesar in the life of Jesus from the Jewish historian

Josephus—as if there were no New Testament at all. Only once that was independently established, would I add on anything from the Gospels. In other words, what can we learn from the historically grounded Jesus apart from the canonical portraits?

That provides us with a third option, of culture *confronted and criticized*, pioneered by the historical Jesus, a culture with a permanent confrontation between God and Caesar, a constant tension between what the New Testament describes as "the world" of divine creation and "this world" of human civilization (Part Three). That critical confrontation is grounded on and empowered by Jesus's nonviolent resistance for distributive justice against the violence of nondistributive injustice.

One concluding thought. It was said, for what it is worth, that the emperor Nero's dying words were: "What an artist dies [in me]." Be that as it may, he had adherents loyal enough to create, celebrate, and even incarnate the hope that he was not finished, but only gone for a time, and would soon return in victorious and avenging triumph.

That legend of Nero Redivivus ("Nero's Return") was so alive in the late first century and is so important, as we shall see, for the book of Revelation in Part One, that I end this Prologue by suggesting another version of Nero's last words: "I shall be back in some form. I will see you soon."

THE THINGS OF CAESAR AND THE THINGS OF GOD

The things of Caesar *give back* (*apodote*) to Caesar.
—Mark 12:17

Give back (*apodote*) therefore the things of Caesar to Caesar.
—Matt. 22:21

Then *give back* (*apodote*) the things of Caesar to Caesar.
—Luke 20:25

BEFORE MOVING INTO JESUS'S OVERLY FAMILIAR STORY, HERE are some questions that allow us to see the events in a new light. Why was Jesus executed? If Jesus went regularly to Jerusalem for Passover, what led to his execution on that final visit? If Jesus went only once to Jerusalem for Passover, why did he go there that single time and how did it lead to his execution?

Either way, this question presses: In the most plausible historical reconstruction—as in a detective story—*what* happened, *why* did it happen, and *how* did it happen that Jesus of Nazareth died publicly, legally, and officially on a Roman cross before the end of Passover at Jerusalem around the year 30? The follow-up question, then, is: What does this tell us about the nature of Jesus's movement?

To understand Jesus's intention, we can focus on his activity and determine his purpose by assessing his strategy at Jerusalem that Passover week. The best guide is to follow the *general* sequence in Mark, the earliest of the four Gospels, certainly the major source for Matthew and Luke and probably for John as well. Without Mark, we have no way to explain—apart from polemics and apologetics—why Jesus was executed on *that specific* Passover. More significantly, without Mark's *general* context, there is no way to explain why Jesus was not arrested for his *specific* activity on (Palm) Sunday, at the earliest, or on Tuesday, at the latest—especially in the tinderbox context of the Temple at Passover in Jerusalem. But why the tinderbox context?

In the close quarters of the Temple at Passover, massed Jewish pilgrims celebrated Israel's deliverance from Egyptian bondage in the ancient past even while they were under Roman bondage in the present. That paradox was particularly evident as they assembled for sacrifice in the Temple, which was overlooked by the Fortress Antonia, a northern attachment that both observed and controlled Temple activity and symbolized their present imperial oppression.

No wonder, then, that two massive riots happened in the Temple at Passover, according to the Jewish historian Josephus. One was in 4 BCE in which "three thousand" were killed and another in around 50 CE in which either "twenty thousand" or "thirty thousand" were killed (*Jewish War* 2.10–13, 223–47; *Jewish Antiquities* 17.213–18; 20.105–12; henceforth abbreviated as *JW* and *JA*).

Furthermore, at Passover, Pilate, the Roman *prefect*, or second-rank governor of southern Israel, was present with extra troops to enforce zero toleration for anything subversive. Pilate, by the way, was not exactly that indecisive character, half Hamlet and half Polonius, portrayed in the Gospel accounts. We know more about him than about any other governor in the first-century Jewish homeland. After a decade in power (26–36), he was finally sent back to Rome by his superior, Vitellius, the *legate*, or first-rank governor of Syria, to defend himself before the emperor Tiberius (*JA* 18.88–89).

With all of that in mind, this Overture concentrates on the first days of Jesus's final week—our Palm Sunday, Monday, and Tuesday—and, within those three days, it focuses on the tribute question during that Tuesday: What did Jesus do on those three days, and how do those actions reveal the intention of his visit and the overall strategy of that week?

On our Palm Sunday, Jesus mounted (pun intended) a public demonstration against Roman imperial control, starting from "Bethphage and Bethany, near the Mount of Olives" and going toward Jerusalem (Mark 11:1). In an *anti*-triumphal entry, he rode into Jerusalem from the east on a donkey in a symbolic subversive demonstration against the Roman governor Pilate, arriving from the west on a stallion. Pilate came from his headquarters at coastal Caesarea to overpower the Passover crowds if necessary. Jesus came from Galilee to empower those same crowds—if possible.

According to Mark, Jesus was greeted as the Davidic Messiah, as a New David: "Many people spread their cloaks on the road, and others spread leafy branches that they had cut in the fields. Then those who went ahead and those who followed were shouting . . . 'Blessed is the coming kingdom of our ancestor David!'" (11:8–10). Why was Jesus not immediately arrested?

On the next day, Jesus conducted the other half of his ongoing single demonstration—this time against Temple-based collaboration with the Roman oppressors. He did not "purify" the Temple; he closed it down by symbolically overturning the tables for its annual taxes, its sacred gifts, and its fiscal supports (Mark 11:15–17).

Quoting the prophet Jeremiah, Jesus invoked God's priority for distributive justice over liturgical worship. Jeremiah and Jesus accused the Temple of having become a refuge, a hideaway, a safe house, "a den" for "robbers" (Mark 11:17), because sacrificial worship inside had supplanted social justice outside (Jer. 7:1–15). That challenge, by the way, almost cost Jeremiah his life (26:1–24). Again, then, why was Jesus not arrested by that second night?

The answer to those two preceding questions is that Mark describes Jesus during those first three days in Jerusalem as *opposed by Jewish authorities* but *protected by Jewish crowds.* (No need, by the way, to demonize those high-priestly authorities. As collaborators, they feared Jesus; according to John 11:48, they said: "Everyone will believe in him, and the Romans will come and destroy both our holy place and our nation"—themselves included!)

On Palm Sunday, as we just saw, Mark detailed the "many people" who welcomed Jesus into Jerusalem. No mention yet of tension with the authorities—but it can be fairly presumed. On Monday, after the Temple incident, both sides appeared in explicit confrontation over Jesus: "When the chief priests and the scribes heard it, they kept looking for a way to kill him; for they were afraid of him, because the whole crowd was spellbound by his teaching" (Mark 11:18). On Tuesday, this conflict between authorities and crowds over Jesus intensified dramatically according to Mark. On that day, Mark has Jesus "win" a series of five debates in Jerusalem's Temple (11:27–12:40) to mirror deliberately the inaugural series of five debates that he "won" in Galilee (2:1–3:6).

During those Temple debates, the authorities included chief priests, scribes, elders (11:27–12:12), Pharisees and Herodians (12:13–17), Sadducees (12:18–27), and scribes again (12:28–40). Against that serried opposition, all that protected Jesus was "the crowd," and Mark mentions them three times that day:

They were afraid of the crowd, for all regarded John as truly a prophet. (11:32)

When they realized that he had told this parable against them, they wanted to arrest him, but they feared the crowd. So they left him and went away. (12:12)

The large crowd was listening to him with delight. (12:37)

That protective screen of supporting "crowds" kept Jesus safe from the authorities even in the Temple itself.

But Jesus also adopted another security measure. He did not stay overnight in Jerusalem. Instead, each day, he came from and returned to a safe location out of sight on the southeastern slopes of the Mount of Olives about two miles from Jerusalem. There, at Bethany, he stayed in the home of Martha, Mary, and Lazarus—probably Judean relatives—a place accurately called al-Eizariya, the Place of Lazarus, today.

Mark emphasizes that Jesus left from and returned to Bethany each of the first three days that Passover week:

[*Sunday*] He entered Jerusalem and went into the temple; and when he had looked around at everything, as it was already late, he went out to Bethany with the twelve. (11:11)

[*Monday*] On the following day, when they came from Bethany, he was hungry. . . . When evening came, Jesus and his disciples went out of the city. (11:12, 19)

[*Tuesday*] In the morning as they passed by, they saw the fig tree withered away to its roots. . . . Again they came to Jerusalem. . . . When he was sitting on the Mount of Olives opposite the temple . . . (11:20, 27; 13:3)

It is only those two items—protective crowds and Jesus's suburban refuge—that explain why he was not arrested by Sunday, Monday, or Tuesday of that Passover week, all according to prearranged security plans.

From that we may draw two conclusions about Jesus's intentions based on his actions that Passover week. He did *not* go to Jerusalem deliberately to be martyred, either as a sacrifice for sin, as in evangelical Protestant theology, or as a model for suffering, as in Roman Catholic theology. He went there because Judean supporters and relatives said something like this: "If you are serious about this *rule of God* movement, take it out of those small villages in Galilee and bring it to the holy city of Jerusalem. Also, bring it here at Passover because of its traditional liberation meaning and also because pilgrim visitors will then carry it everywhere. Furthermore, we can protect you this Passover—in the Temple by day and in Bethany by night."

———

Granted that intentional matrix derived from Jesus's public actions and safety strategies, we can focus next on Jesus in the Temple on (our) Tuesday of that Passover week (Mark 11:27–12:44). On that day, in the Markan context, Jesus was asked a question whose answer was calculated to either strip him of his *protective crowd* or enable the *inimical authorities* to accuse him before Pilate.

Recall that, as just mentioned, Mark frames his life of Jesus between the inaugural debates in Galilee and the terminal ones in Jerusalem. After the five Galilean debates, "The Pharisees went out and immediately conspired with the Herodians against him, how to destroy him" (Mark 3:6). Then, during the five Jerusalem debates, that same combination of scholarly and princely power reappeared against Jesus.

Each of the five Jerusalem debates began with a question. The first one came from "the chief priests, the scribes, and the elders" (Mark 11:27–33). It involved the question of Jesus's authority and, after deflecting it, he rebutted them with the parable of the Wicked Tenants (12:1–11). That led directly into the second question-based debate: "When they realized that he had told this parable against them, they wanted to arrest him, but they feared the crowd. So they left him and went away. Then they sent to him some Pharisees and some Herodians to trap him in what he said" (12:12–13).

In Jerusalem at the end, as in Galilee at the start, the scholarly/religious and princely/political authorities combined forces against Jesus, and a three-step "they/he" dialogue ensued in which, of course, Jesus got the last word:

> *They* came and said to him, "Teacher, we know that you are sincere, and show deference to no one; for you do not regard people with partiality, but teach the way of God in accordance with truth. Is it lawful to pay taxes to the emperor, or not? Should we pay them, or should we not?" (12:14–15a)
>
> But knowing their hypocrisy, *he* said to them, "Why are you putting me to the test? Bring me a denarius and let me see it." (12:15b)
>
> And *they* brought one. (12:16a)
> Then *he* said to them, "Whose image (*eikon*) is this, and whose inscription (*epigraphē*)?" (12:16b)
>
> *They* answered, "Caesar's (*Kaisaros*)." (12:16c)
> *Jesus* said to them, "Caesar's (*ta Kaisaros*) give back to Caesar and God's to God." (12:17ab)

In what follows, each stage in the overall dialogue will be looked at separately, but that is simply for explanatory focus, as the incident must always be seen as a unitary whole.

Taxes and Test (12:14–15). In the first stage of the incident, the question was a rather obvious gotcha—especially in that time and place. The result of a "no" answer, against Roman taxation, was always dangerous, but for Jesus to refute imperial tribute in the Temple at Passover was particularly so, because it focused his opposition on Pilate's political power rather than on Caiaphas's religious power. Luke alone, by the way, makes a refusal to pay Roman taxes part of the accusation against Jesus before Pilate: "We found this man perverting our nation, forbidding us to pay taxes to the emperor, and saying that he himself is the Messiah, a king" (23:1–2).

Granted that a "no" response to Roman taxation was extremely dangerous, a "yes" answer, in favor of Roman taxation, was equally, if differently, dangerous. Jesus would lose the protective screen of his supporters, thereby allowing the authorities to move against him safely. Either response seemed fatal for Jesus.

Image and Inscription (12:16ab). To the gotcha in the opening, Jesus first countered with his own gotcha. Jesus himself did not carry the tribute coin. He asked the group to show him one, questioned them as if he had never seen one before, and forced them to tell him whose "image" and "inscription" were on it. But, at this point, what follows depends on which Roman coin Jesus observed, Mark presumed, and we hearers/readers imagine.

What tribute coin fits best with the exchange in the second section and especially with Jesus's climactic conclusion, "The things of Caesar give back (*apodote*) to Caesar and the things of God to God" (Mark 12:17b, literally)? What coin's inscription might best have generated such a specific distinction between "God" and "Caesar"?[1]

In answering that question in what follows, we need to pay close attention not just to a coin's central "image," but also to its surrounding "inscription," since Jesus explicitly asked about both those elements. Also, for clarity and legibility, schematic drawings are used rather than photos of actual coins, because in some cases the dies were bigger than the blanks or badly centered on them or the coins were simply abraded over time.

The *silver denarius of Tiberius* is the classic example of the tribute coin and is the one usually described, discussed, and depicted in connection with this passage. Mark calls it a "denarius" (*dēnarion*). That is a Latin coin, 11/16 of an inch in diameter, about the size of a US penny or dime, and in value the equivalent of a Greek drachma.

On this coin Tiberius's "image" appears facing right on its front, or obverse, and the surrounding "inscription" reads counterclockwise in abbreviated Latin: TI CAESAR DIVI AVG F AVGVSTVS, or Tiberius Caesar, Son of the Divine Augustus, Augustus.

The back, or reverse, side shows the goddess Pax seated, facing right, with an inverted spear in her right hand and an olive branch in her left. The abbreviated counterclockwise Latin inscription reads: PONTIF MAXIM, or Pontifex Maximus, the "Supreme Bridgebuilder" between earth and heaven—from *pons*, "bridge," and *facere*, "to build" (Figure 1).

There are, however, several intractable problems with that coin as the one observed by Jesus or intended by Mark. First, it is a Latin coin minted at Lyons in faraway Gaul (France)—which explains why none that date before the 60s have ever been discovered in Israel. Second, this denarius is a tiny coin and, on the front, the abbreviated six-word Latin counterclockwise "inscription" would be visually difficult to read, and the reader would have to know Latin case endings to read DIVI AVG F correctly as DIVI AVGVSTI FILIVS.

Finally, and in any case, Mark probably used "denarius" as a general

FIGURE 1
Roman Imperial Coins I.26-30: http://numismatics.org/ocre/id/ric.1(2).tib.30, and
https://www.forumancientcoins.com/numiswiki/view.asp?key=tribute%20penny

term for whatever silver coin those questioners produced—just as the King James Bible used "penny" in its translation. (I grew up in Ireland with the old British coinage of "pounds, shillings, and pence/pennies," indicated by *£, s,* and *d*—*d* from denarii but used for pennies.)

A better candidate for the coin in question is the *silver tetradrachm of Tiberius.* As its name indicates, this coin was worth four drachmas, or four denarii. At an inch in diameter (the size of the US quarter), it was bigger than a denarius and therefore easier to observe. Also, rather than abbreviated Latin inscriptions, it had large unabbreviated Greek ones, which would have been easier to both read and debate.

There are two tetradrachms worth considering—one from the mint in Alexandria, Egypt, the other from the mint in Antioch, Syria— with only ten known examples. On the obverse of both types is the wreathed head of Tiberius; the Egyptian coin reads TIBERIOS KAISAR SEBASTOS (Tiberius Caesar Augustus) and the Syrian coin reads TIBERIOS SEBASTOS KAISAR (Tiberius Augustus Caesar).

The reverse of both coins shows the crowned head of Augustus and, since the following discussion focuses on them, here they are side by side:

FIGURE 2	**FIGURE 3**
Roman Provincial Coins I.5089: https: //rpc.ashmus.ox.ac.uk/coins/1/5089	*Roman Provincial Coins* I.4161: https: //rpc.ashmus.ox.ac.uk/coins/1/4161

As you can see, the clockwise two-word inscription in Figure 2 reads ΘΕΟΣ ΣΕΒΑΣΤΟΣ (THEOS SEBASTOS, God Augustus); the counterclockwise three-word inscription in Figure 3 reads ΘΕΟΣ ΣΕΒΑΣΤΟΣ ΚΑΙΣΑΡ (THEOS SEBASTOS KAISAR, God Augustus Caesar). But before considering which coin type best fits Jesus's specific response, a word about words and especially about titles.

We know that Jesus's title "Messiah" is based on the Semitic word for the Greek term we translate as "Christ." Caesar's title *Sebastos* is the Greek word for the Latin term *Augustus*. *Sebastos* is an adjective from the verb *sebō*, "to worship," and should be properly translated as "worshiped." It is, in fact, the verb used six times in Acts for "God-worshipers" (*sebomenoi*). *Sebastos/Augustus* means "the worshiped one." So Caesar represented not only the military, economic, and political power, but also the ideological or theological power that held together Rome's Mediterranean globalization. It is, therefore, a serious mistake to consider that theological title to be empty court protocol or to dismiss it as merely part of the workings of the ruler cult.

In the last decade of his life, for example, the poet Horace began a literary letter to Augustus in which he noted that ancient heroes like Hercules and Romulus were only divinized after death. To Augustus he said: "Upon you [Augustus], however, *while still among us*, we bestow honors betimes, set up altars to swear by in your name, and confess that nothing like you will hereafter arise or has arisen ever now" (*Epistles* 2.1.15–17).

Granted all that, it is no surprise to find Augustus entitled *Theos Sebastos* (God Augustus) on the reverse side of both tetradrachm coin types. But which is the one best suited within the full account of Mark's tribute debate?

Caesar and God (12:16c–17b). The questioners opened with this trap: "Is it lawful to pay taxes to the emperor, or not? Should we pay them, or should we not?" As we just saw, their "test" was to trap Jesus into an equally dangerous yes or no choice. Jesus's countertrap was to force them into their equally dangerous Caesar-or-God choice, based on his double question about "image" and "inscription."

First, in this third stage of the incident, think about Jesus's question, "Whose image is this?" In the literal Greek text, the questioners had to admit that it is "Caesar's" (*Kaisaros*), and Jesus immediately picked up their word and replied, "Caesar's (*ta Kaisaros*) give back to Caesar." Note, it is not simply "give" or "render" (*dote*), but "give back" or "render back" (*apodote*). That exchange is thus as linguistically appropriate as it is beautifully ambiguous, especially since Jesus did not carry Caesar's coin but they did!

Jesus's reply, "Caesar's *give back* to Caesar," could mean yes, keep Caesar's coin and pay your taxes, or no, return Caesar's coin and do not—because you then cannot—pay your taxes. If you do not accept Caesar's coin, how can you pay Caesar's taxes? No wonder the questioners and/or observers "were utterly amazed at him" (12:17c).

Second, think now about Jesus's question, "Whose inscription is this?" Once Jesus had avoided their clever trap with an even more clever countertrap, he concluded with a profound challenge—especially among Jews, who were aniconic monotheists, under domination by Romans, who were iconic polytheists.

On the obverse of the silver tetradrachm offered as the tribute coin, the Greek "inscription" called Augustus *both* "God" (*Theos*) *and* "Caesar" (*Kaisar*). Augustus was not just *Sebastos*, "the worshiped one," but, lest there be any mistake, he was "the worshiped God." On that coin, as so often elsewhere in Roman imperial theology, Caesar and God were identified.

We can now see why Jesus's final comment brought up "Caesar" and "God." It was because the Syrian coin had already equated them. And, in response, he had quietly denied that equation and serenely separated "the things of Caesar" from "the things of God."

That coin's identification of God and Caesar announced, as it were: *Render to Caesar the things that are God's, and to God the things that are Caesar's*. Jesus's distinction between Caesar and God instead announced: *Render to Caesar the things that are Caesar's, and to God the things that are God's.*

That final quotation from Jesus should never be cited as if it were a stand-alone proverb or aphorism dividing the world between Caesar and God, politics and religion, state and temple/church/mosque. That is to ignore its context, negate its challenge, and betray its meaning.

———————

All of that, however, leaves us with these rather obvious questions: If Caesar and God are not identified, then how are they distinguished? If Caesar and God are not equated, then how are they related? If Caesar and God are neither identified nor equated, how are they associated, accommodated, adapted, assimilated, or acculturated to one another in the actual world in which we all live?

Notice that those five verbs represent the classic slippery slope toward full *acculturation*. By that word I designate deep integration in the surrounding culture so that you swim in it smoothly, unconsciously, and uncritically—like fish in the sea. *Acculturation is the drag of normalcy, the lure of conformity, the curse of careerism that can—under certain leaders, in certain circumstances, at certain times and places—turn some of us into monsters, many of us into liars, and most of us into cowards.*

Next we look, first, at two contradictory New Testament answers to the question of divine rule and human acculturation. One solution is to *demonize acculturation,* as is done in the book of Revelation (Part One). Another solution is to *canonize acculturation,* as in the two-volume book of Luke-Acts (Part Two). Then, granted that dichotomy, what about *radically criticizing acculturation* as the way forward for Christian faith—and human evolution (Part Three)?

PART ONE

CULTURE REJECTED AND DEMONIZED

To demonize others is to fail to learn
the lessons of history.[1]

—Phillip Cole, *The Myth of Evil*

1

GOD SHALL
OVERCOME SOMEDAY

T HE LAST BOOK OF THE CHRISTIAN BIBLE ANNOUNCES IT-
self as: "The revelation (*apokalypsis*) of Jesus Christ, which God
gave him to show his servants what must soon take place; he made it
known by sending his angel to his servant John" (Rev. 1:1). The author
then announces himself as: "I, John, your brother who share with you
in Jesus the persecution and the *rule of God* and the patient endurance,
was on the island called Patmos because of the word of God and the
testimony of Jesus" (1:9). Patmos is, today, a small Greek island off
the southwestern coast of Turkey. John of Patmos likes to emphasize
certain elements by repeating them at the start and finish of his text.
Using that framing style, he identifies himself again later as: "I, John,
am the one who heard and saw these things. And when I heard and saw
them, I fell down to worship at the feet of the angel who showed them
to me" (22:8).

The opening word, *apokalypsis* in the original Greek, or "revelation"
in English translation, promises the unveiling or disclosing of a hidden
or secret content, presumably one that is important, momentous, or
even cataclysmic. But after that single inaugural use of *apocalypse*, the

author prefers to describe the book as *prophecy*, a term that, once again, appears at the start and finish to frame the entire text. At the start, we get this promise: "Blessed is the one who reads aloud the words of the *prophecy*, and blessed are those who hear and who keep what is written in it; for the time is near" (1:3). At the end, we get that same promise, but now tempered with a threat:

> Blessed is the one who keeps the words of the *prophecy* of
> this book. . . . Do not seal up the words of the *prophecy*
> of this book. . . . I warn everyone who hears the words of the
> *prophecy* of this book: if anyone adds to them, God will add
> to that person the plagues described in this book; if anyone
> takes away from the words of the book of this *prophecy*,
> God will take away that person's share in the tree of life
> and in the holy city, which are described in this book.
> (22:7, 10, 18–19)

Those framing promises are a forceful hint that, whatever external enemies exist, there are also internal forces to be praised and/or threatened. But, more to the point, by using the term "prophecy," this book's apocalyptic vision declares itself—defensively and polemically—as belonging to, depending on, and continuing forward the authoritative prophetic vision of ancient biblical tradition.

Furthermore, the author also specifies that prophetic content, again at the start and finish of his book, with these framing details on a coming *what* and a coming *who*. The *what* is described as "what must soon take place" in 1:1 at the beginning and then again in 22:6 at the end, and the *who* as "I will come to you soon" in 2:16 and 3:11 at the beginning and "I am coming soon" in 22:7, 12, 20 at the end. This book's content is about a coming *what* and a coming *who*, both of which are specified as coming *soon*, as an imminent *when*.

How, then, does John's announcement of a coming *what* and a coming *who* connect with previous prophetic announcements of a similar double advent?

Toward the conclusion of his book, John describes climactically what is *coming* as a new and transfigured world summed up within a vision of a new Jerusalem:

> I saw the holy city, the new Jerusalem, coming down out of heaven from God, prepared as a bride adorned for her husband. And I heard a loud voice from the throne saying, "See, the home of God is among mortals. He will dwell with them; they will be his peoples, and God himself will be with them; he will wipe every tear from their eyes. Death will be no more; mourning and crying and pain will be no more, for the first things have passed away."
>
> And the one who was seated on the throne said, "See, I am making all things new.". . .
>
> Then one of the seven angels . . . carried me away to a great, high mountain and showed me the holy city Jerusalem coming down out of heaven from God. (21:2–5, 9–10)

That magnificent vision of "a new heaven and a new earth" (21:1) is both the soaring climax of John's apocalyptic *prophecy* and the deliberate recall of another equally climactic *prophecy* from half a millennium earlier. That is also, of course, why—despite the redundancy—John labels his apocalypse precisely as prophecy and, indeed, as the climactic fulfillment of biblical prophecy.

First, the theme of a new creation and a new Jerusalem recalls the ecstatic chapters added to the book of Isaiah at the time of Israel's Persian restoration from its Babylonian captivity in the late 500s BCE:

> I am about to create new heavens and a new earth; the former things shall not be remembered or come to mind. But be glad

and rejoice forever in what I am creating; for I am about to
create Jerusalem as a joy, and its people as a delight. I will
rejoice in Jerusalem, and delight in my people; no more shall
the sound of weeping be heard in it, or the cry of distress.
(Isa. 65:17–19)

Next, John's promise of tears wiped from every eye, of an end to
death, and of a new Jerusalem recalls this promise of the Persian restoration as a great divine feast for all the nations on the mountain of
Jerusalem:

On this mountain the LORD of hosts will make for all peoples
a feast of rich food, a feast of well-aged wines, of rich food filled
with marrow, of well-aged wines strained clear. And he will
destroy on this mountain the shroud that is cast over all peoples,
the sheet that is spread over all nations; he will swallow up death
forever. Then the Lord GOD will wipe away the tears from all
faces, and the disgrace of his people he will take away from
all the earth, for the LORD has spoken. (Isa. 25:6–8)

For our first glimpse of what John sees as *coming*, we start by going
back—as we just saw John himself doing—into Israel's deepest hopes
for a new and very different world here below. Why was a new world
needed? What would make it new? Who would inaugurate it here
below? When would it happen? How would it happen?

The Hebrew scriptures, and the Christian Old Testament derived from
it, repeatedly describe Israel in idyllic fashion as "a good and broad
land, a land flowing with milk and honey" (Exod. 3:8) or "a land flowing with milk and honey, the most glorious of all lands" (Ezek. 20:6).

Be that as it may, this promised land is located on the Mediterranean's Levantine coast as the connecting link between the continents of Europe, Asia, and Africa. As such, Israel is permanently positioned on the highway of superpower conflict between Mesopotamia and Egypt, Persia and Greece, Parthia and Rome, and repeatedly struggled under the occupation and oppression that resulted from that location.

Furthermore, if your *faith* is in a God who rules the world by distributive justice (for example, Ps. 82), but your *experience* is one of repeated imperial injustice, how do you reconcile that discrepancy or resolve that profound cognitive dissonance? Israel's answer was, in summary: God will overcome—someday!

There would be, *there had to be*, a Great Divine Cleanup of the World, an Extreme Makeover: Cosmic Edition. A just God could only temporarily tolerate an unjust world, a violent earth, and a vitiated creation. There would be, there had to be, a final, last, or eschatological transformation of our earth ("eschatological" simply comes from the Greek word for "last"). An unjust world would have to be justified— *someday*, would have to be transfigured from violent distributive injustice to nonviolent distributive justice—*someday*.

Then, in the late 500s BCE, came a miraculous moment, a euphoric instant, a rhapsodic reversal when it looked as if the world's divine renovation, the earth's eschatological transformation had finally begun. But it began tragically in the Babylonian captivity before it ended ecstatically in the Persian restoration.

In successive deportations between 597 and 581 BCE, the Babylonian Empire took the elite leadership of conquered Jerusalem into exile at Babylonia. But then, in 612 BCE, the Babylonians were defeated by the Persians, whose imperial policy was support and tax rather than defeat and loot. Deported peoples must return home and restore country, religion, and law to become a fitting part of Persia, the greatest empire in the history of the world (Ezra 1:2–3). Think of Cyrus the Great as inventing the Marshall Plan a little ahead of its time!

At that incredible moment, when forced Babylonian exile had become funded Persian return, anything was possible and everything was imaginable. First, God declared Cyrus to be God's "shepherd," to be God's "anointed," or Messiah/Christ, for all the world (Isa. 44:24, 28; 45:1, 13).

Next, travel home was to be a dreamlike passage across the intervening desert. Indeed, that smooth transit was not just for the exiles, but for God returning to Jerusalem: "A voice cries out: 'In the wilderness prepare the way of the LORD, make straight in the desert a highway for our God. Every valley shall be lifted up, and every mountain and hill be made low; the uneven ground shall become level, and the rough places a plain'" (Isa. 40:3–4).

Finally, in this instant of extreme elation, Israel imagined not just a special renewal for itself, but a general one for all the earth. Maybe the exilic sufferings of personified Israel were not justified punishment for national sin—as in standard Deuteronomic theology—but rather vicarious atonement for imperial sin (Isa. 53). And Israel's vicarious atonement had evidently succeeded, as imperialism itself had publicly been "converted" from Babylonian oppression to Persian support. So, if empire could change, might not the world change?

At this transformative moment, Israel imagined a world without war or violence, an earth without bloodshed or fear, a humanity living in safety and security, prosperity and peace. And, as it prepared to restore its country, rebuild its Temple, and remake its Bible, Israel retrojected this later vision into the earlier prophecies of Isaiah in that book's final redaction:

> In days to *come* . . . [God] shall judge between the nations, and shall arbitrate for many peoples; *they* shall beat their swords into plowshares, and their spears into pruning hooks; nation shall not lift up sword against nation, neither shall *they* learn war any more. (2:2, 4)

All of Isaiah 2:2–4 is repeated verbatim in Micah 4:1–3, but Micah adds this line: "They shall all sit under their own vines and under their own fig trees, and no one shall make them afraid" (4:4). It is violence, war, and the fear of both that supports the injustice of possessing another's vines, fig trees, and lands. Thus, if war allows and establishes injustice, justice allows and establishes peace. What came next, however, for tiny Israel and its wider Euro-Asian world was not justice and peace, but greater war, greater violence, and greater fear.

In 331 BCE, the Persian Empire fell to the Greek empire of Alexander the Great, whose fearsome war machine with its phalanxes of double-pointed twenty-foot pikes allowed five rows in the killing zone at the same time. Then, after Alexander's early death in 323, his generals turned on one another, and from 274 to 168 the successor empires of Seleucid Greco-Syria to the north and Ptolemaic Greco-Egypt to the south fought six wars using Israel as a convenient battlefield.

Still and all, despite that escalatory violence or maybe because of it, Israel held fast to its visionary hope in a coming world of distributive justice and universal peace. Prophecy about a nonviolent future held firm—at least for some—despite or because of the trajectory of a violent present.

In the middle of the second century BCE, in the Jewish homeland, the book of Daniel *twice* invoked heavenly judgment and divine condemnation on all prior and contemporary empires—Babylonian, Median, Persian (even Persian!), Greek, and Greco-Syrian (2:32–33, 37–43; 7:1–12). Those transient rules would be replaced by a permanent one, the *rule of God* (2:34–35, 44–45; 7:13–14, 18, 27). (In Appendix A, I explain why "kingdom of God" or "God's kingdom" is always translated and italicized in this book as the *rule of God* or *God's rule*.)

No description—beyond permanence ("forever")—is given for the *rule of God* on earth in Daniel 2 or 7, but a contemporary prophecy from the Jewish diaspora in nearby Egypt furnishes these details about it:

There will be no sword on earth or din of battle, and the earth
will no longer be shaken, groaning deeply. There will no longer
be war or drought on earth, no famine or hail, damaging to
fruits, but there will be great peace throughout the whole earth.
King will be friend to king to the end of the age. The Immortal
[God] . . . will raise up a *rule* for all ages among men. . . .
Prophets of the great God will take away the sword. . . . There
will also be just wealth among men for this is the judgment
and dominion of the great God." (*Sibylline Oracles* 3.751–84,
excerpts)

Finally, after one hundred years of independence under a not en-
tirely acceptable Jewish Hasmonean dynasty, the Romans arrived
under Pompey. As Israel's Romanization began toward the end of the
first century BCE, we have, once again, that abiding hope for peace on
earth from both Jewish homeland and Jewish diaspora.

The *Psalms of Solomon*—eighteen hymns not in the Hebrew Bible
but included in its Greek translation—speak of the *rule of God* (the
what), but in very general terms: "May those who fear the Lord rejoice
in good things, and your kindness be upon Israel under your *rule*"
(5:18), because "we will hope in God our savior; for the might of our
God is forever with pity, and the *rule* of our God is forever over the
nations in judgment" (17:3).

They also speak, again in very general terms, of God's "anointed"
(the *who*) as the Messiah/Christ and the new David-like ruler:

See, O Lord, and raise up for them their king, the son of David,
at the time which you chose, O God . . . he shall be a righteous
king, taught by God, over them, and there shall be no injustice
in his days in their midst, for all shall be holy, and their king the
anointed of the Lord. For he shall not put his hope in horse and
rider and bow, nor shall he multiply for himself gold and silver

for war, nor shall he gather hopes from a multitude of people for the day of war. (17:21, 32–33; see also 18:5–7)

For more details on how "there shall be no injustice" under this coming messianic *rule of God*, we turn, once again, from homeland to diaspora:

> The earth will belong equally to all, undivided by walls or
> fences. It will then bear more abundant fruits spontaneously.
> Lives will be in common and wealth will have no division.
> For there will be no poor man there, no rich, and no tyrant,
> no slave. Further, no one will be either great or small anymore.
> No kings, no leaders. All will be on a par together.
> (*Sib. Or.* 2.319–24)

Two footnotes about that half millennium of visionary hope for an eventual, final, eschatological world of distributive justice on an earth of universal peace. First, whether utopian hope or visionary dream, prophecy about the *rule of God* was never about the "end of the world," about the earth's destruction and humanity's evacuation elsewhere. You could call it the "end of this world as *we know it*," because eschatology is about the radical transformation of civilization's normalcy, moving from injustice to justice, war to peace, violence to nonviolence, destruction to conservation. Think of it not as civilization's return to barbarism, but as its evolution to postcivilization.

Second, it is utterly possible to assess all this biblical expectation of earth's global peace as a delusional dream, a utopian fantasy, the Bible's cosmic equivalent of the Depression's "Big Rock Candy Mountain." But think of trajectory rather than of prophecy and consider the evolution of humanity's escalatory violence in this summary: "From the first chipped stone to the first smelted iron took nearly 3 million years; from the first iron to the hydrogen bomb took only 3,000."[1]

If the dream of a world without war or violence on an earth trans-figured by justice and peace is irrational or delusional, is allowing human violence to escalate as we have done any less irrational and is presuming it will just somehow change any less delusional? *Trajectory*, not prophecy, shows we are a self-endangered species and that *only non-violent resistance* can stop the escalatory spiral of human violence—while there is still time.

Finally, down through those five hundred years from Persians to Romans, the biblical *coming* of earth's transformation is as sure and certain as its *timing* is unsure and uncertain. It will arrive "on that day" (Isa. 2:17), "in days to come" (Mic. 4:1), "in those days and at that time" (Joel 3:1), "at the end of days" (Dan. 2:28; 10:14), or "in those days" (*Psalms of Solomon* 17:44; 18:6). The *what* is clear, but the *when* is vague.

This furnishes some obvious questions for this chapter's next section. Granted that the coming earthly *rule of God* was a five-hundred-year-old prophetic tradition before John of Patmos ever continued its procla-mation, where did he get the apocalyptic revelation that it was coming *soon*? How does John know that the world's utopian transfiguration and the world's eschatological transformation are *imminent*? Where did John get his revelation of *soon*—did he get it from a time before Jesus, from Jesus's time on earth, from a time after Jesus, or from all of those sources together?

Those who opposed with equal dislike both the *baptism of God* move-ment of John and the *rule of God* movement of Jesus still distinguished them with this negative assessment given in Matthew 11:18–19 and Luke 7:33–34:

> John came neither eating nor drinking, and they say, "He has
> a demon"; the Son of Man came eating and drinking, and they

say, "Look, a glutton and a drunkard, a friend of tax collectors and sinners!"

We can set aside those inimical name-calling interpretations, but the basic facts are that John was known for fasting and Jesus for feasting. You *fast*, however, in preparation for *what is coming soon*; you *feast* in celebration for *what has already arrived*.

For Jesus, therefore, the *rule of God* has already arrived on earth. But how is that even remotely credible in a world still ruled by violent injustice, military power, and martial law? Who hears the "Anvil Chorus" as swords become plowshares and spears become pruning hooks? How is Jesus's message not a cruel joke in an Israel under inaugural Romanization?

Mark 1:15, for example, usually translated as "The time is fulfilled, and the *rule of God* has come near," summarizes the message of Jesus. Here is a deliberately wooden translation to make the parallelism more obvious:

| Has | been fulfilled | the *time*, |
| Has | come near | the *rule*. |

Those parallel verbs in Greek in the perfect tense mean that the *rule of God* is not imminently future, but *already present*. But that involves a paradigm shift, a disruptive innovation, a tradition swerve from John the Baptist's preparation for the *rule of God* as *coming* (1:7) to Jesus's celebration of the *rule of God* as *here* (1:15).

For Israel, up to and including John the Baptist, the advent of *God's rule* entailed a transcendental intrusion for which humans could hope, pray, and prepare, but not participate in except by acceptance. For Jesus, the advent of *God's rule* involved both divine and human participation, a two-way covenantal commitment. The difference was between *John's apocalyptic eschatology*, in which God's rule was *imminent*, and *Jesus's collaborative eschatology*, in which it was already *present*.

The paradigm shift involved in Jesus's vision is best seen in the parable of the Mustard Seed, which is one of his shortest but also the only one with two *independent* versions within the New Testament: one in Mark and one in that other source—apart from Mark—used by both Matthew and Luke, which scholars call Q or the Q Gospel:

> With what can we compare the *rule of God*, or what parable will we use for it? It is like a mustard seed, which, *when sown upon the ground*, is the smallest of all the seeds on earth; yet when it is sown it grows up and becomes the greatest of all shrubs, and puts forth large branches, so that the birds of the air can make nests in its shade. (Mark 4:30–32)

> What is the *rule of God* like? And to what should I compare it? It is like a mustard seed that *someone took and sowed* in the garden; it grew and became a tree, and the birds of the air made nests in its branches. (Q/Luke 13:18–19)

First, it is immediately startling to describe the *rule of God* on earth not as an immediate, full-scale, all-at-once cataclysmic transformation, but as a normal, familiar, and everyday growth process from small to large. Nobody ever suggested *that* understanding in Israel's preceding eschatological tradition! Still, even granted growth, is that growth process dependent on divine intervention or on divine and human collaboration?

Second, mustard comes in two varieties—either wild or cultivated—as was well known in Jesus's first-century context. The Roman naturalist Pliny the Elder, for example, noted: "Though mustard will grow without cultivation, it is considerably improved by being transplanted; but on the other hand, it is extremely difficult to rid the soil of it when once sown there, since the seed when it falls germinates immediately" (*Natural History* 19.170).

Jesus chose cultivated rather than wild mustard, as my italics indicate in both passages above. *Wild* mustard—or, indeed, any other *wild* plant—here would be an appropriate image for a development or growth process controlled exclusively by God. But *cultivated* mustard requires human cooperation, first to transplant and then to control.

For Jesus's paradigm shift in his people's eschatological expectation, the *rule of God* is already here or, better, has always been here, but in a growth process that *only* succeeds by divine *and* human cooperation. Call Jesus's vision participatory, collaborative, or, more simply, covenantal eschatology.

You would think that, after that parabolic summary of Jesus's vision, any use of "near now" or "coming soon" for *God's rule* would have been respectfully buried and replaced by "here now" or "already come." But think about this statement: "Truly I tell you, there are some standing here who will not taste death until they see that the *rule of God* has come with power" (Mark 9:1). Go back to the Mustard Seed parable once more and focus on it as a *growth process* not just from small to large, but from seed to tree, beginning to end, advent to consummation.

First, Jesus proclaimed that the advent or beginning of *God's rule* on earth was not a divine intervention coming soon, but a divine and human collaboration already—and maybe always—available. But did he also say that the consummation or end of *God's rule* on earth was coming soon? That depends on whether such sayings as, for example, Mark 9:1 or Matthew 10:23 come from the historical Jesus, the tradition about Jesus, or the evangelists on Jesus.

Next, here's a possible explanation of what happened. Jesus's followers heard that Mustard Seed parable, but focused not on *how* it would grow from small to large by their participation but on *when* it would be consummated by divine intervention. They transferred that *coming soon* from the *rule's* start to a *coming soon* of the *rule's* end. Instead of living under the *rule*, or even as an excuse to keep from accepting the *rule*, hearers asked about how long it would be before its climactic consummation. In any case, and whether started by or after Jesus, the presumption that *God's rule* on earth was/is a short-term program rather than an open-ended movement and the delusion that the consummation of earth's transformation is *coming soon* are already present in Paul of Tarsus, John of Patmos, and much of the New Testament.

A *soon-coming* consummation avoids participation, denies collaboration, prevents commitment, and thereby nullifies the *rule of God* as present on earth and a challenge to earth. Put another way, biblical apocalyptic is what happened when biblical prophecy changed its focus from the *signs of the times* to the *times of the signs*.

All of that leaves us with one rather obvious question for the next chapter: How and why does John of Patmos create confusion by repeating for the end and consummation of *God's rule* on earth the same term, "coming," that had been used for its beginning, its advent? Why is that term "coming" so important for him?

In ordinary everyday language, a "coming" implies an absence. It presumes that the *what* or *who* to come is absent. Hence, we often hear of a Second Coming or Return of Christ as the content of John's apocalyptic revelation. But is that what is implied by "coming" in his book? If not arrival after absence, does John envision the *coming of what was not absent*? If so, what understanding of "coming" justifies that paradoxical usage? More specifically, when John proclaimed the *coming of what was already there*, did he presume some contemporary model that made his message both possible for him and credible for others?

2

THE COMING OF
WHAT IS ALREADY
PRESENT

JOHN OF PATMOS DESCRIBES *GOD'S RULE* AND GOD'S MESSIAH as already present, as having already come: "The rule of the world *has become* the *rule* of our Lord and of his Messiah, and he will reign forever and ever" (Rev. 11:15). And again: "*Now have come* the salvation and the power and the *rule* of our God and the authority of his Messiah" (12:10).

Hence the question for this chapter is: Why and how can John announce the *coming* of what is *already here*? We have, in fact, to expand that question to: Why and how can John announce the coming of what is *always* here—for example, God?

To accredit Moses as the leader of Israel's liberation from Egyptian slavery, God said to him: "You shall say to the Israelites, 'I AM has sent me to you'" (Exod. 3:14). With such an abiding and transcendental name as "I AM," you could easily think of the biblical God as the one "who was, who is, and who will be." That is not, however, how John glosses the existence of God.

He invokes the first two temporal indices of divine presence like this: "Lord God Almighty, who are and who were" (Rev. 11:17) or as "the "Holy One, who are and were" (16:5). Then instead of adding on "who will be" to complete the triadic divine eternity, John concludes like this:

> Grace to you and peace from him who is and who was and *who is to come*, and from the seven spirits who are before his throne. (1:4)

> "I am the Alpha and the Omega," says the Lord God, who is and who was and *who is to come*, the Almighty. (1:8)

> Day and night without ceasing they sing, "Holy, holy, holy, the Lord God the Almighty, who was and is and *is to come*." (4:8)

For John, therefore, the *rule of God* is *already* present, the Messiah/ Christ is *already* present, and, God—certainly—is not just *already* but *always* present. John's message is not about the initial state or advent but about the final state or consummation of *God's rule* on earth as "coming soon." Still, why is that word "coming" so insistent, emphatic, and repetitive in Revelation?

Furthermore, there are tandem statements made by God and Christ, both at the start and the end of John's book—in another example of his favorite literary device of framing:

> *God*: "I am the Alpha and the Omega." (1:8)
> *Christ*: "I am the first and the last." (1:17)

> *God*: "I am the Alpha and the Omega, the beginning and the end." (21:6)
> *Christ*: "I am the Alpha and the Omega, the first and the last, the beginning and the end." (22:13)

As you probably know, alpha (our letter A) and omega (our letter Z, as it were) are the first and last letters of the Greek alphabet. Hence that emphatic "I am" for both God and Christ is a claim of permanent presence, not of any departure and return or arrival after absence—not for God and not for Christ.

Hence, therefore, this more specific question: Does John's preference for "coming" derive from some contemporary model useful for imagining the consummation of God's Messianic/Christic *rule* on earth? Does some controlling model necessitate the use of "coming," exemplify its content, and facilitate its credibility?

As a prefatory remark, note that our English word "coming"—*parousia* in Greek and *adventus* in Latin—can range in contextual meaning from a casual visit by a friend, to an official visitation by an inspector, to a formal state visit by a ruler. And, for the recipients, each of those contacts could be restorative or punitive, consoling or threatening, good news or bad news. Here is a classic example of each option by Alexander the Great.

In November of 333 BCE, Alexander defeated Darius of Persia at Issus in northwestern Syria and, in the following spring, marched southward down the Levantine coast toward Egypt. First Tyre—for seven months—and then Gaza—for two—refused to surrender to his triumphant "coming" (*parousia*), and for that lack of submissive "reception" (*apantēsis*) those cites were besieged and devastated, their inhabitants enslaved or slaughtered.

According to the story—parable rather than history—in Josephus's *Jewish Antiquities*, Alexander was "in haste to go up to the city of Jerusalem," but the high priest Jaddus "was in an agony of fear, not knowing how he could meet (*apantēsei*) the Macedonians, whose king was angered by his former disobedience" (11.326) in maintaining loyalty to Darius over Alexander (11.317–20).

In his dilemma, Jaddus ordered sacrifices for divine protection and received this response that same night:

God spoke oracularly to him in his sleep, telling him to take courage and adorn the city with wreaths and open the gates and go out to meet them (*literally*, make the *hypantēsin*, or reception), and that the people should be in white garments. . . . And, after doing all the things that he had been told to do, he awaited the coming (*parousian*) of the king. (11.327–328)

As Alexander approached the city, Jaddus "went out with the priests and the citizens . . . making the reception (*hypantēsin*)" on Mt. Scopus (11.329). All went well, of course. Alexander prostrated himself before God, "gave his hand to the high priest and, with the Jews, entered the city," sacrificed in the Temple, and recognized that the book of Daniel had prophesied his victory over Persia (11.336–37; in Daniel 8, written in the 160s BCE).

Josephus's parable of divine protection shows that the coming (*parousia*) of an imperial conqueror can lead to either urban celebration or urban slaughter. It all depends on whether the city resists or submits, defends its walls or opens its doors. Everything depends on the public ritual of submission and the proper reception (*apantēsis*).

Both Paul of Tarsus and John of Patmos adopted that model of imperial visitation to imagine and announce the coming consummation of *God's rule* on earth. I look at Paul on Christ's "coming soon" in the rest of this chapter and then turn to John in the next chapter.

In the early 50s CE, local but lethal opposition in Thessalonica, capital of Rome's Macedonia province, forced Paul to flee south to Corinth, capital of its adjacent Achaia province. Concern for that persecution's effect on his Thessalonian converts—and maybe some defensive guilt at his own flight—had him stop at Athens to send

Timothy back for news. Timothy reported that all was well, but brought back a question from the Thessalonians, a query not so much abstractly theological or distantly eschatological as profoundly human and deeply personal.

They had understood from Paul that the consummation of *God's rule* would occur in their lifetime but what, now, about loved ones who had just died under persecution? Would "those who have died" (1 Thess. 4:13) be at some sort of disadvantage when the climactic culmination came? Paul's obvious answer could have been—but was not—like the response to that same general question asked later in another context.

In a book written around 100 CE, after the destruction of the Temple and the devastation of Jerusalem, a Jewish seer asks this plaintive question about those already dead before the end of time: "O Lord, you have charge of those who are alive at the end, but what will those do who lived before me, or we, ourselves, or those who come after us?" The answer from God is: "I shall liken my judgment to a circle; just as for those who are last there is no slowness, so for those who are first there is no haste" (4 Ezra 5:41–42).

At the end all will arise together simultaneously without any precedence one way or another. Paul could have simply replied that same way by denying any precedence for either the living or the dead but, instead, as a consolation for his bereaved questioners, he replied positively, that the dead would have a special advantage:

> For this we declare to you by the word of the Lord, that we
> who are alive, who are left until the coming (*parousian*) of the
> Lord, will by no means precede those who have died. For the
> Lord himself, with a cry of command, with the archangel's call
> and with the sound of God's trumpet, will descend from heaven,
> and the dead in Christ will rise first. Then we who are alive,
> who are left, will be caught up in the clouds together with them

to meet (*apantēsin*) the Lord in the air; and so we will be with
the Lord forever. (1 Thess. 4:15–17)

Notice that twice repeated is "we who are alive" as an indication that
Paul expects to be alive at the *rule*'s climactic moment. Be that as it may,
what makes that consolation credible to the Thessalonians are those two
Greek words—*parousia* for "coming" and *apantēsis* for "meeting."

In that context, those words are technical terms for the ceremonial
protocol involved in meeting the coming of a conquering general, important official, imperial emissary, or, especially, the emperor himself.
During a time of war, this protocol was a ceremony of submission and
surrender; during a time of peace, it was a ceremony of festivity and
celebration. In both cases, and because of its origins in surrender, the
city gates were opened wide and all of the town's dignitaries, dressed
in their finest and whitest garments, went outside the gates to greet
the coming visitor.

Paul presents Christ's "coming" (*parousia*) in 1 Thessalonians within
this well-known matrix of imperial visitation and its appropriate "meeting" (*apantēsis*). Apart from that use just seen in 1 Thessalonians 4:15,
Paul also mentions "our Lord Jesus at his coming (*parousia*)" in 2:19,
"the coming (*parousia*) of our Lord Jesus with all his saints" in 3:13, and
"the coming (*parousia*) of our Lord Jesus Christ" in 5:23.

This traditional model of imperial visitation gives Paul the following
five parallels in answer to his Thessalonian questioners. First, as with
imperial visitation, the coming of Christ does not derive from a preceding absence—as some sort of Return or Second Coming—but is an
explicit apparition, a climactic manifestation, an epiphanic revelation
of a permanent presence.

Second, within the vaunted Pax Romana ("Roman peace"), the
"golden age" of Roman imperialism that began with Augustus, nobody alive in Paul's Thessalonica had experienced an imperial visitation as other than a time of festival and rejoicing, an event of

congratulation and celebration. That common peaceful and joyful experience of imperial *parousia* is what Paul presumed in writing to the Thessalonians, and later to the Corinthians:

> Christ the first fruits, then at his coming (*parousia*) those who belong to Christ. Then comes the end, when he hands over the [earthly] *rule* to God the Father, after he has destroyed every ruler and every authority and power. For he must reign until he has put all his enemies under his feet. The last enemy to be destroyed is death. . . . When all things are subjected to him, then the Son himself will also be subjected to the one who put all things in subjection under him, so that God may be all in all. (1 Cor. 15:23–28)

Christ's *parousia* is therefore an occasion for rejoicing, a festival of success, and a ceremony of congratulation.

Third, as the citizens had to go outside their city to meet the emperor, so the Thessalonians would have to go outside their world "up in the clouds . . . to meet (*apantēsin*) the Lord in the air" (1 Thess. 4:17). They are simply going outside the world to meet its Ruler.

Fourth, in that imperial model, the coming one was first greeted outside but then accompanied inside the city. Alexander "gave his hand to the high priest and, with the Jews, entered the city" of Jerusalem in the legend cited above. For the Thessalonians, after that meeting in the air, among the clouds, outside the world, Paul does not imagine continuing upward with Christ to heaven, but rather moving "back inside," downward with Christ to a transfigured earth.

Fifth, since the tombs of the most honored dead lined the road leading to the city gates, in any imperial visitation they were the first to "greet" the emperor on his official arrival (think, for example, of the north road into Turkey's ancient city of Hierapolis). This brilliant insight from his imperial *parousia/apantēsis* model allowed Paul to assure the Thessalonians convincingly that the martyrs, as their most honored dead, would greet Christ first, after which the living would then do so.

Paul's scenario for the consummation of *God's rule* on earth was brilliantly reassuring for his disconsolate Thessalonians. It was also utterly plausible within the Pax Romana. For about eighty years after the victorious accession of Caesar Augustus as imperial *princeps*—first among equals, with all the equals dead—Roman urbanites had not known any *parousia* or *adventus* that did not entail congratulatory celebration and peaceful festivity.

Imperial coming as a time for urban rejoicing is depicted, for example, in the image of a fully oared galley, surrounded by the motto ADVENTUS AVG[V]STI, on coins minted at Corinth to celebrate the arrival there of the emperor Nero in 67 CE. Furthermore, an imperial *parousia* or *adventus* is an extremely appropriate model for Christ's coming for the following reason.

An imperial coming and reception was never simply a political or even religious event; it always had divine or transcendental connotations. *Parousia* has overtones of *epiphany*, of the manifestation of a divinity always present, the coming of one not absent beforehand. Here is a classic example of this coming/epiphany of one always divinely present.

At Trier in 291, an anonymous orator offered a birthday eulogy to Maximian Augustus, ruler of the Western Roman Empire. In this panegyric, Maximian's transalpine arrival into Italy is described as a divine epiphany:

> When from each summit of the Alps your deity first shone
> forth, a clearer light spread over all Italy. . . . Some god was

arising from those mountain tops, or by these steps descending
from heaven. . . . People invoked not the god transmitted
by conjecture but a visible and present Jupiter near at hand;
they adored Hercules not as a stranger but as the Emperor.
(*Panegyrici Latini* 11.10.4–5)

Since an imperial arrival was a divine epiphany, a present arrival did
not involve a preceding absence, as this birthday accolade insists:

Although Jupiter himself holds the highest point of heaven
above the clouds and above the winds sitting in perpetual
light, nevertheless his deity and mind spread through the
entire earth. I now make bold to proclaim about each of you
[emperors]: wherever you are, even if you retire to one place,
your divinity abides everywhere, all lands and all seas are
filled with you. (11.14.2–4)

And, of course, apart from transcendental ubiquity, imperial coins,
statues, and inscriptions made the divine emperor present everywhere
across the empire.

———————

As we just saw, the *parousia* of Christ for the Thessalonians—on the
western shores of the Aegean Sea after almost a century of the Pax
Romana—was easily imaginable and immediately credible as a joyful
and peaceful occasion. Who there had ever experienced an imperial
visitation as other than an occasion for celebration and feasting, sacrifices and entertainments?

Although John never uses the Greek word *parousia* for Christ's climactic presence, his reiterated term "coming" presumes and evokes that
same model of imperial visitation. John writes to seven urban commu-

nities on the eastern side of the Aegean Sea—in modern Turkey: "to Ephesus, to Smyrna, to Pergamum, to Thyatira, to Sardis, to Philadelphia, and to Laodicea" (Rev. 1:11).

A first question: Within that mode of imperial coming, does John imagine the climactic consummation of God's Messianic/Christic *rule* happening like Alexander's celebration at Jerusalem or like Alexander's slaughter at Tyre and Gaza?

Our first probe toward an answer focuses on John's favorite term for Christ—*the Lamb*—a term he uses almost thirty times throughout the book of Revelation. This figure is introduced as "a Lamb standing as if it had been slaughtered" (5:6); then referred to twice later as "the Lamb that was slaughtered" (5:12; 13:8); and twice again by "the blood of the Lamb" (7:14; 12:11). That first mention identifies this Lamb as Christ crucified ("slaughtered") and resurrected ("standing" up alive, not lying down dead).

Still, this crucified and resurrected Lamb moves swiftly from "slaughtered" to slaughtering: "No one in heaven or on earth or under the earth was able to open the scroll or to look into it" except the Lamb (5:3). The Christ/Lamb opens the first four seals on the scroll and releases four horses and riders to devastate the earth:

> *A white horse!* Its rider had a bow; a crown was given to him, and he came out conquering and to conquer.
>
> *Another horse, bright red*; its rider was permitted to take peace from the earth, so that people would slaughter one another; and he was given a great sword.
>
> *A black horse!* Its rider held a pair of scales in his hand . . . saying, "A quart of wheat for a day's pay . . ."
>
> *A pale green horse!* Its rider's name was Death, and Hades followed with him; they were given authority over a fourth of the earth, to kill with sword, famine, and pestilence, and by the wild animals of the earth. (6:2, 4, 5–6, 8)

Two points about those infamous four horsemen. First, earth's devastation starts with weapon, crown, and conquest—*conquering* is the thread that runs through the rest of what follows. *Conquest* is followed by *slaughter* and then by *famine*; finally *Death* crowns and completes the whole terrible troop. But the leader of the foursome is conquest.

Second, and this point is even more significant: It would be possible to mention those four horsemen neutrally, as a simple description of past and present time or, ironically, as a short history of civilization, a brief record of human progress. The four might even have been portrayed as what God allows or even how God punishes sin. But that is not what John does.

Instead, he announces: "The Lion of the tribe of Judah, the Root of David, has conquered, so that he can open the scroll and its seven seals" (5:5). Then, after that prelude, John introduces the Lamb for the first time (5:6), and it is this Lamb that opens those first four seals (6:1, 3, 5, 7) and releases the riders to devastate a quarter of the earth (6:8). For John, the nonviolent slaughtered Lamb becomes the violent slaughtering Lamb.

Finally, lest there be any way around that conclusion, the Lamb himself is explicitly and directly named later as the slaughterer: "The Lamb will conquer them, for he is Lord of lords and King of kings, and those with him are called and chosen and faithful" (17:14). There are no intervening horsemen to distract from the Lamb's direct action there—or here:

> There was a white horse! Its rider is called Faithful and True, and in righteousness he judges and makes war. . . . From his mouth comes a sharp sword with which to strike down the nations, and he will rule them with a rod of iron; he will tread the wine press of the fury of the wrath of God the Almighty. On his robe and on his thigh he has a name inscribed, "King of kings and Lord of lords." (19:11, 15–16)

Christ, wearing "a robe dipped in blood" leads "the armies of heaven . . . on white horses" (19:13–14), and it is impossible not to remember that the first horseman also rode a white horse and "came out conquering and to conquer." (Did John not notice or not care about that coincidence—or deliberately intend it?) Be that as it may, what comes before and after that war scene (19:11–16) is an even more terrible scenario, which frames it.

Before the war scene, a lovely festival scene in 19:1–10 announces that "the marriage of the Lamb has come, and his bride has made herself ready" (19:7). An angel proclaims: "Blessed are those who are invited to the marriage supper of the Lamb" (19:9). After that introduction, readers presume that a wedding scene will come next. But we do not hear more about this wedding until much later when John sees "the holy city, the new Jerusalem, coming down out of heaven from God, prepared as a bride adorned for her husband" (21:2). Only then do we meet "the bride, the wife of the Lamb" (21:9; 22:17). But in Revelation 19, instead of an expected wedding scene, we get that war scene.

After the war scene, and indeed as its continuation, in 19:17–21, "the kings of the earth with their armies gathered to make war against the rider on the horse and against his army" but "were killed by the sword of the rider on the horse, the sword that came from his mouth" (19:19, 21).

Then, in a shocking transformation of the "wedding supper of the Lamb" (19:7, 9), an angel "called to all the birds that fly in midheaven, 'Come, gather for the great supper of God, to eat the flesh of kings, the flesh of captains, the flesh of the mighty, the flesh of horses and their riders—flesh of all, both free and slave, both small and great.' . . . And all the birds were gorged with their flesh" (19:17–18, 21).

As we saw at the start of the last chapter, Isaiah 25:6–8 depicted God's eschatological *rule* on earth as a splendid feast for "all peoples . . . all nations" and as a wiping "away the tears from all faces." For John, however, that consummation entails no feast *for* all the nations; instead, it is a feast *of* them for all the vultures.

Finally, as we also saw at the start of the last chapter and is often emphasized by commentators, John concludes Revelation with his own magnificent variation on Isaiah's description of the finally transformed earth: "See, the home of God is among mortals. . . . They will be his peoples" (21:3; note the plural "peoples"). It is a glorious conclusion, a marriage of heaven and earth, but located on earth rather than in heaven. That earthly location is emphasized by the framing phrases about "the holy city, the new Jerusalem, *coming down* out of heaven from God" (21:2, 10).

Still, ever, and always, this wedding feast is also a victory feast, and here is another metaphor for that battle victory—here is the "Battle Hymn of Revelation":

> The angel swung his sickle over the earth and gathered the vintage of the earth, and he threw it into the great wine press of the wrath of God. And the wine press was trodden outside the city, and blood flowed from the wine press, as high as a horse's bridle, for a distance of about two hundred miles. (14:19–20)

Isaiah had foreseen "a feast of well-aged wines . . . of well-aged wines strained clear" (25:6), but John has blood for wine, and you wade to that glorious wedding feast through a sea of blood.

Here, then, is the rather obvious question for our next chapter. After about eighty years of the Pax Romana, Paul could credibly use the model of imperial visitation for the peaceful consummation of *God's rule* on earth and Christ's coming/*parousia* for celebratory congratulations.

But how, after another fifty or so years of that same Pax Romana, can John persuasively present his magnificently peaceful vision of Christ's *coming* in Revelation 21:1–5, 9–10, but only after having first passed through "blood . . . as high as a horse's bridle, for a distance of about two hundred miles" (14:20)? How can Christ, the imperial "King of kings," be plausibly portrayed in that Roman context as the Lamb, slaughtered but slaughtering?

Where, within the contemporary experience of Rome's emperor-style coming, does John get that vision of Christ, the rider on the white horse, from whose "mouth comes a sharp sword with which to strike down the nations, [whom] he will rule . . . with a rod of iron," and who "will tread the wine press of the fury of the wrath of God the Almighty" (19:15)?

How can John, unlike Paul, persuasively describe Christ's coming with repeated scenes of extreme violence, with almost hypnotically repeated scenarios of ghastly slaughter?

Summarily and bluntly, for the next chapter: What *model* does John presume and use as the hopefully persuasive matrix for his vision of victory? What *model* made it possible for him to communicate his message and sound credible to his audience within the triumphant Pax Romana?

3

THE ONCE AND FUTURE BEAST

TWICE, AND ONLY TWICE, IN THE ENTIRE BOOK OF REVELA-
tion, John pauses and directly addresses his readers with these
peremptory warnings:

> This calls for wisdom: let anyone with understanding calculate
> the number of the beast, for it is the number of a person. Its
> number is six hundred sixty-six. (13:18)

> This calls for a mind that has wisdom: the seven heads are seven
> mountains on which the woman is seated; also, they are seven
> kings. (17:9)

Having reached those places, readers are over halfway through the
book, and it seems a little late to call for understanding and wisdom
from recipients already reeling under the kaleidoscopic onslaught of
John's ever-changing metaphorical imagery. But, granted that, we must
still pay special attention to those two texts in their immediately surrounding contexts.

For what is such special insight needed at those particular places? And do they both refer to the same mysterious subject? Furthermore, how will wisdom and understanding about them help answer this chapter's question about John's model for his vision of Christ's coming as an imperial devastation despite the exultant Pax Romana?

––––––––

On Revelation 13:18. To begin, reread that former admonition once more and notice its triple structure: the *number* of the beast is the *number* of a person is the *number* 666. In what follows, we will look at the identity of the person coded 666 and why that person is termed "the beast" or, better, "the Beast."

How do we establish the identity of that person coded by the number 666? It depends on a process called *gematria* (invented—to my mind—by people with too much time on their hands—sorry!). Gematria assigns numerical values to letters, so that a word always has a numerical equivalent. The twenty-two letters and five letter variants of the Hebrew alphabet, for example, are assigned gematria numbers as follows: the first nine letters get numbers 1–9, the next nine letters get numbers 10–90 (by 10s); and the final nine letters get numbers 100–900 (by 100s).

Based on that Jewish tradition, the imperial person coded by the number 666 is the emperor Nero, who ruled from 54 to 68 CE. His full titular name was Nero Claudius Caesar Augustus Germanicus, which is abbreviated in English as NERO CAESAR or in transcribed Hebrew as NRWN QSR. Then, according to Hebrew gematria, N is 50, R 200, W 6, N 50, Q 100, S 60, and R 200, so Nero Caesar is cumulatively identified as 666.

That mode of alphanumerical cipher may seem strange to us, but its usage is confirmed by the *Fifth Sibylline Oracle*, a Jewish apocalypse contemporary with the Christian one of John. This text needs some introduction, as it will be of great comparative significance throughout this chapter.

First, in the triangular pendentives above the windows of Michelangelo's magnificent Sistine Chapel are five female figures called sibyls—one each from Persia, Egypt, and Rome, but two from Greece, including the most famous of them all, the ecstatic oracular prophetess at Delphi. Interspersed with those unnamed female sibyls are seven named male prophets—Jonah, Jeremiah, Ezekiel, Joel, Zechariah, Isaiah, and Daniel. For Michelangelo, prophets and sibyls, Jews and Gentiles, that is, the whole world, both foretold and awaited the advent of *God's rule* on earth.

Sibyls were the Gentile equivalent of the Jewish prophets, and both kinds of visionaries announced the future under divine inspiration. Although oracles, or pronouncements, by sibyls were originally a Gentile creation, from 100 BCE to 600 CE they were adopted and adapted by the Jewish and Christian traditions, which produced their own *Sibylline Oracles*. (We met two Jewish *Sibylline Oracles* in Chapter 1.)

The *Fifth Sibylline Oracle* begins by recounting the "woeful history of the Latin race" from its origins to the late second century (*Sib. Or.* 5.1). In this list, imperial rulers are not identified directly by name, but indirectly by their first initials given numerically in Greek gematria. Nero is described as "one who has fifty as an initial" (*Sib. Or.* 5.28). Once again N is given the number 50 by gematria in Hebrew—or Greek. Well over a hundred years later, another—but pro-Roman—Jewish author copied that section on the emperors and identified Nero once again as "another man, of the number fifty" (*Sib. Or.* 12.78).

Granted, then, that 666 codes the Roman emperor Nero, why is he also the Beast? Is that just nasty name-calling (they go low, we go lower)?

In the Christian Bible the Beast appears twice in Daniel (7:6, 11), but then reappears over thirty times throughout Revelation. The first teaser mention is as "the beast that comes up from the bottomless pit" (11:7;

see also 17:1), but then, after that semi-introduction, the Beast appears a dozen times in Revelation 13, where, as we just saw, it is climactically identified as the emperor Nero (13:18).

We begin, therefore, with John's biblical basis in Daniel 7. In Daniel's night vision, "Four great beasts came up out of the sea, different from one another. . . . The first was like a lion, . . . a second one, that looked like a bear, . . . another appeared, like a leopard" (Dan. 7:2–6). Those beasts represent three great past empires:

The lion is the Babylonian or Chaldean Empire (7:4), ruled by Nebuchadnezzar (2:1–5:18) and Belshazzar (5:1).

The bear is the Median Empire (7:5), ruled by the alleged "Darius the Mede" (5:31; 11:1) or "Darius . . . a Mede" (9:1).

The leopard is the Persian Empire (7:6), represented by "Cyrus the Persian" (6:28) or "Cyrus of Persia" (10:1).

Based on Daniel's vision, John "saw a beast rising out of the sea, having . . . seven heads. . . . And the beast that I saw was like a leopard, its feet were like a bear's, and its mouth was like a lion's mouth" (Rev. 13:1–2). In Daniel, three predatory wild beasts designated successive empires, but John combined all three into his single sea beast, namely, the Roman Empire itself.

But then John immediately shifts the imagery from the Roman Empire in general to a particular part of it: "One of its heads seemed to have received a death-blow, but its mortal wound had been healed" (13:3). One head of the Beast designates one emperor of the Roman Empire— but which one, and why is he described as surviving a fatal wound?

In the next section, John moves from "sea beast"—the Roman Empire—to "land beast"—the Roman emperors: "I saw another beast that rose out of the earth. . . . It exercises all the authority of the first beast on its behalf" (13:11–12). But, once again, John moves immediately from emperors in general to that same particular emperor singled out before (13:3). This land beast:

> makes the earth and its inhabitants worship the first beast, whose mortal wound had been healed. (13:12)

and

> deceives the inhabitants of earth, telling them to make an image for the beast that had been wounded by the sword and yet lived. (13:14)

This special emperor was mortally wounded and yet is healed and alive. The Beast morphs from Roman Empire as sea beast to Roman emperors as land beast but, in both cases, moves immediately to focus on one emperor described as wounded but healed and finally identified as Nero (13:18). In other words, for John, the Beast is an imperial conglomerate involving the Roman Empire in general, the Roman emperors in particular, and the emperor Nero as a special case.

But how and why is Nero the emperor described as mortally wounded yet healed and alive? Hold that question, as we turn next to the second of those twin admonitions seen at the start of this chapter (13:18; 17:9).

On Revelation 17:9. At this point we move beyond any double identification such as mortally wounded yet healed/alive to a striking triple identification:

> The beast that you saw *was, and is not, and is about to ascend* from the bottomless pit and go to destruction. And the

inhabitants of the earth, whose names have not been written
in the book of life from the foundation of the world, will be
amazed when they see the beast, because it *was and is not and is
to come.* (17:8)

In framing phrases, the Beast is identified now as "was, and is not, and
is about to ascend" and "was and is not and is to come."

Next, we get that call for wisdom (17:9) and are then told of how
that just-identified beast/emperor fits into a sequence of eight kings/
emperors: "They are seven kings, of whom five have fallen, one is living,
and the other has not yet come; and when he comes, he must remain
only a little while. As for the beast that was and is not, it is an eighth
but it belongs to the seven, and it goes to destruction" (17:9–11).

Scholars intensely debate how to identify that imperial sequence
primarily because it *might* help date the writing of the book. A good
option is that the five dead emperors are Augustus, Tiberius, Caligula,
Claudius, and Nero; the living one is Vespasian, and the coming briefly
reigning one is Titus.

In other words, John wants us to conclude that he is writing under
Vespasian (69–79), prophesying—correctly!—the future brief reign of
Titus (79–81), and therefore foretelling—also correctly—everything
else about the future as well. Maybe John is writing under the actual
eighth emperor, Domitian (81–96), but, if so, Domitian is of no interest
to him. Be that as it may, for here and now, we focus on these three
parallel descriptions:

The beast that . . . was, and is not, and is about to ascend from
the bottomless pit and go to destruction. (17:8a)

The beast [that] was and is not and is to come. (17:8b)

The beast that was and is not, it is an eighth but it belongs to
the seven, and it goes to destruction. (17:11)

The Beast here, once again—and granted the required interpretive "wisdom"—refers to Nero. But now the question is even more complicated: How is Nero the emperor who was wounded mortally yet is healed/alive? How is he the emperor who "was and is not and is to come" ("come," *parestai* in Greek, from which we also get *parousia*)? How is he the emperor who is both inside the first seven emperors as their fifth and outside the first seven emperors as their eighth—at the same time?

The answer to those questions takes us back to those Jewish *Sibylline Oracles* in general, to the *Fifth Sibylline Oracle* in particular, and to the strange legend of Nero's Return, or *Nero Redivivus*—literally "Nero Alive Again," although "Nero Still Alive" would be more accurate according to the legend.

Populist leaders who depart this world under mysterious circumstances with missions unfinished often generate legends in which they are not actually dead but hidden away pending a future return. Also, such legends often morph from historical possibilities into mythical options or even eschatological hopes with national or even cosmic dimensions.

Classic examples are the unhistorical fifth/sixth-century King Arthur as the "once and future king" and the historical twelfth-century Holy Roman Emperor Frederick Barbarossa as the "sleeping hero" awaiting revival in a forested mountain cave. But why would John even imagine Nero as the once and future emperor, as the imperial Beast "[that] was and is not and is to come"? Why is John interested in Nero's Return or in "Nero Still Alive"?

Why, after 64, when Nero slaughtered Christians for causing the great Roman fire, would any Christian want him *still alive*? Why, after 66, when Nero sent sixty thousand soldiers to attack Israel, would any Jew want him *still alive*? Why, after 69, when he escaped senatorial execution by suicide, would any Roman want him *still alive*? Why would anyone anywhere want Nero *back alive*?

Answer: The Greek East did not see Nero as did the Latin West, and it was able to imagine him *still alive* and returning east to west against Rome itself. Watch, then, how a legend is born.

In 63, Nero negotiated a compromise to end the Roman-Parthian war over Armenia and that peace endeared him at least to Parthia.

In 67, Nero lived the entire year in Greece. He participated in the most important festival games in both lyre contests and chariot races (he always won!). He started the daunting technical challenge of cutting a canal through the Isthmus of Corinth; and, as he departed, he freed Greece from paying taxes to Rome. All of that endeared him at least to Greece—high and low alike.

In 68, Nero committed suicide and, within a year, the stories of Nero's Return (Nero Redivivus) were born. It started immediately on a historical level with a first imposter claiming to be the real Nero returning from the east.

In 69, "Achaia and Asia were terrified by a false rumor of Nero's arrival. The reports with regard to his death had been varied, and therefore many people imagined and believed that he was alive" (Tacitus, *Histories* 2.8). After traveling eastward to raise a rebellion, this unnamed pseudo-Nero was eventually captured and executed. But, whether for safety or irony, his body was then shipped back to Rome (2.9).

In 79, as Titus replaced his father, Vespasian, as Roman emperor, "a false Nero appeared, who was an Asiatic named Terentius Maximus. He resembled Nero both in appearance and in voice (for he too sang to the accompaniment of the lyre). He gained a few followers in Asia and in his advance to the Euphrates attached a far greater number. He finally sought refuge with Artabanus, the Parthian leader, who, because of his anger against Titus, both received him and set about making preparations to restore him to Rome" (Cassius Dio, *Roman History* 66.19.3).

That was a far fuller and much more dangerous incarnation of the legend: the still-alive Nero traveled from the Roman Empire across the Euphrates to the Parthian Empire—Rome's only imperial opponent—and planned a war between Parthia and Rome to restore him to his throne.

In 88, Dio Chrysostom summed up those Nero imposters with this laconic comment: "Even now everybody wishes he were still alive. And the great majority do believe that he is, although in a certain sense he has died not once but often along with those who had been firmly convinced that he was still alive" (*Discourse 21: On Beauty* 9).

In the 90s, when a still-alive Nero would have been in his sixties, it was still possible to imagine his historical return with Parthian armies to devastate Rome. The *Fourth Sibylline Oracle*, written in that decade, says:

> A great king will flee from Italy like a runaway slave unseen and unheard over the channel of the Euphrates. . . . Then the strife of war being aroused will come to the west and the fugitive from Rome will also come, brandishing a great spear having crossed the Euphrates with many myriads. (4.119–20, 137–39)

Most scholars date John's apocalypse to that same decade, so that we have the legend of Nero's Return in both a Jewish and a Christian text from that same time. It is clear, of course, that, for both writers, their inclusion of Nero's Return was born not of their love for him, but of their hope that he might lead Parthia to devastate Rome—*soon*.

Still, by the early decades of the second century, Nero would be securely dead and his return—if maintained—had to morph from a historical event into a myth or even an eschatological hope. The *Fifth Sibylline Oracle*, written in the 120s, has five separate sections on Nero's Return as if, almost obsessively, it cannot get away from it. Also, climactically, the fifth section elevates Nero; his battleground is no longer merely imperial war—now it's eschatological conflict.

Just to remind you, all of this prepares us to understand why Nero is so important in John's Revelation and where he gets his model for Christ's cataclysmic *parousia, adventus,* or coming. Here is a swift survey of the *Fifth Sibylline Oracle's* five sections about *Nero's Return.*

In the first section, Nero, coded as "one who has fifty as an initial," is described as

> a terrible snake, breathing out grievous war, who one day will lay hands on his own family and slay them, and throw everything into confusion, athlete, charioteer, murderer, who dares ten thousand things. He will also cut the mountain between two seas and defile it with gore. (5.28–32)

Those are the standard attributes of Nero in the *Fifth Sibylline Oracle*: he murdered his mother, Agrippina, in 59, competed in Greek festival games, and attempted to create the Corinthian canal. It concludes: "Even when he disappears, he will be destructive. Then he will return declaring himself equal to God" (5.33–34).

In the second section, Rome is warned: "The Persian will . . . destroy your land . . . a savage-minded man . . . with a full host numerous as sand, bringing destruction on you" (5.93–97). But then the text takes on transcendental or eschatological overtones: "The one who obtained the land of the Persians will fight and, killing every man, he will destroy all life so that a one-third portion will remain for wretched mortals" (5.101–3). He will only be stopped by a messianic opponent, "a certain king sent from God against him" (5.108).

In the third section, "a great king of great Rome, a god-like man from Italy, will cut the ridge of the isthmus . . . playing at theatricals. . . . He will flee from Babylon [Rome] . . . come to the Medes and the king of the Persians. . . . On his appearance the whole creation was shaken" (5.143, 147, 152). Once again there are eschatological overtones, but Nero is especially indicted for starting the war that ended in the destruction of Jerusalem's Temple.

In the fourth section, Greece is singled out for special destruction: "Corinth, bewail the mournful destruction within you. . . . The one who is now fleeing deceitfully . . . who formerly cut out the rock with ductile bronze . . . to him God gave strength to perform things like no previous one of the kings. . . . Murder and terrors are in store for all men" (5.214–21). There are again cosmic and universal overtones, but also special mention of what Nero started against Jerusalem, "the great city and righteous people," in 69 (5.226).

In the fifth and climactic section, the pseudohistorical is absorbed into the eschatological quite completely. It begins by announcing: "There will come to pass in the last time . . . a war that will throw the world into confusion and be deceptive in guile. A man who is a matricide will come from the ends of the earth [Rome] in flight and . . . will destroy every land and conquer all. . . . Blood will flow up to the bank of deep-eddying rivers, . . . fire will rain on men from the floors of heaven . . . to destroy at once all kings and noble men" (5.361–80).

But then, after a detailed description of the return of Nero morphing into terrible eschatological warfare, the conclusion is serenely magnificent: "Then the piteous destruction of war will cease and no longer will anyone fight with swords or iron or with weapons at all, which will no longer be lawful. A wise people which is left will have peace, having experienced evil so that it might later rejoice" (5.381–85).

In that whole section, Nero is no longer imagined as simply the leader of the Persian/Parthian Empire in a historical attack against the Roman Empire. Instead his coming involves an eschatological onslaught against evil before the establishment of *God's rule* on earth (5.381–85).

On June 9 in 68, the thirty-year-old Nero, helped by his secretary and witnessed only by him, committed suicide in flight outside Rome. The year 68 saw the dismal end of the hundred-year-old Julio-Claudian dynasty, and the year 69 saw four emperors violently competing for power. In the eastern Roman Empire, the response was to deny Nero's death, assert his flight across the Euphrates, and expect his imminent return with Persian/Parthian forces to destroy Rome. As that legend developed through imposters and morphed from a historical to an eschatological hope, Nero's Return was ready at hand for John to use in his Messianic/Christic apocalypse. But why does he want it and how does he use it?

First, God is identified by a title containing three time elements: "who is and who was and who is to come" (Rev. 1:4, 8; 4:8). Nero is also identified by a title with three time elements: "was, and is not, and is" (17:8a, 11) and "was and is not and is to come" (17:8b). There is a deliberate similarity between those threefold titles, but God's "was and *is*" is obviously superior to Nero's "was and *is not*."

Next, Christ is "a Lamb standing as if it had been slaughtered" (5:6) and "the Lamb that was slaughtered" (5:12; 13:8). That juxtaposition of "standing" and "slaughtered" points to Christ as crucified and resurrected and, despite a double mention of "the blood of the Lamb" (7:14; 12:11), that slaughtered Lamb is very much—and very violently—alive (17:14). But, even granted that superiority, why does John make that comparison?

Nero, of course, is the Beast who "received a death-blow, but its mortal wound had been healed, . . . the beast whose mortal wound had been healed, . . . the beast that had been wounded by the sword and yet lived" (13:3, 12, 14). Nero, dead by "sword," and Christ, dead by "crucifixion" (11:18), are both dead yet alive, but of course Nero is but a caricature of Christ, who says, "I was dead, and see, I am alive forever and ever; and I have the keys of Death and of Hades" (1:18). Still, once again, granted that transcendental superiority of Christ over Nero, why does John even make linguistic parallels between them?

This is where we see the answer to this chapter's main question. Unlike those Jewish apocalypses before and after it, John's Christian apocalypse does not celebrate Nero, slain yet alive, *coming soon* as avenger on Rome and destroyer of evil. Instead, he uses it as a *model* to make credible the Lamb, slain yet alive, *coming soon* as avenger on Rome and destroyer of evil.

Within the general matrix of the Pax Romana, the legend of Nero's Return gives John a perfect *model* for an imperial *parousia/adventus/* coming that includes both the devastation of the Roman Empire on a historical level and the destruction of evil on an eschatological level. Not Nero's Return, or Nero Redivivus, but Christ's Return, or Christus Redivivus, is what is "coming soon" (1:1; 2:16; 3:11; 22:6, 7, 12, 20).

The Roman focus of the *Fourth Sibylline Oracle* is on apocalyptic vengeance for what Rome did to the Jewish people and their Temple in the great war of 66–74. Although this oracle imagines a future "happy mankind on earth . . . that will reject all temples" (4.24–27), it still indicts Rome for "an evil war . . . upon Jerusalem from Italy" and for "sacking the great Temple of God" (4.115–16). It describes Titus, then emperor-to-be, as "a leader of Rome who will come to Syria and burn the Temple of Jerusalem with fire, at the same time slaughter many men and destroy the great land of the Jews with its broad roads" (4.125–27; see also 5.397–413).

John has no interest whatsoever in Jerusalem's *physical* Temple, which was destroyed by Titus in August of 70. That event cannot explain the ferocity of the divine vengeance he prophecies for the Roman Empire.

Instead, as we have already seen, John imagines a completely different *spiritual* temple in Revelation. First, the archetypal temple of God is in heaven: "the temple of my God" (3:12), "the temple of God" (11:1), "God's temple in heaven" (11:19), "the temple in heaven" (14:17), "the temple of the tent of witness in heaven" (15:5). In heaven too is that temple's "golden altar" before God (8:3; 9:13).

Next, that heavenly temple appears on earth not as a Christian building in any one place, but as the Christian community united across every place. That is why *all* Christians are priests in this living temple-as-community (1:6; 5:10).

Finally, and climactically, John "saw the holy city, the new Jerusalem, coming down out of heaven from God" (21:1–2). But in this new Jerusalem on a new earth, "I saw no temple in the city, for its temple is the Lord God the Almighty and the Lamb" (21:22), and all Christians everywhere are priests of this transcendental temple on earth.

John's visions of implacable divine vengeance on Rome derives not from its destruction of God's *physical* Temple and its slaughter of the *Jewish* people, but from Rome's destruction of God's *spiritual* temple and its slaughter of the *Christian* people. That is why John gives us this terrible image of slaughtered Christians:

> I saw under the altar the souls of those who had been
> slaughtered for the word of God and for the testimony they
> had given; they cried out with a loud voice, "Sovereign Lord,
> holy and true, how long will it be before you judge and avenge
> our blood on the inhabitants of the earth?" They were each
> given a white robe and told to rest a little longer, until the
> number would be complete both of their fellow servants and
> of their brothers and sisters, who were soon to be killed as they
> themselves had been killed. (6:9–11)

Sometimes in reading Revelation, you get the impression that slaughtering Christians is Rome's major imperial activity. Rome ordered that "those who would not worship the image of the beast be killed" (13:15) and "was drunk with the blood of the saints and the blood of the witnesses to Jesus" (17:6). Really?

On the other hand, the author of Revelation identifies himself as "I, John, your brother who share with you in Jesus the persecution, . . . was on the island called Patmos because of the word of God and the testimony of Jesus" (1:9). John was not executed but exiled to Patmos, and only one other named Christian was executed: "Antipas my witness, my faithful one, who was killed" (2:13).

In the light of all this, we are left with one rather searing—and very contemporary—question about the book of Revelation. If there was no Roman slaughter of Christians under Domitian in the immediate past, *why does John invent it to justify a divine slaughter of Romans under Christ in the imminent future?*

We begin the answer to that ultimate question—the solution to John's basic purpose, and the meaning of Revelation's intention—in the next chapter and complete it in the final chapter of Part One.

4

AMONG THESE DARK
SATANIC HILLS

T HE METAPHORICAL ADVERSARY KNOWN AS THE BEAST IS, AS just seen, an imperial conglomerate involving the Roman Empire, the Roman emperors, and especially the emperor Nero as Nero Redivivus, or Nero Returning, the once and future emperor, "the beast [that] was and is not and is to come" (Rev. 17:8b).

Two other metaphorical adversaries appear in close conjunction with the Beast. The Beast had "ten horns and seven heads; and on its horns were ten diadems, and on its heads were blasphemous names" (13:1). Two associated protagonists manifest similar endowments of heads, horns, diadems, and names.

The first character is the *Red Dragon, the Ruler of the Beast*. It "appeared in heaven," "a great red dragon, with seven heads and ten horns, and seven diadems on his heads" (12:3). People "worshiped the dragon, for he had given his authority to the beast" (13:4).

The second character is the *Great Whore, the Rider of the Beast*. She is "the great whore who is seated on many waters, . . . a woman sitting on a scarlet beast that was full of blasphemous names, and it had seven heads and ten horns" (17:1, 3).

The Dragon, the Beast, and the Great Whore are linked together by each having ten horns and seven heads The Dragon and the Beast are linked by having either seven or ten diadems. The Beast and the Whore are linked by having "blasphemous names." In Revelation, those very special qualifications unite to hold closely together the Dragon, the Beast, and the Whore—in that order of precedence.

Based on that unholy trinity, here are the questions for this chapter: What is the Dragon? Who is the Whore? How do the Dragon and the Whore help toward understanding the ferocious violence described in the book of Revelation—first by Rome against Christ and soon by Christ against Rome?

———

We begin with the Dragon, the Ruler of the Beast. Twice in Revelation, the great Red Dragon is identified by three other names in the same sequence: "serpent," "Devil," and "Satan" (note indefinite and definite pronouns below):

> The great dragon was thrown down, that ancient *serpent,*
> who is called *Devil* and *the Satan*, the deceiver of the whole
> world—he was thrown down to the earth, and his angels were
> thrown down with him. (12:9)

> He seized the dragon, that ancient *serpent,* who is *Devil* and *the
> Satan*, and bound him for a thousand years. (20:2)

John presumes two earlier tales about this dragon, the Dragon as serpent and the Dragon as the Satan, and, in retelling them, he deliberately turns them upside down theologically. Although he also fuses them smoothly into a single saga, they are separated here for purposes of clarity.

The first of John's two intertwined tales focuses on the *Dragon as the serpent* and, in the process, presents a Christian *subversion* of an older imperial tradition.

In Greco-Roman mythology, Zeus, king of the gods, impregnated the mortal woman Leto and thereby aroused the jealousy of his wife, the goddess Hera. She sent Python, a serpent-dragon living at the earth's center, in pursuit of Leto in order to slay her offspring at birth. But Leto's twins, the divine Apollo and divine Artemis, were born safely, and Apollo slew Python in revenge for his failed attack on Leto. Apollo, of course, was the divine father of Caesar Augustus and the god of order, prophecy, and truth.

Think of four acts: birthing mother, attacking monster, saved off-spring, and divine triumph, and watch how John retells that Roman mythopoetic tale as a Christian one.

The *birthing mother* is now "a woman clothed with the sun, with the moon under her feet, and on her head a crown of twelve stars. She was pregnant and was crying out in birth pangs, in the agony of giving birth" (12:1–2). Individual Leto is now the communal personification of the people of God.

The *attacking monster* is now "a great red dragon, with seven heads and ten horns, and seven diadems on his heads, . . . [who] stood before the woman who was about to bear a child, so that he might devour her child as soon as it was born" (12:3–4). The serpent-dragon Python is now the serpent-dragon Satan.

The *saved offspring* is "a son, a male child, who is to rule all the nations with a rod of iron. But her child was snatched away and taken to God and to his throne" (12:5). This is God's Messiah, born of the Messianic/Christic people of God.

The *divine triumph* is not now Apollos's, but Christ's: "Now have come the salvation and the power and the *rule* of our God and the authority of his Messiah" (12:10).

There is, of course, a searing polemical irony in that parallel. In

Roman symbolism, Apollo, representing heavenly and superhuman imperial order, overcame Python, representing earthly and subhuman cosmic disorder. In Christian symbolism, God's Messiah/Christ of course represents heavenly and superhuman divine order, but the figure representing earthly and subhuman cosmic disorder that he overcomes is now *Rome*.

The second of John's two intertwined tales focuses on the *Dragon as the Satan* and, in the process, presents a Christian development of an older biblical tradition. That development takes the Satan through four roles: cosmic inspector, humanity's tempter, rebel angel, and enemy within, to become a major protagonist in John's apocalyptic scenario.

In the book of Job, God is imagined presiding over a celestial court in heaven rather like the Persian emperor at Persepolis on earth. Among those celestial courtiers is the Satan, God's attorney general for earthly affairs, a *cosmic inspector*. "One day the heavenly beings came to present themselves before the LORD, and the Satan also came among them. The LORD said to the Satan, 'Where have you come from?' The Satan answered the LORD, 'From going to and fro on the earth, and from walking up and down on it'" (Job 1:6–7). At this stage, the Satan is a servant of divinity and a spy on humanity. (Note that "the Satan" is a role with a title while "Satan" is the personal name of an individual!)

The Satan as God's attorney general can easily morph into an *agent provocateur*, an undercover agent who entraps or provokes humans to sin, *humanity's tempter*. Compare these two accounts of David counting the Israelites to determine taxation rates: The earlier account says that "the anger of the LORD was kindled against Israel, and he incited David against them" (2 Sam. 24:1). But the later revision exculpates God and says instead that "Satan stood up against Israel, and incited David to count the people of Israel" (1 Chron. 21:1).

The Satan as *rebel angel* appears in the *Life of Adam and Eve*, an extrabiblical writing from the end of the first century. Adam asks Satan why he pursues and deceives him. Satan explains that, after humans were created in God's image and likeness—according to Genesis 1:26—all the angels were ordered to worship them. But Satan said: "I will not worship one inferior and subsequent to me. . . . I will set my throne above the stars of heaven and will be like the Most High" (*Life* 14.3; 15.3). For that, Satan and all other angels who refused to worship humans were cast out of heaven forever.

Watch next how John retells that story:

> War broke out in heaven; Michael and his angels fought against
> the dragon. The dragon and his angels fought back, but they
> were defeated, and there was no longer any place for them
> in heaven. The great dragon was thrown down, that ancient
> serpent, who is called Devil and the Satan, the deceiver of the
> whole world—he was thrown down to the earth, and his angels
> were thrown down with him. (Rev. 12:7–9)

John speaks not only of angelic insubordination and rebellion, but of transcendental heavenly warfare. But John makes an even more profound development in this ancient tradition of the Satan and his fallen angels: it is not the ascendancy of Adam but of *Christ* that causes the rebellion of the Satan in heaven. As the triumphant Christ ascends to heaven, the recusant Satan descends to earth.

Cast down from heaven to earth, the Satan is granted predatory control here below "for one thousand two hundred sixty days" (11:3; 12:6) or "for forty-two months" (11:2; 13:5) or "for a time, and times, and half a time" (12:14). Whether given in days, months, or years, that is simply taken from "a time, two times, and half a time" in Daniel (7:25; 12:7) and means three and a half years.

Since the time span between Jesus's departure to heaven and return to earth already far exceeded any such literal time span, a year, two years, and half a year must be taken symbolically to mean a very short time. For John, three and a half is a cipher for "short."

Still, "Woe to the earth and the sea, for the devil has come down to you with great wrath, because he knows that his time is short!" (Rev. 12:12). "Short" is the time span for earthly persecution, for making "war on . . . those who keep the commandments of God and hold the testimony of Jesus" (12:17).

Similarly, with the Satan's next time span. After those three and a half years of earthly predation, an angel "seized the dragon, that ancient serpent, who is Devil and the Satan, and bound him for a thousand years" (20:2). But, when the thousand years are ended, the Satan is released from his prison (20:3, 7) as if on parole. But, because of his intransigent evil, "the devil . . . was thrown into the lake of fire and sulfur," where he "will be tormented day and night forever and ever" (20:10).

When three and a half years are given as the time of persecution from Jesus's departure to his return and one thousand years are given as the time of vindication thereafter, those numbers must be read not temporally and chronologically but symbolically and comparatively to mean "a very short time" of earthly suffering against "a very long time" of heavenly triumph.

The Satan is also the *enemy within*. From its experience of great empires from the Assyrians to the Babylonians, Israel knew all about overwhelming military domination. But with the Greeks and Romans such imperial domination also involved overweening cultural ascendancy. And, although military power controls you *externally*, cultural power invades you *internally*. Thence these *cultural* challenges: Could you be a good Jew and a good Greek at the same time? Could you be a good Christian and a good Roman at the same time? What about that slippery slope of adaptation, accommodation, assimilation, acculturation?[1]

Elaine Pagels, a religious historian at Princeton University, argues: "This greatest and most dangerous enemy did not originate, as one might expect, as an outsider, an alien, or a stranger. Satan is not the distant enemy but the intimate enemy—one's trusted colleague, close associate, brother."[2] The Satan is—far more dangerously—the one who accommodates from within rather than the one who oppresses from without. The Satan is the outsider already inside.

Phillip Cole, a social philosopher at the University of the West of England (Bristol), agrees that Satan is the archetypal *rebel within*, the transcendental model for *internal revolt*, for what politics calls the "traitor" and religion calls the "heretic." Opponents or enemies are often—unfortunately—called demonic or diabolical, but it is especially the *insider enemy* that is termed satanic, the internal betrayal that is attributed to Satan:

> Satan became increasingly important as a figure, the ultimate enemy in that he had been a trusted friend in heaven before his fall, one of the highest angels. He represents, therefore, one of the most dangerous of enemies, the enemy within. . . . The figure of Satan emerges at its most intense within communities which consider themselves to be under threat, not from an external enemy, but from an internal one, the kind of enemy who threatens to transform the identity of that community and change it into something else, and the kind of enemy who appears to be a close and loyal ally but turns out to be plotting this kind of destruction.[3]

I am completely persuaded by Pagels and Cole on the special role of the Satan as the *enemy within*, the community member whose internal identity gives external enmity a local habitation and a name. That raises, however, a particular problem for the book of Revelation. Pagels concludes: "Christians dreaded Satan's attacks from outside—that is, from hostile pagans—but many of them believed that even more dangerous were Satan's forays among the most intimate enemies of all—other Christians."[4] Is Revelation an exception to or a supreme example of the Satan as the enemy within? Does John think of the

Satan *especially*—even if not exclusively—as the intimate enemy, the member who allows and embodies the outside enemy inside?

Hold those questions for an answer in the next chapter. But always remember that the Satan originally became *God's intimate enemy in heaven* before being cast down to become *an intimate enemy on earth*. In heaven, before on earth, the Satan was the transcendental traitor, the leader of the rebel angels, an apostate general of the heavenly hosts. The Satan was the *intimate enemy*—of God.

We turn next to add some more questions to those we are holding by looking at the final protagonist in John's unholy trinity of the Dragon, the Beast, and the Whore.

———————

The character of the Great Whore, the Rider of the Beast, is introduced as "the great whore . . . a woman sitting on a scarlet beast that was full of blasphemous names, and it had seven heads and ten horns" (17:1, 3). We already know that the Beast is the Roman Empire, its emperors, and especially Nero Returning. The identity of the Great Whore is revealed by two very clear clues. (But wonder immediately why John's imagery turns here from bestial metaphors to pornographic misogyny.)

The first clue is in a verse we've already seen: "This calls for a mind that has wisdom: the seven heads are seven mountains on which the woman is seated; also, they are seven kings" (17:9). At that earlier point, we focused our wisdom on those "seven kings." Here we focus it on those "seven mountains."

It actually does not take much wisdom to recognize that a woman seated on "seven mountains" or hills is Rome itself, capital city of the Roman Empire. In Virgil's epic masterpiece, the *Aeneid*, Anchises prophesies to his son Aeneas in Hades that "glorious Rome shall extend her empire to earth's end . . . and shall embrace seven hills with a single city's wall" (6.781–83). His slightly younger contemporary Propertius wrote of Rome as "the city set on seven hills which presides over the whole world" (*Elegies* 3.11.57). John, obviously, sees Rome atop its seven hills in a somewhat different light.

The second clue to the identity of the Great Whore is that "on her forehead was written a name, a mystery: 'Babylon the great, mother of whores and of earth's abominations'" (Rev. 17:5). John calls Rome, capital city of the Roman Empire, by the code name of Babylon, capital city of the Babylonian Empire—for two reasons. One reason is that, as the Babylonian Empire destroyed Israel's First Temple in 587 BCE, so the Roman Empire destroyed its Second Temple in 70 CE. *Rome as Babylon is the destroyer.* Another reason is that, as the city of Babylon fell to Cyrus the Great of Persia in 539 BCE, so Rome as Babylon is surely doomed and, as it were, "fallen, fallen" already. *Rome as Babylon is destroyed.*

First, then, Rome, "the great city that rules over the kings of the earth" (17:18), is the *destroyed destroyer* and, even before it is named "the great whore" (17:1), it is named Babylon and its doom is thereby set: "Fallen, fallen is Babylon the great! She has made all nations drink of the wine of the wrath of her fornication" (14:8); and again: "God remembered great Babylon and gave her the wine-cup of the fury of his wrath" (16:19).

Next, John names Rome as "the great whore" so that it brackets (17:1; 19:2) all of Revelation 18, a ferocious taunt poem on the fall of Rome as "Babylon, the mighty city" (18:10b) or, again and again, as "the great city" (18:10a, 16, 18, 19, 21).

Finally, we have "kings of the earth" mentioned repeatedly through-out Revelation from 1:5 to 21:24. With them we also get "the magnates and the generals and the rich and the powerful, and everyone, slave and free" (6:15) or "captains . . . the mighty . . . horses and their riders . . . both free and slave, both small and great" (19:18).

But there is one other category we never get alongside those "kings of the earth" except in Revelation 18. There, the fate of "the great whore" known as Babylon the Great gives double space and emphasis to *merchants* (18:3, 11, 15, 23) over *kings* (18:3, 9). Look, to begin with, at this verse:

> The kings of the earth
> have committed fornication with her,
> The merchants of the earth
> have grown rich from the power of her luxury. (18:3)

That poetic diptych gives parallel space to kings and merchants, but it is only an evenly balanced headline or overture to what follows immediately:

> The kings of the earth, who committed fornication and lived in luxury with her, will weep and wail over her when they see the smoke of her burning; they *will stand far off, in fear of her torment*, and say, "*Alas, alas, the great city*, Babylon, the mighty city! *For in one hour* your judgment has come." (18:9–10; recall 17:2)

I have italicized three key phrases in that dirge because John repeats those expressions—twice—as he turns next from kings to merchants:

> The merchants . . . who gained wealth from her, *will stand far off, in fear of her torment*, weeping and mourning aloud, "*Alas, alas, the great city*, clothed in fine linen, in purple and scarlet, adorned with gold, with jewels, and with pearls! *For in one hour* all this wealth has been laid waste!" (18:15–17)

That seems initially like another equal emphasis on kings and merchants—in that same sequence—but then, as John continues, he focuses our attention far more on the merchants than on the kings.

After those land merchants, John turns to the sea merchants and uses the same set of three formulaic expressions (italicized once again):

> All shipmasters and seafarers, sailors and all whose trade is on the sea, *stood far off* and cried out as they saw the smoke of her burning . . . *"Alas, alas, the great city,* where all who had ships at sea grew rich by her wealth! *For in one hour* she has been laid waste." (18:17–19)

Kings of the earth, merchants of the earth, and merchants of the sea are all described with that same set of formulaic phrases. But, obviously and deliberately, merchants, distinguished as land traders and sea traders, get double space over kings.

Think, for a moment, about the reality of commercial trade in the Mediterranean globalization of the imperial Roman economy. First, Roman rule created something radically new—a *territorial* empire, with its legions located all around the imperial periphery. Inside that *cordon sanitaire*, safety and security manifested the Pax Romana quite visibly.

Second, that internal peace certainly facilitated and fostered *local* commercial trade both rural and urban. But not even Rome's sixty thousand plus miles of paved roads could make the long-haul transport of heavy merchandise a financially feasible project. Rivers could better handle some types of long-range commerce and, of course, the giant state-insured grain ships from Alexandria could furnish the daily food dole for Rome.

Finally, therefore, John's distinction between land merchants and sea merchants fits well into the "economy" of the Roman Empire. In both cases, the emphasis was on high-priced luxury goods for the Roman aristocracy but, certainly, the sea traders could bring the large-bulk items that were impossible for the land traders.

Hold on to that general commercial matrix as we return to John, where the Great Whore, the city of Rome, dominates the text from 17:1 to 19:2. Within that context, as just seen, "merchants" (18:3, 11, 15, 23) receive more emphasis than "kings" (18:3, 9) and "trade" (18:17, 22) more attention than "rule" (17:18; 18:7). Also, recall that the Great Whore rides the great Beast (17:3) and "that no one can buy or sell who does not have the mark, that is, the name of the beast or the number of its name" (13:17).

John's vision of Roman commerce as prostitution was not, by the way, original. Isaiah said: "Tyre . . . will return to her trade, and will prostitute herself with all the kingdoms of the world on the face of the earth" (23:17). As Tyre for Isaiah then, so Rome for John now.

From all the data in this chapter on the Satan as the outside enemy already inside and the Whore as the focus of trade, commerce, and business, we get the following hypothesis to be tested in the next and final chapter in Part One.

First, as we know so well from Revelation 13:1–18 and 17:3–17, John's special name for Rome as empire is simply the Beast—a predatory epithet derived clearly from Daniel 7:2–7. As "sea beast" the Beast represents the empire; as "land beast," the emperors; and the return of Nero is the Beast in particular. One single feral title is adequate for the Roman Empire, the whole and its parts, from 11:7 through 20:10. Still, despite all that, John creates his own new and separate term for Rome as a city even though, as capital of the empire, it is already part of the Beast.

Recall what Daniel did in a somewhat similar situation. Daniel describes the Greek empire of Alexander the Great as "a fourth beast, terrifying and dreadful and exceedingly strong . . . different from all the [imperial] beasts that preceded it, and it had ten horns" (7:7). Then, the Greco-Syrian sub-empire of the Seleucids is caricatured as "another

horn . . . a little one coming up among them" (7:8). That allows Daniel
to maintain consistently the predatory metaphor of empire as beast.

John, however, does not call Rome as city "the lair of the beast,"
but, as we saw, "the great whore . . . on [whose] forehead was written a
name, a mystery: 'Babylon the great, mother of whores and of earth's
abominations'" (Rev. 17:1, 5). In other words, he creates a whole new
and very different metaphor for Rome as city.

Second, therefore, think of the basic difference between the two
metaphors of the Roman Empire as Beast and the city of Rome as
Whore. The Beast is about violence; the Whore is about sex. The Beast
is about predation, subjection, domination, and oppression; the Whore
is about temptation, enticement, seduction, and inducement. The Beast
takes wealth—unwillingly as far as the client is concerned; the Whore
receives wealth—willingly as far as the client is concerned. Summarily,
the Beast attacks you, but the Whore attracts you.

Third, map atop that basic metaphorical distinction between Beast
and Whore that other distinction between king and merchant, or ruler
and trader, just seen in Revelation 18:

> The merchants of the earth weep and mourn for her, since
> no one buys their cargo anymore, cargo of gold, silver, jewels
> and pearls, fine linen, purple, silk and scarlet, all kinds of
> scented wood, all articles of ivory, all articles of costly wood,
> bronze, iron, and marble, cinnamon, spice, incense, myrrh,
> frankincense, wine, olive oil, choice flour and wheat, cattle and
> sheep, horses and chariots, slaves—and human souls. (18:11–13)

In John's pornographic metaphor all those merchants and traders
supplying goods for sale in Rome—especially those easily transport-
able luxury goods—are but clients heading for a whorehouse. Their
"cargo" adorns the Great Whore, "the woman . . . clothed in purple
and scarlet, and adorned with gold and jewels and pearls, holding in

her hand a golden cup full of abominations and the impurities of her fornication" (17:4).

Power flows *from* Rome, the imperial capital city, to the provinces, but "cargo" flows from the provinces *to* Rome. For John, royal power going out from Rome and—especially—mercantile trade coming into Rome are simply "fornication" at the central bordello of the Roman Empire (14:8; 17:2, 4; 18:3, 9; 19:2).

Fourth, we get a very strong hint that John's audience is already attracted by commercial contacts with the city of Rome, is already involved in trade as fornication: "Come out of her, my people, so that you do not take part in her sins, and so that you do not share in her plagues" (18:4).

Finally, we can bring together the two parts of this chapter. In the first half, we saw that the Satan is a special biblical and Christian term for an outside evil already inside the community. It is the intimate enemy, the external and inimical agent already accepted internally by at least some members of the group in question.

In the second half of this chapter we saw exactly how the Satan had successfully infiltrated John's communities. It was not the lure of Roman imperial theology, but the seduction of Roman imperial commerce. Was it possible to be a good Christian at Ephesus and a good trader at Rome? Could you be a faithful Christian and the "artisan of any trade" with Rome (18:22)?

What better way to repudiate the attraction of imperial economy than to describe it as the seduction of a brothel? What better way to condemn participation in imperial commerce than to describe it as fornication? What better way to offset Rome as a lure for luxury trade than to describe it as "the great whore who is seated on many waters, with whom the kings of the earth have committed fornication, and with the wine of whose fornication the inhabitants of the earth have become drunk" (17:1–2)?

John is, of course, absolutely against any Christian accommodation to Roman imperial theology and its "blasphemous names" (13:1; 17:3) or "blasphemous words" (13:5). But that is surely not an actual problem for him or his communities. Neither does he indicate that accommodation to Roman military or political power is a pressing problem requiring stern refutation.

Instead, here is the question or hypothesis for the final chapter of Part One. Does a *commercial* relationship with the city of Rome, already in force, constitute for John the first step along the slippery slope from accommodation through adaptation and assimilation to acculturation—with each of those terms as slippery as the slope itself? Is the major purpose of the Apocalypse, the basic intention of John, and the primary message of the book of Revelation a ferocious polemic against incipient *commercial* association with imperial Rome?

To stop that incipient acculturation immediately, John luridly describes Rome's recent history of slaughtering Christians (libel against Rome) and the imminent future in which Christ will slaughter Romans (libel against God). Who would acculturate with a regime so diabolical and so doomed?

5

THE LONGEST LIE

THE WORLD OF JOHN'S REVELATION IS AWASH IN "BLOOD."
There is, first of all, the execution of Jesus the Christ, who was
"pierced" (1:7), "crucified" (11:8), and "clothed in a robe dipped in
blood" (19:13). Thereafter, that "blood of the Lamb" (7:14; 12:11) is emphasized as salvific for Christians. They are "freed . . . ransomed . . .
washed" by it and "have conquered" through it (1:5; 5:9; 7:14; 12:11).

Next, there is the blood of Christians murdered—apparently wholesale—by the Roman Empire. Rome is "drunk with the blood of the
saints and the blood of the witnesses to Jesus" (17:6), and in it "was
found the blood of prophets and of saints, and of all who have been
slaughtered on earth" (18:24).

Finally, in vengeance, God causes the universe itself to become
blood-soaked: "The full moon became like blood" (6:12); "hail and fire,
mixed with blood" burned a third of the earth and "a third of the sea
became blood" (8:7, 9); "the waters [were turned] into blood; . . . the
sea . . . became like the blood of a corpse, and every living thing in the
sea died; . . . and the springs of water they became blood" (11:6; 16:3,
4). Finally, to sum it all up, comes this terrible climactic metaphor:
"The wine press was trodden outside the city, and blood flowed from
the wine press, as high as a horse's bridle, for a distance of about two
hundred miles" (14:20).

What can justify—or at least explain—that vision of imminent dev-astation for "a *fourth* of the earth" (6:8), or, better, for "a *third* of the rivers . . . waters . . . sun, moon, stars . . . humankind" (8:10–12; 9:15, 18), or, better still, for *all* "the earth" (16:1–21)?

Recall that, in heaven, "the souls of those who had been slaughtered for the word of God" asked, "How long will it be before you judge and avenge our blood on the inhabitants of the earth?" They were told to wait for those "who were soon to be killed as they themselves had been killed" (6:9–11). John sees a blood-drenched empire as Rome's past slaughterhouse for Christians and God's future slaughterhouse for Romans:

> Because they shed the blood of saints and prophets, you [God] have given them blood to drink. It is what they deserve! (16:6)

> Render to her as she herself has rendered, and repay her double for her deeds; mix a double draught for her in the cup she mixed. (18:6)

> God has judged the great whore who corrupted the earth with her fornication, and he has avenged on her the blood of his servants. (19:2)

For John, the justification—or at lease explanation—of God' action in Christ is this: in the immediate past *Rome has slaughtered Christians* and in the imminent future *God will slaughter Romans*. It is a response of blood for blood and slaughter for slaughter. It is calibrated vengeance, appropriate reprisal, proportionate revenge, and retributive justice.

The structural logic of John's vision is this: *the history of Rome's past violence against Christians justifies the prophecy of Christ's future violence against Romans.* But that sequential reciprocity between Rome's action and God's reaction raises this fundamental question: Is it *historically* accurate that the Roman Empire—as policy or practice—slaughtered Christians during the first century or especially at its end?

―――――――――

In past biblical scholarship, that question was answered quite affirmatively. Here, for example, is an extreme but classic assertion from the New Testament scholar Sir William Mitchell Ramsay. He traveled extensively in Greece and Turkey in the early 1880s, wrote *The Letters to the Seven Churches of Asia* in 1904, and spoke of a "Flavian persecution" that extended from Vespasian through Titus to Domitian (69–96) and ended only under Trajan (98–117):

> The Flavian persecution was not a temporary flaming forth of cruelty: it was a steady, uniform application of a deliberately chosen and unvarying policy. . . . The Christians were to be annihilated. . . . Domitian was not a mere capricious tyrant . . . his narrow intensity . . . may be gathered from his portrait taken from one of his coins.[1]

That is immediately followed by a coin showing the bust of Domitian facing right and designated "Figure 5: Domitian the persecutor."

The argument of scholars like Ramsay went like this: John's Revelation was written *under* the emperor Domitian (81–96)—or at least between 90 and 110. But John describes imperial slaughter of Christians. Therefore, Rome *must have* slaughtered Christians under or after Domitian. You recognize, of course, the perfect circularity of that argument.

In present biblical scholarship, a growing consensus emphatically questions that circular argument's final conclusion. The problem is this historical one: there is *no evidence* that Christians were slaughtered or even persecuted under Domitian and, more important, there is *strong evidence against it*—before, during, and after Domitian.

Think, for example, about two sets of letters written under the emperor Trajan in the early second century. One set is from a Christian martyr who traveled westward by land *to* Rome; the other is from an imperial legate who traveled eastward by sea *from* Rome.

First, from the Christian side. Probably around 110, Ignatius, bishop of Antioch in Syria, was taken by a band of soldiers as a bound captive destined for wild beasts in the arena at Rome. As he traveled across Asia Minor, he wrote seven letters, six to the churches of Ephesus, Magnesia, Tralles, Rome, Philadelphia, and Smyrna. Then, since he "could not write to all the churches because of [his] sudden sailing from Troas to Neapolis," he wrote a final letter to Polycarp, "bishop" of Smyrna, asking him to send letters or messengers to the churches "on the road in front of [him]" (Ign. *Pol.* 8).

John of Patmos wrote seven letters to seven churches in western Asia Minor (Rev. 1:11); Ignatius of Antioch wrote six letters to six churches in western Asia Minor. Three of those churches were the same; Ephesus, Smyrna, and Philadelphia received a letter from each writer.

John wrote, as we saw, of "those who had been slaughtered for the word of God" (6:9) and of "the blood of prophets and of saints, and of all who have been slaughtered on earth" (18:24), but not a hint of any such murderous Roman ferocity appears in Ignatius's letters to those same regions.

Instead of mentioning past *external* Roman persecution, Ignatius focuses on the present *internal* Christian organization. His vision is to establish a "bishop" (*episcopos* in Greek) as a single "monarchical" authority in each church, instead of, say, a board of multiple elders (*presbyteroi* in Greek). Indeed, it *may* have been public conflict between supporters and opponents of his program that caused the Roman governor to have him condemned locally but executed at a distance. In any case, as Ignatius travels to martyrdom in Rome, the major problem for the churches of western Asia Minor is not past external persecution but present internal dissension—to be solved by having the plural "presbytery . . . attuned to the bishop as the strings to a harp" (Ign. *Eph.* 4).

Ignatius, for example, uses the term "beasts" (*thyria*) literally for those that await him in the Roman arena and metaphorically for the soldiers who accompany him there. But he can also use that predatory metaphor like this:

> There are some who make a practice of carrying about the
> Name with wicked guile, and do certain other things unworthy
> of God; these you must shun as wild beasts (*thyria*), for they
> are ravening dogs, who bite secretly, and you must be upon
> your guard against them, for they are scarcely to be cured.
> (Ign. *Eph.* 7)

Like John of Patmos, Ignatius of Antioch praises the Ephesians because they rejected false teachings: "Some from elsewhere have stayed with you, who have evil teaching; but you did not allow them to sow it among you, and stopped your ears" (Ign. *Eph.* 9).

Still, as you read through all of Ignatius's letters and especially the one to the church at Rome, you cannot glimpse a single hint of the past human "slaughter" of Christians by Romans alleged by John to justify a future divine slaughter of Romans by Christ. In summary, that past event did not happen—*ever*; that future event did not happen—*soon*.

Next, from the Roman side. In 110, the emperor Trajan sent Pliny the Younger as legate to Bithynia-Pontus, a Roman province on the Black Sea's southern coast, to remedy financial mismanagement by the two preceding governors, whom Pliny had successfully defended against charges of corruption. (Maybe Trajan had an ironic sense of humor?) Although Pliny died there in 113, he managed to write 121 letters to Trajan, and among them is the first account by a Roman aristocratic official of the ritual life and legal status of the Christian community in a provincial city (*Letters* 10).

Pliny was the nephew and adopted son of the learned encyclopedist Pliny the Elder, friend of the emperor Vespasian. The uncle was himself a high-level lawyer in Rome who had taken part in the trials of three other provincial governors (apart from those two mentioned above for the nephew). Yet despite aristocratic family connections, vast legal experience, and historian associates of note, when Pliny the Younger first encountered troublesome Christians in Bithynia-Pontus, he wrote his concerns to Trajan: "I have never participated in trials of Christians. I therefore do not know what offenses it is the practice to punish or investigate, and to what extent" and "whether the name itself, even without offenses, or only the offenses associated with the name are to be punished" (*Letters* 10.96).

In reply, Trajan approves Pliny's procedures, says it is "not possible to lay down any general rule to serve as a kind of fixed standard," and then proceeds to lay down three of them:

> They are not to be sought out; if they are denounced and proved guilty, they are to be punished, with this reservation, that whoever denies that he is a Christian and really proves it—that is, by worshiping our gods—even though he was under suspicion in the past, shall obtain pardon through repentance. But anonymously posted accusations ought to have no place in any prosecution. For this is both a dangerous kind of precedent and out of keeping with the spirit of our age. (*Letters* 10.97)

It is flatly impossible to reconcile imperial slaughter of Christians—as either policy or practice—with complete ignorance about them by an aristocratic lawyer as highly placed and well-connected as Pliny the Younger. Once again, and this time from the Roman side, John's scenario just never happened.

At this point, of course, a second question presses in inexorably: If Rome did not slaughter Christians, *why does John claim*—insistently and ad nauseam—*that it did*? If Rome did not act like a Red Dragon, a fearsome Beast, and a Great Whore, *why does John use such metaphors to describe it*? The answer to that question will establish a proposal for the authorial intention of John, the rhetorical strategy of Revelation, and the meaning of the last book of the Christian Bible.

The first step in understanding John's authorial strategy focuses on the inaugural *presence* of those seven letters in Revelation 2–3; notice that, from small items to large segments, John's programmatic number is clearly "seven." In his book it appears over fifty times, from twice in 1:4 to thrice in 21:9.

Some *sevens* appear only in one or two locations: "seven flaming torches" (4:5a), "seven horns" (5:6), "seven eyes" (5:7), "seven trumpets" (8:2, 6), "seven thunders" (10:3, 4), "seven diadems" (12:3), "seven mountains" (17:9), and "seven kings" (17:9, 11). Some *sevens* reappear multiple times: "seven heads" (12:3; 13:1; 17:3, 7, 9), "seven spirits" (1:4; 3:1; 4:5; 5:6), and especially "seven angels" (8:2, 6; 15:1, 6, 7, 8; 16:1; 17:1; 21:9). Some *sevens* structure and integrate larger sections: "seven seals" (4:1–8:5), "seven trumpets" (8:2–11:18), and especially "seven bowls with seven plagues" (15:5–16:21; 21:9).

John's obsessive use of *sevens* emphasizes his sense of totality and finality, prophetic conviction, and cosmic certitude—from the old "heavens and earth" of creation in Genesis 2:1 to "the new heaven and new earth" of Revelation 21:1. Still, in all those teeming *sevens*, the first set in Revelation 2–3—the seven letters to the churches—stands out as emphatically primordial.

First, those seven letters even get their own subsets of sevens: "seven spirits" (1:4; 3:1), "seven stars" (1:16, 20; 2:1; 3:1), and "seven golden lampstands" (1:12, 20; 2:1). Those last two items are explained in climactic sevens by Christ himself: "The mystery of the seven stars that you saw in my right hand, and the seven golden lampstands: the seven stars are the angels of the seven churches, and the seven lampstands are the seven churches" (1:20).

Next, the seven letters in Revelation 2–3 form an opening frame for the whole book, because John never mentions "church(es)" again until this comment at the end of the book, which forms the closing frame: "It is I, Jesus, who sent my angel to you with this testimony for the churches" (22:16).

Furthermore, John signals the importance of the letters to the individual churches by using opening and closing formats with only very minor variations. They start: "To the angel of the church in [*place*] write: These are the words of [*description of Christ*]." They continue as Christ *praises* and/or *blames* the recipients in a declaration that begins "I know . . ." They end: "Let anyone who has an ear listen to what the Spirit is saying to the churches. To everyone who conquers, I will give [*transcendental rewards*]." These letters form a textually initial and formally similar set of seven even among the multiplied examples yet to come.

————————

The second step in understanding John's authorial strategy focuses on the *content* of those seven letters in Revelation 2–3. In many cases, content that was quite clear to the original recipients is not at all clear to us today. The plan is not to work through all seven letters in sequence, but to focus on *five linkages* between and across the letters. Using those linkages, we can move from John's most general and implicit comments to his more specific and explicit ones. Finally, from that process will come an understanding of John's basic purpose in this primordial seven among all the succeeding sevens in Revelation.

A first linkage is between the churches of Sardis (3:1–6) and Laodicea (3:14–22). First, at Sardis: "You have still a few persons in Sardis who have not soiled their clothes; they will walk with me, dressed in white, for they are worthy. If you conquer, you will be clothed like them in white robes" (3:4–5). Next, at Laodicea: "You say, 'I am rich, I have prospered, and I need nothing.' . . . I counsel you to buy from me gold refined by fire so that you may be rich; and white robes to clothe you and to keep the shame of your nakedness from being seen" (3:17–18).

The common linkage is the general language denoting impurity, "soiled clothes" and "shame of nakedness," and the promise of purity, "clothed in white robes." In Revelation "white robes" are, of course, the vesture of heavenly purity (4:4; 6:11; 7:9, 13, 14).

Also, to be "rich"—literally and economically—is not a good situation in John's eyes. Recall how "the merchants of the earth have grown rich from the power of her [doomed Rome's] luxury" and "all who had ships at sea grew rich by her wealth" (18:3, 19).

A second linkage is between the churches of Ephesus (2:1–7), Smyrna (2:8–11), and Philadelphia (3:7–13). All three letters make a pointed reference to "those who say they are . . . but are not." The Ephesians are praised for scrutinizing: "You cannot tolerate evildoers; you have tested those *who claim to be* apostles *but are not*" (2:2). Because they are termed "apostles," these "evildoers" are opponents from inside the community rather than from outside it.

The indictments, similar in form and content, against Smyrna and Philadelphia, however, mention "Jews." To Smyrna, John writes: "I know the slander on the part of those who say that they are Jews and are not, but are a synagogue of Satan" (2:9). And to Philadelphia: "I will make those of the synagogue of Satan who say that they are Jews and are not . . . bow down before your feet" (3:9). Against whom are those accusations directed? The answer from scholarship is contested and divided between two major options.

One option imagines an *outside* attack ("slander") by the local *Jewish* synagogue against the local *Christian* church. Even if that *outside* option were basically accurate, it would have to be rephrased as a dispute between non-Messianic/Christic Jews in the local synagogue and Messianic/Christic Jews—like John—in the local church.

The other—and far more likely—option is an *inside* controversy within those two urban Messianic/Christic churches. This view reminds us that western Asia Minor was Paul's territory before it was John's (1 Cor. 15:32; 16:8; Acts, passim). If Paul's Gentile and especially God-fearer converts were inside those churches, John could easily call them pseudo-Jews and Satan's synagogue. He would also judge intermarriage with them to be "fornication," or *porneia*.

That scholarly option is confirmed, for me, by the parallel between pseudo-apostles and pseudo-Jews, which indicates insider, not outsider, problems. Also, of course, by what comes up below in the fifth and final linkage.

A third linkage is between the churches of Ephesus (2:1–7), Pergamum (2:12–17), and Thyatira (2:18–29). Here we get much more information, but it also demands some general knowledge of both the Old Testament biblical matrix and the Roman urban matrix. Watch how the linkage works.

Christ tells the Ephesian community: "This is to your credit: you hate the works of the Nicolaitans, which I also hate" (2:6). At Ephesus, we have no idea who this group is or what they advocate, but we get more information about them at Pergamum. The letter to Pergamum says: "I have a few things against you: you have some there who hold to the teaching of Balaam, who taught Balak to put a stumbling block before the people of Israel, so that they would eat food sacrificed to idols and practice fornication. So you also have some who hold to the teaching of the Nicolaitans" (2:14–15).

That links the "works of the Nicolaitans," rejected at Ephesus (2:6), to "the teaching of the Nicolaitans," accepted by at least "some" at Pergamum (2:14–15). Furthermore, we now have content for the Nicolaitan position: it concerns "eating food sacrificed to idols and practicing fornication."

Finally, in the letter to Thyatira, Christ's accusation is: "I have this against you: you tolerate that woman Jezebel, who . . . is teaching . . . my servants to practice fornication and to eat food sacrificed to idols" (2:20). That is the same indictment seen in the letter to Pergamum, but in reverse order as "practicing fornication and eating food sacrificed to idols."

In other words, John's subject in all three churches is "fornication and eating food offered to idols," which is refused at Ephesus (2:6), but accepted at both Pergamum (2:14–15) and Thyatira (2:20). Hold, for now, this question: Why are Christians debating for and against "fornication and eating food offered to idols," and what exactly is meant by it?

A fourth linkage is between the churches of Pergamum and Thyatira. Those indictments for both "fornication" and "eating idol food offerings" are likened to Old Testament incidents concerning Balaam (Num. 22–24) and Jezebel (1 Kings 16–2 Kings 9). What do we learn from those stories that may assist with John's concern in his churches?

Although Balaam refused to curse Israel as it passed through Moab during its exodus from Egypt to Canaan in Numbers 22–24, what happened next is a less positive picture of Balaam:

> While Israel was staying at Shittim, the people began to have sexual relations with the women of Moab. These invited the people to the sacrifices of their gods, and the people ate and bowed down to their gods. Thus Israel yoked itself to the [god] Baal of Peor, and the LORD's anger was kindled against Israel. (Num. 25:1–3)

Although it is never mentioned in that story, Balaam is later held responsible for Israel's Moabite defection. Those who did not succumb to it "killed Balaam son of Beor with the sword," because "these women here, on Balaam's advice, made the Israelites act treacherously against the LORD in the affair of Peor" (Num. 31:8, 16; see also Josh. 13:22).

Notice that the two features of the "affair of Peor" are "sexual relations" with the women of Moab (*ekporneusai*, from *porneuō*) and "eating sacrifices" with Baal, god of Moab. I understand that as describing an Israelite-Moabite *acculturation* involving the obvious features of bed and board, marriage and meal. The term "sexual relations" (*porneuō*, verb, or *porneia*, noun) might indicate casual fornication, but it more likely refers to ethnic intermarriage or *any type* of marital irregularity—as judged from some observer's viewpoint.

The "Jezebel" mentioned in Revelation 2:20 could be the actual name of a Thyatiran woman, but it seems unlikely, as it is hard to imagine anyone using a name so suffused with biblical infamy. As with Balaam at Pergamum, so with Jezebel at Thyatira, John is directing us to another Old Testament parallel.

In the mid-800s BCE, "[King] Ahab son of Omri . . . took as his wife Jezebel daughter of King Ethbaal of the Sidonians, and went and served Baal, and worshiped him" (1 Kings 16:30–31). In this ethnic Israelite-Canaanite marriage, Queen Jezebel naturally expected the court to accept her native religious traditions, with worship of the Canaanite God Baal at least alongside that of the Israelite God Yahweh.

God commanded the prophets Elijah and Elisha to engineer a violent regime change to replace the dynasty of Omri with that of Jehu. (As so often, then and now, violent regime change in that part of the world did not work: they removed Ahab—who was bad—and obtained Jeroboam II—who was worse.). Once again, we have a prophetic condemnation of acculturation, this time of an Israelite-Canaanite one involving ethnic intermarriage.

A fifth linkage, between the churches of Smyrna (2:8–11), Pergamum (2:12–17), Thyatira (2:18–29), and Philadelphia (3:7–13), is the specific mention of the Satan in each of their letters. Of the eight mentions of the Satan in Revelation, only three indict him by that name for his empowerment of the Roman Empire against God (12:9; 20:2, 7). The other five mentions of the Satan appear here within these four letters (2:9, 13ab, 24; 3:9).

Recall what we saw earlier about the Satan as the *intimate enemy* first of God in heaven above and then of God's people here below on earth. This linkage indicates that, as the intimate enemy, the outside antagonist is already inside those communities—whether accepted or rejected—but how?

From that intricate web of linkages, we can conclude that, as John sees it, the basic overall problem in those seven churches is acculturation with regard to mixed marriages and pagan sacrifices. But how exactly did such acculturation work with regard to idol offerings and mixed marriages? Why were those items so attractive in those churches, and how did they get accepted by at least some members there?

Think, to begin with, how assistance within extended families and the support within village kinship could disappear completely for urban immigrants around the Roman Empire. Also, think about slaves who never had a family or freed slaves whose patrons were no longer alive. How did people—from day workers to freed slaves—survive in the great anonymous cities of the Roman Empire, where living conditions resulted in much disease and death, demanding a constant influx of rural immigrants? (Scholars have suggested that 7–17 percent of the population lived with some material security, while 80–90 percent lived barely above, generally on, or even below the subsistence level.)

The solution turned Roman society into what one scholar has called "a world of associations." Groups formed voluntary associations (*collegia*) on the basis of common *cultic*, *ethnic*, *commercial*, *local*, or *domestic* interests to provide for the welfare of their members. With their own rules and sanctions, fees and fines, set meetings, set meals, and rit-ual funerals, they usually had a patron deity and hopefully a financial sponsor as well. Commerce-based, trade-based, or occupation-based associations, for example, were like craft guilds for artisans, traders, and merchants, and their common meals both bonded the association internally and advertised it externally.

What Paul of Tarsus or John of Patmos called a Christian *ekklesia*, or "church," would have appeared to outsiders as basically a cultic *collegium*. But what if Christian artisans, traders, or merchants wanted also to participate in occupational *collegia* besides their own Christ-based cultic *collegium*?

If Christians became members of non-Christian trade guilds, how did Christians navigate through the necessary rituals for a patron deity or around the obligatory celebrations for a sponsor's feast days? What if a trade association met in a temple on those very special occasions? Was participation in an association's meals—in either content or location—*simply a justifiable accommodation or a disastrous acculturation to Roman paganism?*

That question of trade guilds and association meals did not just arise for John and his churches in Asia Minor. It had arisen earlier for Paul at Corinth on the other side of the Aegean Sea. Paul himself was an ar-tisan in the workshop of Prisca and Aquila, who moved from Rome to Corinth (Acts 18:1–3), Corinth to Ephesus (Acts 18:18, 19, 26; 1 Cor. 16:), and Ephesus back to Rome (Rom. 16:3).

In 1 Corinthians, Paul had to face decisions about trade guilds and craft associations, as did John, and on a much more personal level. Read through all of 1 Corinthians 7–10, for example, and pay special atten-tion to what Paul advises on "sexual immorality," or *porneia* (7:2; 10:8), and "idol offerings," or *eidōlothyta* (8:1; 10:19). His decision on mixed marriages (7:12–16) and his "Don't ask, don't tell" advice on idol offer-ings are open, hopeful, and liberating. Even his warning not to scan-dalize more conservative members ends with this truculent comment:

"Why should my liberty be subject to the judgment of someone else's conscience" (10:29).

Still, around fifty years after Paul, John's seven letters judge all of that Pauline advice not as valid accommodation, but as disastrous acculturation or, more simply, as "Satanic" influence already *within* the community.

All of that leaves us with one final set of questions: Is John's attitude of *absolutely no accommodation* with Romanization and, especially with the seductive lure of trade advantages in craft guilds, applicable *only* to those seven letters at the start of his book? John has already said that the loss of trade contacts and commercial opportunities is why "artisans" and "merchants" mourn over the final fate of Rome (Rev. 18:3c, 11, 15, 22, 23). Is *absolutely no acculturation* a far wider theme or even the dominant theme of John's Revelation? Is that what best explains the author's basic intention and the book's overall rhetorical strategy?

John's radical *no acculturation* with the seductive *pornography* of Rome's commercial globalization can be seen as spreading from those seven letters to pervade his entire Revelation, a conclusion confirmed in both the form and content of his book—but especially the content.

First, the *form* of the letter. Our letters—if we send such things anymore—are relatively formulaic at the start and finish with regard to four items: the *recipient* ("Dear Mary") and *greeting* ("Hope all is well") at the start, and the *farewell* ("With best wishes") and *sender* ("John") at the end.

Ancients letters had these formulaic elements as well, except that the *sender*, *recipient*, and *greeting* appeared at the beginning and only the *farewell* appeared at the end. (You can easily check that system, by the way, in all of Paul's letters.) Watch how this works for Revelation as a whole.

The *sender* is "John," and the *recipient* is "the seven churches that are in Asia" (1:4a). John later elaborates on the occasion of the letter by reporting Christ's command to him: "Write in a *book* what you see and send it to the seven churches, to Ephesus, to Smyrna, to Pergamum, to Thyatira, to Sardis, to Philadelphia, and to Laodicea" (1:11). Notice that this specifies the entire book as a single letter—apart from the seven individual letters to the churches and even if they were not present!

Next comes the *greeting*: "Grace to you and peace from him who is and who was and who is to come, and from the seven spirits who are before his throne, and from Jesus Christ, the faithful witness, the firstborn of the dead, and the ruler of the kings of the earth" (1:4–5). Finally, John's *farewell* picks up and repeats "grace" from the greeting: "The grace of the Lord Jesus be with all the saints. Amen" (22:21).

Revelation is an encyclical epistle, a circular letter sent by John from the offshore island of Patmos to cities on the mainland of Asia Minor. The courier first moved northward from Ephesus through Smyrna to Pergamum and then, turning southeastward, from Thyatira through Sardis and Philadelphia to Laodicea.

That overall epistolary format is not in any way surprising, and neither is the idea of having it couriered on a circuit of multiple cities. What is surprising, however, is including those *seven individual letters* for each of the recipient cities *within the encyclical letter to them all*. That creates a certain oscillation from those seven letters to the overall letter at least on the level of form.

Second, the *content* of the letter. The Greek verb *planaō*, "to deceive or beguile," is first used for Jezebel at Thyatira: "You tolerate that woman Jezebel, who . . . is teaching and deceiving/beguiling (*plana*) my servants" (2:20). After that first usage, the accusation of "deceiving" is reserved for the Dragon (20:3, 8, 10), the Beast (3:14), the Whore (18:23), and a new personification called the False Prophet (19:20). That arches the theme of *deception* from one end of Revelation to the other. It also integrates Jezebel into the highest echelons of earth's deceivers and raises the question: Who or what exactly is the False Prophet?

In answer, think how the theme of *prophecy* pervades Revelation. Although the opening word of John's book is "apocalypse," that term never appears again. Instead, he speaks thereafter about the "words of the prophecy" (1:3), the "spirit of prophecy" (19:10), or, especially, the "words of the prophecy of this book" (22:7, 10, 18, 19). He also mentions "God's servants the prophets" (10:7; 11:18), "the blood of saints and prophets" (16:6), "saints and apostles and prophets" (18:20), and, again, "the blood of prophets and of saints" (18:24).

Next, John reproaches the church at Thyatira for tolerating "that woman Jezebel, who calls herself a prophet" (2:20). Think of her—for John—as a pseudo-prophet like the pseudo-apostles at Ephesus or the pseudo-Jews at Smyrna and Philadelphia—all of whom are inside and not outside those Christian communities (2:2, 9; 3:9).

Then, after presenting three major metaphorical personifications in the Dragon, the Beast, and the Whore, John introduces a new major personification called the False Prophet:

> I saw three foul spirits like frogs coming from the mouth of the dragon, from the mouth of the beast, and from the mouth of the *false prophet*. (16:13)

> The beast was captured, and with it the *false prophet* who had performed in its presence the signs by which he deceived those who had received the mark of the beast and those who worshiped its image. These two were thrown alive into the lake of fire that burns with sulfur. (19:20)

> The devil who had deceived them was thrown into the lake of fire and sulfur, where the beast and the *false prophet* were, and they will be tormented day and night forever and ever. (20:10)

Those are the only three times the False Prophet appears by that name in Revelation. Notice, however, that it never appears there alone. It is either with the Beast (19:20) or with both the Dragon/Devil and the Beast (16:13; 20:10).

Who or what exactly is the False Prophet? And does John point us to the answer by framing his book with *deception* and *false prophecy* from a person at the start to a personification at the end?

We already saw John's first unholy trinity in the Dragon, the Beast, and the Whore. The Dragon is the Satan or the Devil (2:9–10; 12:9); the Beast is the Roman Empire, its emperors in general, and Nero Returning in particular (13:3, 18); and the Whore is the city of Rome, especially as lure for luxury trade from provincial cities (18:3c, 11, 15, 23). Strictly speaking, however, the Whore is seated on the Beast (17:3) and is already part of the Beast as the capital city of the Roman Empire. Eventually, therefore, John collapses the Whore back into the Beast and creates a new and final unholy trinity in the Dragon, the Beast, and the False Prophet.

In John's thinking, the Dragon and the Beast attack his churches from outside, the Whore seduces them also from outside, but the False Prophet is the Dragon, the Beast, and the Whore as already within the church, as already inside the community. *The False Prophet is acculturation itself.* Furthermore, using his favorite framing technique at the book's start and finish, acculturation as the False Prophet is inaugurally present with Jezebel at Thyatira (2:20) and then ultimately personified on a level with, but totally dependent on, the Dragon, the Beast, and the Whore (19:20; 20:10).

For John, there remain these three: the Satan, the Beast, and the False Prophet, that is, demonic evil, Roman Empire, and acculturation between Messianic/Christic life and Roman imperial normalcy—but the greatest, most immediate, and most internal threat is that final one.

We can now answer *together* both the basic question of this chapter—namely, why does John describe a slaughter that never happened?—and propose an understanding of John's rhetorical strategy and his book's overall purpose.

Revelation paints a glorious picture of heavenly transcendence centered on the throne of God:

> I heard the voice of many angels surrounding the throne and the living creatures and the elders; they numbered myriads of myriads and thousands of thousands. . . . Then I heard every creature in heaven and on earth and under the earth and in the sea, and all that is in them, singing, "To the one seated on the *throne* and to the Lamb be blessing and honor and glory and might forever and ever!" (5:11, 13)

The "throne of God," mentioned about forty times in Revelation, is like an insistent theme from 1:4 to 22:3.

Furthermore, that magnificent vision of heavenly transcendence becomes a gift of earthly immanence:

> I heard a loud voice from the *throne* saying, "See, the home of God is among mortals. He will dwell with them; they will be his peoples, and God himself will be with them; he will wipe every tear from their eyes. Death will be no more; mourning and crying and pain will be no more, for the first things have passed away." And the one who was seated on the *throne* said, "See, I am making all things new." (21:3–5)

That rhapsodic scenario makes the "throne" of the Satan (2:13), which undergirds the "throne" of the Beast (13:2; 16:10), look like a bad joke. But, of course, that rather serene contrast is more the outer frames than the inner content of Revelation.

In the inner content, John's vision is repeated in ever differing images, but with this underlying and reciprocal logic: *in the imminent future Christ will slaughter Romans because in the immediate past Rome slaughtered Christians.* That vision makes an understandable appeal to the human instinct for a vengeful reckoning of retributive justice. It leaves us, however, with these final questions: Is John's prophecy of the imminent future a mistake and his history of the immediate past a lie? Is Revelation all radically false? If so, why was it ever written?

The first part of John's reciprocal vision was a *prophecy* about the imminent future. As we know—and knew by the fourth century—it was a wildly wrong forecast of what actually happened with regard to *when* and especially with regard to *what.* The Roman Empire was not destroyed *by* Christ, but was converted *to* Christ. John's promise of imminent ("soon") slaughter by Christ was *historically* wrong.

But was that promise also *theologically* wrong? Does Christus Redivivus acting as Nero Redivivus turn the Christ of the gospel into the anti-Christ of the apocalypse? For myself, the answer is yes, because this apocalyptic Christ is not the gospel Christ. Rome executed Jesus for nonviolent resistance against its own imperial violence (John 18:36), and Jesus's nonviolent resistance was exercised in imitation, manifestation, and incarnation of a nonviolent God (Matt. 5:45; Luke 6:35).

The *rule of God* on earth was for Jesus—and Paul after him—an alternative to the *rule of Rome* on earth. But they asserted it as an ongoing confrontation rather than as an imminent destruction. The book of Revelation replaces good news with fake news.

Be that as it may, the second part of John's reciprocal vision was a *history* about the immediate past. But, then, as the modern consensus of scholarship holds and as we argued earlier, there was no such imperial persecution—let alone wholesale slaughter—of Christians before, during, or after Domitian. (What Nero did to Roman "Christians" after the Great Fire of 64 was a savage personal aberration, *not* an imperial global policy.)

Acculturation to Roman ways is the possibility—no, better, the already dawning actuality—that sears John's vision at its core and gives him the authorial intention and rhetorical strategy for Revelation. He sees urban trade for artisans and merchants as already the Roman camel's nose inside the Messianic/Christic tent. With craft associations come meals (idol offerings) and marriages (fornication) that facilitate further acculturation.

In response, he deliberately portrays Roman imperialism as so ferociously evil, so obscenely murderous, so pornographically seductive, and so imminently doomed that nobody could, would, or should even imagine the slightest accommodation to it. Call it accommodation or adaptation or assimilation or acculturation, it is all alike for John, and he paints it as so evil that one must surely avoid even the first fatal dance with Romanization.

In the meanwhile, the (alleged) persecution is only for a *short* period and vindication is for a *far longer* time, and, on the model of an imminently returning Nero, John portrays an imminently returning Christ with a cosmic slaughter, a vintage trampled out in blood, and a feast for vultures.

Concluding Unscientific Postscript on Revelation. You were historically wrong, John. You were wrong that Romans slaughtered Christians in the immediate past. You were wrong that God would slaughter Romans in the immediate future. You did see, however, how economy subverts theology or, better, becomes theology.

Revelation is simply the demonization of acculturation with Rome. The imperial city of Rome is the Whore of Babylon and will "soon" be replaced by the new Jerusalem as the Bride of Christ (21:2). That is one view, an absolutely extreme view. What, however, about the opposite and equally extreme view? What if somebody imagined not a new Jerusalem replacing the old Rome, but a new Rome replacing the old Jerusalem? That is what comes next in Part Two.

PART TWO

CULTURE
ACCEPTED
AND
CANONIZED

And so we came to Rome.
—Acts 28:14

6

CREATING A COUNTERNARRATIVE

BOTH THE JEWISH HISTORIAN JOSEPHUS AND THE ROMAN historian Tacitus gave concise summaries of the Christian narrative that, despite rhetorical differences, agree very closely on the basic sequence of events.

In his *Jewish Antiquities*, from the 90s, Josephus outlines the history of Christianity as a *narrative* sequence of four events:

> [Movement] About this time there lived Jesus, a wise man, *if indeed one ought to call him a man*. For he was one who wrought surprising feats and was a teacher of such people as accept the truth gladly. He won over many Jews and many of the Greeks. *He was the Messiah (ho christos houtos ēn).*

> [Execution] When Pilate, upon hearing him accused by men of the highest standing amongst us, had condemned him to be crucified,

> [Continuation] those who had in the first place come to love him did not give up their affection for him. *On the third day*

*he appeared to them restored to life, for the prophets of God had
prophesied these and countless other marvelous things about him.*

[Expansion] And the tribe of the Christians, so called after him,
has still to this day not disappeared. (18.63–64)

The general scholarly consensus today is that Christian copyists
interpolated the three italicized portions, but the rest comes from
Josephus. Politely noncommittal and prudently inoffensive, that authentic core text suffices for the present discussion.

Tacitus, in his *Annals*, written in the 110s, records Rome's imperial
history from Tiberius through Nero and gives a brief history of Christianity using the same four successive *narrative* stages as Josephus twenty
years earlier:

[Movement] Christus, the founder of the name,

[Execution] had undergone the death penalty in the reign of
Tiberius, by sentence of the procurator Pontius Pilatus, and the
pernicious superstition was checked for a moment,

[Continuation] only to break out once more, not merely in
Judaea, the home of the disease,

[Expansion] but in the capital itself, where all things horrible or
shameful in the world collect and find a vogue. (15.44)

That was the official Roman narrative about Christianity in the first
years of the second century. Also, apart from its neutral or nasty rhetorical overtones, it was a perfectly true and absolutely accurate narrative.

There were also, of course, sweeping polemical indictments.
Tacitus, as just seen, called Christianity a "pernicious superstition."

That precise evaluation agrees with one by Pliny the Younger, imperial governor of Bithynia-Pontus, on the southern coast of the Black Sea, who called Christianity "a depraved, excessive, and contagious superstition" in 111 (*Letters* 10.96). It also agrees with the assessment of Suetonius, gossip, historian, and secretary to the emperor Hadrian, for whom Christianity was "a new and evil superstition" in 122 (*Nero* 16.2).

At the start of the second century, therefore, contemporary texts accused earliest Christianity of superstitious content and described its inimical advent. Faced with two such textual attacks, what textual defenses were created by Christian intellectuals as that century progressed?

On the one hand, Christian apologists wrote texts publicly defending their religion against accusations of superstition. St. Justin Martyr, born in 100 at Flavia Neapolis—modern Palestinian Nablus—and beheaded in 165 at Rome, addressed his defense to the emperor Antoninus Pius and the Senate and people of Rome. He wrote it in 156 "on behalf of those of all nations who are unjustly hated and wantonly abused, myself being one of them" and made, for example, this telling rebuttal of Rome's accusation of superstition:

> When we say also that the Word, who is the first-birth of
> God, was produced without sexual union, and that He, Jesus
> Christ, our Teacher, was crucified and died, and rose again,
> and ascended into heaven, we propound nothing different from
> what you believe regarding those whom you esteem sons of
> Jupiter . . . Mercury, Aesculapius, Bacchus, Hercules, the sons
> of Leda, Dioscuri, Perseus, Bellerophon, Ariadne . . . and the
> emperors who die among yourselves, whom you deem worthy
> of deification, and in whose behalf you produce someone who
> swears he has seen the burning Caesar rise to heaven from the
> funeral pyre. (*First Apology* 21)

If Roman stories about divine conceptions and heavenly ascensions were religion and not superstition, why were similar Christian stories superstition and not religion? Rome's polemical accusations against Christianity at the start of the second century were countered by similar apologetic rebuttals throughout the following decades.

On the other hand, apart from attacking Christianity as a superstition—new, evil, depraved, excessive, contagious, and pernicious—what about the brief early history of Christianity presented by Josephus and Tacitus? Christ, "the founder of the name," the creator of the Christian movement, died by legal and public *Roman* execution: "Pilate . . . had condemned him to be crucified" (Josephus); Christ had "undergone the death penalty in the reign of Tiberius, by sentence of the procurator Pontius Pilatus" (Tacitus).

However nasty the rhetoric, Tacitus's story was an accurate summary that, although written in the 110s, ended with Christianity at Rome in the 60s. Its core was the simple truth: there was a movement over there; Romans executed its founder, but it continued and spread even to Rome itself. How did Christian writers recover from that Roman narrative of Christian origins?

Only an alternative pro-Christian story, a plausible *counternarrative*, could offset Rome's anti-Christian story. Even if it too were written around the same time as Tacitus's summary version, in the early decades of the second century, it could and should end with Christianity at Rome *in the 60s*. That, of course, is a precise description of Luke-Acts as a unified two-volume narrative written to counter the Roman version.

As an aside, "controlling the narrative" is the purpose of Luke-Acts, and that authorial intention raises basic questions about whether it is telling the truth, the whole truth, and nothing but the truth. Are there different ethical constraints on omissions or inaccuracies about insiders than there are for those about outsiders when you are defending your version of the story? Is false witness *for oneself* somehow excusable since the commandment only forbids false witness *against another* (Luke 18:20; Acts 6:13)? Those questions will remain a constant presence as this and the next chapters look at Luke-Acts.

———

In the small, official, and closed library known as the Christian New Testament, the third text is called the Gospel According to Luke and the fifth one is named the Acts of the Apostles. Even a cursory glance at their dedications indicates that the two volumes form some sort of intentional unity. The former begins: "I too decided . . . to write an orderly account for you, most excellent Theophilus" (Luke 1:3); and the latter starts by looking backward: "In the first book, Theophilus, I wrote about all that Jesus did and taught" (Acts 1:1). But what type of authorial unity is involved in those two books? And why is that important—then and now?

Imagine, for example, the difference between a backward-looking and a forward-looking unity of authorial intention and textual integration. A *backward-looking* unity means that the Gospel According to Luke was written as a complete text unto itself, and only after it was completed and/or published, did its author conceive, execute, and publish the Acts of the Apostles. In that scenario, it would be possible or even inevitable to make certain backward connections as, for example, where that second dedication looks backward to the first one. Luke would be a book planned and completed in itself before Acts was later planned as a sequel (as with the two movies, *Jaws* and *Jaws 2*; the title *Jaws 1* never existed).

A *forward-looking* unity means that those two volumes were originally conceived, outlined, executed, and published as a unified whole. They were never intended to be named independently or physically separated, as they are now within the closed New Testament. To read them as book-plus-sequel denies their authorial intention, negates their textual integrity, and guarantees misunderstanding of their original meaning.

But why was it so easy to create that separation? If Luke-Acts was originally a single text, why was it composed in two smaller volumes rather than in one larger volume? A comparison with a similar text from around the same general time may help to answer that question.

———

In the early 90s, Josephus's *Jewish Antiquities* gave a magisterial account of his people's ancient traditions and historical experiences. When that pro-Jewish apologetic provoked anti-Jewish reaction during the following decade, Josephus added to later editions of *Jewish Antiquities* a powerful polemic against all such cultivated Greek despisers of Judaism. Although it was originally an *untitled* appendix to his *Jewish Antiquities*, that addition eventually became known as *Against Apion*.

That later title is rather inadequate, since Apion of Alexandria does not appear until the second half of the book (2.1–144). Also, apart from Apion, Josephus's attack makes sweeping criticisms of Greek historiography and all its anti-Jewish libels and slanders. In any case, what we now call *Against Apion* is a two-volume treatise, and that raises exactly the same question I just asked about Luke-Acts: Why did Josephus present his *Against Apion* as two smaller volumes rather than as a single larger volume?

The author himself gives us a hint at the end of *Against Apion*'s first volume: "This book however, having already run to a *suitable length*, I propose at this point to begin a second, in which I shall endeavor to supply the remaining portion of my subject" (1.320). But how does Josephus decide on a suitable length and know he has now reached it?

That "suitable length" is not about the limits of message but of medium, not about the limits of content but of technology. Our word "volume" comes from *volumen*, the Latin word for "scroll." The number of volumes in a work, that is, the number of scrolls needed for it, was dictated by the physical constraints of the medium itself.

Scrolls made from papyrus or paper were more delicate, not as strong as scrolls made from parchment or leather—like those found in 1947 in the caves northwest of the Dead Sea. In a papyrus scroll, individual sheets were glued together, and the text continued sheet by sheet, but only on the inside. (A papyrus *codex*, sheets bound together like our books, had writing on both sides of the sheets.)

The suitable length of a papyrus scroll was determined by two physical factors. A scroll could not be so large that a reader could not comfortably unroll it with one hand while rerolling it with the other. It also could not be so large that its glued seams would simply split under the strain of its rolled-up pressure. So, in general, if you purchased an empty papyrus scroll, it would be around thirty feet long—for purely practical reasons.

Josephus's polemic against Gentile slander was long enough to require two scrolls, hence two volumes, even though it was a text conceived, planned, written, and published as a single work. Furthermore, to avoid the possibility that his two-volume work might get separated, Josephus makes clear textual links *forward* and *backward* between the two scrolls/volumes of *Against Apion*.

First, there is the common dedication to the "most excellent Epaphroditus" (1.1) and to "my most esteemed Epaphroditus" (2.1). Next, recall that already cited last sentence of the first scroll: "This book however, having already run to a suitable length, I propose at this point to begin a *second*, in which I shall endeavor to supply the remaining portion of my subject" (1.320). This links to the first sentence of the second scroll: "In the *first* volume of this work, my most esteemed Epaphroditus, I demonstrated the antiquity of our race . . ." (2.1).

Then, the entire two-scroll/volume work ended with this linkage to the opening dedication of each one (1.1 and 2.1): "To you, Epaphroditus . . . I beg to dedicate this and the preceding book" (2.296).

Finally, of course there was the continuing subject of both scrolls in their defense of the "extreme antiquity of our Jewish race" (1.1; 2.1) and in refuting the "malicious calumnies" (1.2) and "lying statements" (2.6) about it.

Obviously, therefore, Josephus's *Against Apion* was planned, written, and published as a single two-volume work. Nobody, of course, has ever suggested otherwise. It occupied two scrolls/volumes as a physical necessity, but it was never divided into two works, never filed separately in some library, and never called a single-volume *book* and its single-volume *sequel*. It lives its literary life as the unity it always was.

Against Apion is used here, of course, as a counterexample of what happened to that other two-volume work later separated into the Gospel According to Luke and the Acts of the Apostles.

The author's purpose in planning, care in writing, and intention in publishing Luke-Acts as a unified two-volume work was ignored when it was separated in place and by name within the Christian New Testament. And, of course, that is an official library where locations are absolute, titles are perpetual, and mistakes are frozen in place forever. Still, to repeat from above, what is at stake here is how such separation has obscured the vision of the author, negated the integrity of the text, and guaranteed that readers will misunderstand its message.

It will take this chapter and the next three to vindicate that Luke-Acts was originally intended and must be interpreted as a single unified whole. This present chapter presents only a preliminary introduction to that reading. Do we find not just backward-looking but forward-looking unity in Luke-Acts? Was each planned and written as part of a whole? Do we find strong indications in the content of Luke that its author was already writing with Acts in mind?

First, with regard to *backward-looking* unity, the two-volume Luke-

Acts has textual links very similar to those just seen in the two-volume *Against Apion*. The first volume of Luke-Acts is addressed to "most excellent Theophilus" (Luke 1:3), using the same Greek term for "most excellent" as in *Against Apion* 1.1. Then, the second volume of Luke-Acts links backward to that dedication by beginning, "In the first book, Theophilus . . ." (Acts 1:1). This person is not known anywhere else, but the name means "God lover." Those common dedications link the two volumes at least by this backward connection.

Second, what about a *forward-looking* connection? There is clear transitional linkage forward from the end of the first to the start of the second volume. This leaves us in expectation at the end of Luke for something to come at the start of Acts. Watch how that process works.

At the end of Luke, Jesus tells his followers: "I am sending upon you what my Father promised; so stay here in the city *until* you have been clothed with power from on high" (24:49). This is a command not to stay permanently in Jerusalem, but to stay *temporarily* until the advent of a divinely promised heavenly power. At that point, readers are left not only anticipating a future moment, but wondering about what it means. Think of it as a literary cliffhanger in a serial story.

Then, at the start of Acts, that pledge is recalled, repeated, and explained, but is still left awaiting fulfillment and completion:

> While staying with them, he ordered them not to leave
> Jerusalem, but to *wait* there *for* the promise of the Father.
> "This," he said, "is what you have heard from me; for John
> baptized with water, but you will be baptized with the Holy
> Spirit not many days from now. . . . You *will receive* power
> when the Holy Spirit has come upon you." (1:4–5, 8)

The Father's promise is the Spirit's power, and its advent is fulfilled in what we call Pentecost, an event described visibly only in Acts 2 in the entire New Testament. Jesus, "exalted at the right hand of God, and having received from the Father the promise of the Holy Spirit, he has poured out this that you both see and hear." (2:33)

The forward-looking connection from promise in Luke 24:49 to fulfillment in Acts 1:4–5, 8 is the *first of seven* such major indications that Luke-Acts was originally planned, written, and published as a conceptually unified two-volume book, so that authorial intention cannot be understood independently for each one but only for both together.

Let me compare that claim with the alternative conclusion in the magisterial work of the late Jesuit scholar Joseph A. Fitzmyer, writing first on the Gospel According to Luke and then on the Acts of the Apostles in the Anchor Bible commentary series.[1]

In the Preface to his commentary on Luke from 1981, Father Fitzmyer speaks of "the Lucan Gospel as only one part of a two-volume work" and repeats that "two-volume" designation on the next page.[2] But in the following section, "The Current State of Luke Studies," he starts to use—and keeps on thereafter—the word "sequel" for Acts.

Similarly, at the start of his Acts commentary from 1985, Father Fitzmyer speaks of "a unity of conception that dominates the two-volume work." He also refers to Luke's "two-volume narrative monograph" and his "two-volume monographical account of the Jesus-story." But he also reverts to his more standard description of Acts as a sequel: "Luke . . . is the sole evangelist to compose a sequel to his Gospel."[3]

A two-volume work, however, is not the same as a one-volume work and its one-volume sequel in authorial intention, textual purpose, or readerly understanding—not for *Against Apion* and not for Luke-Acts. Indeed, as Father Fitzmyer acknowledges: "Despite the wide-spread admission of the common authorship of Luke-Acts, rare is the modern interpreter who has attempted to compose a commentary on the two volumes precisely as two volumes dominated by a single conception."[4]

In the remaining chapters of Part Two, we look at Luke-Acts precisely "as two volumes dominated by a single conception," as a unified and integrated two-volume work conceived, structured, written, and published as such under one single authorial vision.

––––––––––

It will take all of Part Two to prove that interpretation completely but, for the rest of this chapter, we look at two preliminary examples—one very small and one very large—to see how *forward-looking* connections work in Luke-Acts.

The first probe concerns the last word in Luke 1:1–4 and the last word in Acts 28:31 (in Greek). Luke 1:1–4 was described by Father Fitzmyer, for example, as "the Lucan prologue . . . the introduction to the two volumes . . . [which] has to be so understood, as is generally recognized among commentators today."[5] If Luke 1:1–4 is the official introduction to all of Luke-Acts, that whole two-volume production must have been there in authorial intention from the start.

In Luke 1:1–4, a single long sentence with each of its three phrases in a two-strophe pattern, Luke proclaims his credentials with regard to both historical research and literary style:

> *Since many* have undertaken to set down an orderly account
> (*diēgēsin*) of the events that have been fulfilled among us,
> just as they were handed on to us by those who from the
> beginning were eyewitnesses and servants of the word,
>
> *I too* decided, after investigating everything carefully from the
> very first,
> to write an orderly account (*kathexēs*) for you, most excellent
> Theophilus,
>
> *so that* you may know the truth (*asphaleian*)
> concerning the things about which you have been instructed.

Notice, to begin with, the sequence "Since many . . . I too . . . so that." Commentators are correct to emphasize the balanced elegance of that pattern, but I want to discuss, rather, the logical consistency of that content. To say, "Since many have written orderly accounts, I am going to do the same" doesn't follow logically. The "since" construction leads readers to expect that the speaker will write something better, more accurate, or at least different from the orderly accounts that have already been written—not that the speaker *too* will write an orderly account. Bluntly, what does this prologue project that has not already been done? What does Luke-Acts claim to add to past work?

To clarify this problem, look one final time at Josephus's prologue to his two-volume *Against Apion*, and note that its pattern is parallel to the one in Luke-Acts, but its logic is comparatively better:

> *Since* . . . a considerable number . . . discredit . . . my history of our antiquity . . .

> *I* consider it my duty to devote a brief treatise to all these points . . .

> *in order* to convict our detractors of malignity and deliberate falsehood . . .

There the logic is clear: "Since many attack, I will defend." Indeed, in any such prologue you expect other authors who have acted incorrectly, incompletely, or inadequately to be counterpointed by an author who will now write correctly, completely, or fully. (I am doing that implicitly right now myself, and that "Since they did . . . , I will now do . . ." structure is a common introduction to doctoral dissertations!)

There is, however, a third phrase in the formal prologue to Luke-Acts and, since the previous other writers and the current writer both work with "orderly accounts," this must be what is promised as especially worthwhile in the book to follow. Here, to repeat, is its translation: "so that you may know the truth concerning the things about which you have been instructed" (Luke 1:4). For its author, Luke 1:4 summarizes the purpose, explains the intention, and justifies the existence of Luke-Acts.

That concluding "so that" phrase simply creates another logical problem, however. If "many have undertaken to set down an orderly account of the events that have been fulfilled among us, just as they were handed on to us by those who from the beginning were eyewitnesses and servants of the word," how does Theophilus—and any others—*not* "know the truth concerning the things about which" they have been "instructed"? Is that, however, a problem with the ancient logic or only with the modern translation of Luke 1:4?

The original Greek word order of that verse reads: "so that you may know, concerning the things about which you have been instructed, the *asphaleia*." The key word is put in the final place, and this climactic position makes a proper translation of *asphaleia* extremely significant both for the logic of Luke 1:1–4 and the general purpose of Luke-Acts itself.

An online survey of about forty translations shows "truth" and "certainty" as the two most common translations for *asphaleia* in Luke 1:4. Others are "soundness," "well-foundedness," "security," "reliability," and "verity." Once again, I repeat my objection: Does Luke-Acts mean to claim that, despite all those writings that went before it, only here and now does one finally attain certainty or truth about Christianity? (What would Paul think about that insult?)

Furthermore, the word *asphaleia* is only used two other times in the entire New Testament, once in Acts and once by Paul:

> We found the prison securely locked (literally, in full *asphaleia*) and the guards standing at the doors, but when we opened them, we found no one inside. (Acts 5:23)

> When they say, "There is peace and security (*asphaleia*)," then sudden destruction will come upon them, as labor pains come upon a pregnant woman, and there will be no escape! (1 Thess. 5:3)

My conclusion is that the logic of Luke 1:1–4 is perfectly valid once its final and climactic word *asphaleia* is translated *not* within the religious world of secure truth about gospel accuracy, but *within the political world of secure safety from Roman power*. Luke 1:1–4 promises to tell the story as fully and responsibly, as others have already done, but to do so emphasizing that Christianity is a religion safe from, safe under, and safe within the power of the Roman Empire. Luke writes to reassure his readers that they are safe and secure not just as Christians, but as *Roman* Christians.

As a vindication of that reading and a preparatory probe into the intentional unity of Luke-Acts, we move from the final word of the prologue—*asphaleia* as "safety"—to the final word of Luke-Acts itself. It says of Paul, who is in Rome awaiting trial: "He lived there two whole years at his own expense and welcomed all who came to him, proclaiming the *rule of God* and teaching about the Lord Jesus Christ with all boldness and without hindrance" (28:30–31).

That "without hindrance" translates the single Greek word *akōlytōs* ("unhindered") and that is, in both senses, the final word from Luke-Acts. The last word of the prologue ("safety") looks to the last word of the whole two-volume work ("unhindered"). In its prologue, Luke-Acts promises as good an account of "of the events that have been fulfilled among us" as others had done before him. But he will do so by emphasizing the political "safety" (*asphaleia*) of a Christian faith "unhindered" (*akōlytōs*) by Roman imperial power.

The forward-looking connection from "safety" in Luke 1:4 to "unhindered" in Acts 28:31 is the *second of seven* such major indications that Luke-Acts was originally planned, written, and published as a conceptually unified two-volume book.

We look next at two parallel stories, one about Jesus and one about Paul, one at the climactic conclusion of Luke, the other at the climactic conclusion of Acts. They exemplify what Luke imagines as Christianity's *unhindered safety* from, with, and under Roman imperial authority. They also indicate that the trial scene of Jesus in Luke was already looking *forward* to the parallel ones of Paul in Acts.

First, Luke gives an account of Jesus on trial before Pilate. He is accused especially by the "chief priests," but they are also accompanied by the "crowds" or the "scribes" or the "leaders, and the people" (Luke 23:4, 10, 13).

As happens so often, Luke's authorial intention is indicated most clearly by how he alters his Markan source. In Mark, the only comment Pilate makes about Jesus's innocence or guilt is this question: "'Why, what evil has he done?'" (Mark 15:14). But in adopting Mark on Pilate, Luke turns that *question* about innocence into a triple *assertion* of innocence:

> "I find no basis for an accusation against this man." (Luke 23:4)

> "You brought me this man as one who was perverting the people; and here I have examined him in your presence and have not found this man guilty of any of your charges against him." (23:14)

> A third time he said to them, "Why, what evil has he done? I have found in him no ground for the sentence of death; I will therefore have him flogged and then release him." (23:22)

In case readers are not counting carefully, Luke even adds in that "third time" for climactic emphasis.

Furthermore, Luke—and only Luke—has Pilate send his prisoner to Herod Antipas because Jesus "was a Galilean . . . under Herod's jurisdiction . . . who was himself in Jerusalem at that time" (23:6–7). But "Herod with his soldiers treated him with contempt and mocked him; then he put an elegant robe on him, and sent him back to Pilate" (23:11).

Luke's contempt and mockery by *Herodian* soldiers is his far gentler version of the torture and mockery by *Roman* soldiers in Mark 15:16–20—otherwise completely omitted by Luke. Pilate has *not* found Jesus guilty and, as he admits, "Neither has Herod, for he sent him back to us. Indeed, he has done nothing to deserve death" in Herod's view (Luke 23:15).

Finally, as a footnote to those official declarations of Jesus's innocence by Pilate and Herod, Luke makes one more deliberate alteration of his Markan source. Such deliberate changes in the Markan text by Luke are, as we see quite often in Part Two, *a very significant index of authorial purpose and intention.*

At the death of Jesus, Mark says, "When the centurion, who stood facing him, saw that in this way he breathed his last, he said, 'Truly this man was God's Son!'" (15:39). Luke changes that to a final assertion of innocence: "When the centurion saw what had taken place, he praised God and said, 'Certainly this man was innocent'" (23:47).

In Jerusalem, therefore, toward the end of Luke, Jesus is declared innocent by *three* levels of Roman authority: by Pontius Pilate as a local governor, by Herod Antipas as a client ruler, and by that unnamed centurion as a military officer. My suggestion is that, with Jesus on trial, Luke expanded on Pilate (three times "innocent"), added in Herod Antipas ("not guilty"), and changed the centurion's declaration (to "innocent"), because he was *looking forward to and preparing for* a similar three-level vindication of Paul—from military officers (plural), a client ruler, and a provincial governor.

The core accusation against Paul comes, once again, from the "chief priests" accompanied by the "leaders of the Jews" or the "elders of the Jews" (Acts 25:2, 15). But now those legal strategies are primarily a cover for a conspiracy to "kill" Paul—and that word rings like a death knell throughout this entire section (21:31; 23:12, 14, 21, 27; 25:3; 26:21). "The Jews" work by legal accusation only because illegal assassination fails.

Next, Paul—like Jesus—is declared innocent on those same three levels of Roman authority, but each one is now slightly higher in degree of imperial power. First, as Jesus was declared innocent by a *centurion*'s voice (Luke 23:47), so Paul is declared innocent by a *tribune*'s letter from Claudius Lysias at Jerusalem to the governor Felix at Caesarea, and it is cited completely and verbatim (Acts 23:26–30). "I found," writes the tribune, "that he was accused concerning questions of their law, but was charged with nothing deserving death or imprisonment" (23:29). A tribune, by the way, commanded a thousand soldiers and was superior to a centurion, who commanded one hundred (21:32; 22:25–26; 23:17, 23).

Paul is not only innocent. He is important enough to warrant a guard of "two hundred soldiers, seventy horsemen, and two hundred spearmen" with "mounts for Paul to ride, and to take him safely to Felix the governor" (23:23–24).

Second, when Festus replaces Felix as governor, he concurs with the tribune's judgment of innocence:

> When the accusers stood up, they did not charge him with any of the crimes that I was expecting. Instead they had certain points of disagreement with him about their own religion and about a certain Jesus, who had died, but whom Paul asserted to be alive. . . . But I found that he had done nothing deserving death; and when he appealed to his Imperial Majesty, I decided to send him. (25:18–19, 25)

Festus, by the way, is now governor over the territories once divided between Pilate and Antipas, and his declaration of innocence is thus intensified on that level as well.

Third, as the Herodian client prince Antipas agreed with the governor

Pilate on Jesus's innocence, so now the Herodian client king Agrippa II concurs with the governor Festus on Paul's innocence. Agrippa II, the last of the Herodian dynasty, was "king" of Ituraea and Trachonitis—once the territory of Herod Philip (Luke 3:1). He and his widowed sister Bernice "arrived at Caesarea to welcome Festus" as the new governor (Acts 25:23), and after hearing Paul's defense,

> The king got up, and with him the governor and Bernice and those who had been seated with them; and as they were leaving, they said to one another, "This man is doing nothing to deserve death or imprisonment." Agrippa said to Festus, "This man could have been set free if he had not appealed to the emperor." (26:30–32)

Luke's *narrative* logic is presumably that, although declared innocent at Caesarea, the ongoing threat of assassination from Jerusalem forces Paul to insist on imperial trial at Rome. In any case, in Luke's entire scenario "the Jews" are riotous and murderous villains, while the Roman authorities are fair, just, impartial, and legal.

The forward-looking connection from three levels of Roman authority asserting Jesus's innocence in Luke (23:4, 14, 22; 23:11, 15; 23:47) to the same asserting Paul's innocence in Acts (23:26–30; 25:18–19, 25; 26:30–32) is the *third of seven* such major indications that Luke-Acts was originally planned, written, and published as a conceptually unified two-volume book.

———

This chapter presented some initial probes toward confirming Part Two's hypothesis that Luke-Acts was initially imagined, originally planned, inaugurally outlined, and finally published as a conceptually unified two-volume book—just like Josephus's *Against Apion*.

That hypothesis will need continual confirmation as we proceed and also have its implications clarified. As that happens and when it *has* happened, you will understand how wrong it is to read Luke as a stand-alone text followed by Acts as a stand-alone sequel connected only by having the same author and same sponsor. That separation betrays the author's intention, the book's plan, the text's meaning, and the readers' response.

We have begun our exploration of Luke-Acts as a two-volume unified *book*; in the next chapter, we look at the *author* of this two-volume work. What can we know about this person and how does any such authorial knowledge confirm or negate the intended unity of Luke-Acts?

An author may be identified *externally*, from outside the text, or *internally*, from inside it. For example, in this book's Part One, the author of Revelation was internally identified at its start and finish as "John, your brother . . . who heard and saw these things" (1:1, 4, 9; 22:8). Also, an author may be identified *explicitly*—as just seen—or *implicitly*, by drawing conclusions about character or personality, time or place, purpose or meaning from inside the text itself.

In the following chapter, we begin with explicit and external evidence about the author of Luke-Acts before moving—*primarily*—to internal and implicit evidence. That latter evidence focuses on special emphases in Luke-Acts seen by watching how it changes its sources or deviates from parallel versions.

7

"WHOM PAUL HAD TAKEN WITH HIM"

THE AUTHOR OF LUKE-ACTS IS NOT IDENTIFIED EXPLICITLY *inside* that text—as was John inside Revelation. But is the author of Luke-Acts identified explicitly *outside* that text itself? Are there any external documentary claims about the author who wrote the two-volume book? The answer develops over the next three successive steps.

First, among the seven authentic letters from the historical Paul is one to Philemon reminding him that he can no longer own his newly converted slave Onesimus. Paul is imprisoned and chained to a guard in—probably—the governor's jail at Ephesus. In any case, he is allowed on-site supporters and names them: "Epaphras, my fellow prisoner in Christ Jesus, sends greetings to you, and so do Mark, Aristarchus, Demas, and Luke, my fellow workers" (23–24). At that moment, at least, a Luke is among Paul's companions.

Next, two letters written after Paul's death but fictionally attributed to him mention that same name. Pseudo-Paul tells the Colossians: "Luke, the beloved physician, and Demas greet you" (4:14). And in another pseudo-Pauline letter, he complains: "Only Luke is with me" (2 Tim. 4:11). Is that the same Luke mentioned in Philemon? A different person named Luke? Or a deliberate reference to a name found in Philemon in order to establish verisimilitude in the two pseudo-Pauline letters, a deliberate connection to make the "Pauline" authorship of them more believable? The last seems most likely.

Finally, from outside the New Testament, we have a list of its books with comments on their authors in a manuscript known today as the Muratorian Canon. This fragmentary catalogue was written in Greek around 170, translated into Latin and copied into a random collection of early Christian texts in the 700s, passed from St. Columbanus Abbey Library at Bobbio to Cardinal Borromeo's Veneranda Biblioteca Ambrosiana (Ambrosian Library) at Milan in the early 1600s, and "discovered" there by Father Ludovico Antonio Muratori in 1740.

Despite its fragmented state, eccentric grammar, irregular script, and—of course—competing scholarly emendations, the Muratorian Canon's two and a half pages are extremely precious from a historical viewpoint. Even with the start and finish missing, it contains the earliest description of the New Testament's small library of books.

The extant text of the Muratorian Canon starts with the red-lettered title "The Third Book . . . the Gospel According to Luke" and continues with this information:

> Luke, that well-known (*iste*) physician, after the ascension of Christ, whom Paul had taken with him as one learned in the law (*iuris studiosum*), composed in his own name, according to the general belief. Yet he himself had not seen the Lord in the flesh; and therefore, as he was able to determine events, so indeed he begins to tell the story from the birth of John. (VBA, Codex 101, folios 10–11, lines 2–8)

The phrase "that well-known physician" gives no more information and is probably derived from "Luke, the beloved physician" of Colossians 4:14. That other comment about Luke is rather surprising—as if Paul would have needed another one "learned in the law" besides himself.

Then, after a red-lettered title for "The Fourth of the Gospels, of John," and after some commentary on John, the Canon turns to:

> The Acts of All the Apostles written in one book. For "most excellent Theophilus," Luke recorded only the individual events that took place in his presence (*sub praesentia eius singula*), as shown clearly by his omitting the martyrdom of Peter as well as the departure of Paul from the city [of Rome] when he journeyed to Spain. (lines 34–38)

Since "Luke recorded only the individual events that took place in his presence," the author of Acts is writing only what he has seen and heard. As Paul's companion—from Philemon—Luke is a disciplined eyewitness author.

That shows clearly what is at stake in all that authorial identification. With the author of Luke-Acts—and especially of Acts itself—as a companion of Paul, he is an accredited author/ity on what he describes and narrates. He is writing fact, not fiction, not even fact-based fiction. He is writing history, not a historical novel nor even a historical parable.

Further, apart from that *external* evidence, there is also *internal* evidence that the author of Luke-Acts was a companion of Paul for at least half of Acts. Here is that evidence.

Internal evidence about the author of Luke-Acts arises from four locations in Acts where the text shifts abruptly from the more usual third-person ("he/him") stories *about* Paul to a surprising first-person ("we/us") story in which the speaker is *with* Paul—in Acts 16:10–17; 20:5–15; 21:1–18; 27:1–28:16. Those "we/us" sections, replete with detailed times and places, are a travel diary kept by someone who was Paul's companion—at least for the second half of Acts.

First of all, it is not as if this travel companion just jumps in and out of Paul's life four times at random. Instead, those four "we/us" sections indicate that Luke-Acts is using a coherent narrative sequence from a well-kept travel diary replete with precise times and exact places.

The first shift to a "we/us" section, in Acts 16:10–17, is especially important for understanding this travel diary from a Pauline companion. Paul is at Alexandria Troas on the northwestern Aegean coast of modern Turkey—note the first shift from "he" to "we":

> During the night Paul had a vision: there stood a man of
> Macedonia pleading with him and saying, "Come over to
> Macedonia and help us." When *he* had seen the vision, *we*
> immediately tried to cross over to Macedonia, being convinced
> that God had called us to proclaim the good news to them.
> (16:9–10)

The story then continues in the "we" format across the northern Aegean Sea from Troas in modern Turkey, past Samothrace island, to Neapolis in modern Greece, that is, from Asia to Europe. The "we" journey ends at Philippi, "a leading city of the district of Macedonia and a Roman colony" (16:12).

Behind that dreamed request by a Macedonian is a real human invitation by a live Macedonian to cross over from Troas to Philippi. This unnamed *Philippian* was Paul's sponsor or even a patron for an introduction to Philippi, and he was also the travel diarist behind the "we/us" sections in Acts.

Paul himself refers to this incident somewhat differently by saying: "When I came to Troas to proclaim the good news of Christ, a door was opened for me in the Lord; but my mind could not rest because I did not find my brother Titus there. So I said farewell to them and went on to Macedonia" (2 Cor. 2:12–13).

Identifying Paul's traveling companion as a Philippian is strengthened when the second "we/us" section, in Acts 20:5–15, begins in that same city—note the shift from "he/him" to "we":

> He [Paul] was about to set sail for Syria when a plot was made against *him* by the Jews, and so *he* decided to return through Macedonia. . . . But *we* sailed from Philippi after the days of Unleavened Bread, and in five days *we* joined them in Troas, where *we* stayed for seven days. (Acts 20:3–6)

I propose, therefore, that that this fellow traveler lived in Philippi, that he first accompanied Paul there from Troas probably as his sponsor, that he stayed in Philippi when Paul continued on from Macedonia to Achaia, and that he rejoined Paul in Philippi on Paul's way back to Troas and on to Jerusalem.

The third "we/us" section begins with "When *we* had parted from" Miletus—then on the Aegean coast (21:1)—and ends with "When *we* arrived in Jerusalem, the brothers welcomed us warmly" and "Paul went with us to visit James; and all the elders were present" (21:17–18). (Acts never explains why James is so important, but Paul does in Galatians 1:19 by naming him as "James the Lord's brother.")

The fourth "we/us" section begins: "When it was decided that *we* were to sail for Italy, they transferred Paul and some other prisoners to a centurion of the Augustan Cohort, named Julius" (27:1). Paul is now traveling from Caesarea to Rome as a prisoner under guard. This final "we/us" section continues through ship changes and a shipwreck and ends: "When *we* came into Rome, Paul was allowed to live by himself, with the soldier who was guarding him" (28:16).

In summary, those four "we/us" sections represent a travel diary from Troas to Philippi (16:10–17), Philippi to Miletus (20:5–15), Miletus to Jerusalem (21:1–18), and finally Jerusalem to Rome (27:1–28:16).

Those four units give Acts 16–28 a skeletal structure and travel diary sequence into which, for example, special events and especially lengthy Pauline speeches could be inserted: to the Athenians on the Areopagus (17:22–31); to the Christian elders at Miletus (20:16–38); to the Jewish people in Jerusalem—with, once again, a murderous reaction when "Gentiles" are mentioned (22:1–22); and to the Roman authorities at Caesarea Maritima, first before the governor Felix (24:10–21) and then before his successor Festus, along with Herod Agrippa II and his sister Bernice (26:2–23).

It is possible—*but not very probable*—that the Luke in Philemon is the author of Luke-Acts, was with Paul at least for the sea travels in Acts 16–28, and kept a detailed travel diary on them. It is also possible—*and much more probable*—that among the sources available to the *unknown* author of Luke-Acts was a travel diary from one of Paul's *unknown* Philippian companions/sponsors in Acts 16–28.

Still, and much more important, despite the Muratorian Canon's *external* claim of Luke as an eyewitness, the *internal* evidence of Acts is that, although its author has excellent *information* about Paul, his *interpretation* is regularly non-Pauline, pseudo-Pauline, or even anti-Pauline. That is especially evident in how and why that author changes his sources.

———

Here is a simple but extremely paradigmatic example of that process in Acts, a test-case comparison of the same incident told first as *information* by Paul and then as counter-information by Acts. The incident concerns the rather memorable story of Paul's secret exit from Damascus.

On the one hand, Paul, "boasting" of his "weakness" to his Corinthian critics, mocks himself with this tiny anecdote:

> In Damascus, the governor under King Aretas guarded the city of Damascus in order to seize me, but I was let down in a basket

through a window in the wall, and escaped from his hands.
(2 Cor. 11:32–33)

The Roman army awarded a wall-crown (*corona muralis*) to the first soldier *over* the wall into a besieged city. In delicate self-mockery, Paul admits he was the first one *out through* the wall of Damascus! And that story fits very well with both Pauline autobiography and Nabatean history.

Paul records that after his divine call to "proclaim Christ among the Gentiles," he "went away at once into Arabia, and afterwards . . . returned to Damascus" (Gal. 1:16–17). He even swears to it: "In what I am writing to you, before God I do not lie!" (1:20). Since he was commissioned for the Gentiles, he immediately went south of Damascus to the nearest Gentiles—the Nabatean Arabs ruled by Aretas IV Philopatris, whose capital was Petra, the poet's "rose-red city half as old as time."

Unfortunately for Paul, ongoing tensions on the border between Antipas's *Jewish* Perea and Aretas's *Arabian* Nabatea broke into open warfare in the fall of 36, and "in the ensuing battle," according to Josephus, "the whole army of Herod Antipas was destroyed" (*JA* 18.114). Aretas then grabbed control—at least temporarily—of Damascus, and its *Arab* governor moved to arrest the *Jew* Paul. That brought Paul's Arabian mission to an abrupt end after only three years (33–36), and he then fled south to Jerusalem (Gal. 1:17). All of that makes excellent historical, geographical, and biographical sense.

On the other hand, Luke, who must have known that story either from generally known oral tradition or from Paul's own account, retells it like this:

> After some time had passed, the Jews plotted to kill him, but
> their plot became known to Saul. They were watching the gates
> day and night so that they might kill him; but his disciples took

him by night and let him down through an opening in the wall, lowering him in a basket. (Acts 9:23–25)

Both versions agree on *through* the wall and *down* in a basket, but for Paul it is Arab political authorities who want "to seize him," while for Luke it is Jewish religious authorities who want "to kill him"— mentioned twice.

Bluntly, "the Jews" never did nor could control the gates and walls of Arab Damascus. Luke's version is historically implausible, politically impossible, and theologically malicious. Watch, therefore, very, very carefully how Luke-Acts handles "the Jews" throughout the rest of this book.

Furthermore, Luke dates Paul's Damascus exit immediately after his conversion from Pharisaic Jew to Messianic/Christic Jew in 33 (Acts 9:22, 26) rather than at the end of his Arabian mission in 36 (Gal. 1:18). For Luke, there never was an independent God-sent *apostolic* mission (from *apostellein*, "to send") by Paul in Arab Nabatea.

For here and now, I emphasize only the *fact* of rather than the *reason* for Luke-Acts's libel against the Damascus Jews because, whoever he is, the author of Luke-Acts has his own historical, geographical, biographical, and theological vision, which is *fundamentally divergent from or even inimical to that of the apostle Paul.* That divergence between Luke's Paul and Paul's Paul will be confirmed repeatedly and intensively as Part Two continues.

At this point, we move to internal and indirect information about that author's *character.* Think, for example, how you can read an anonymous op-ed piece and, without knowing a name, discern information about the writer's character like religious vision, political affiliation, general education, and disposition (either polite or rude, calm or angry, etc.).

Is there any internal evidence in Luke-Acts that gives information about its author's character? Does the author—implicitly, indirectly, obliquely, maybe even unconsciously—ever sign textual autographs anywhere in Luke-Acts? Does the author leave personal fingerprints anywhere in that two-volume work?

The author of Luke-Acts does in fact leave autobiographical DNA in the text—quite emphatically if quite indirectly. We work toward that character identification in three steps. The first two concern changes Luke makes in his Markan source in preparation for what will appear in Acts. Granted those changes as matrix, the third step is where this author's character becomes most evident—and significant.

The first step looks at the omission of Mark 7–8 in Luke as a preparation for presenting its content later in Acts 10–11. Recall that, with regard to both sequence and content, Mark is the major source for Luke, and changing it in major ways is a basic indication of an intention. It also shows, of course, that even when writing Luke that author was already imagining Acts.

In Mark, Jesus declares to the crowds: "There is nothing outside a person that by going in can defile, but the things that come out are what defile" (7:15). He then repeats to his disciples: "Whatever goes into a person from outside cannot defile. . . . It is what comes out of a person that defiles" (7:18, 20). This obviously nullifies any Jewish kosher food traditions.

After that theological justification for Jewish and Gentile inclusiveness in food, Mark sends Jesus on a "mission" to the Gentiles in 7:24–8:9. He travels northward up the Levantine coast to Tyre and Sidon (7:24, 31) and then concludes in a circle inland and southward to the cities of the Decapolis (7:24, 31).

Mark continues this symbolic Gentile "mission" by including a second multiplication of loaves and fishes, this one for Gentiles (8:1–9), parallel to the one for Jews earlier (6:35–44). Mark's climax is Jesus's insistence to his uncomprehending disciples that there is more than enough food for both Jews and Gentiles to eat together (8:14–21)— even if the disciples need to be healed from blindness to see it (8:18, 22–26).

But as Luke followed Mark as his major source, he omitted all of Mark 7:1–8:26. He copied Mark 6:44 in his own 9:17, but his 9:18 jumps ahead to the text that Mark has in 8:27. In other words, Luke omitted both the *theory* and the *practice* of a "Gentile mission" by Jesus. Why? In order to initiate it for the first time in Acts, where it is *justified for* and then *practiced by* Peter, and *not* Paul, despite its "happening" after Paul's vocation at Damascus (Acts 9). In Acts, both the *theory* and the *practice* of radical inclusivity are recorded twice—first as they happen to Peter at Joppa and then as Peter describes them at Jerusalem.

The *theoretical justification* for Jewish/Gentile inclusivity by the invalidation of kosher tradition occurs when a hungry Peter falls into a trance and sees "something like a large sheet" lowered from heaven containing all sorts of animals, reptiles, and birds (Acts 10:9–12; 11:5–6). Next comes the following dialogue/manifesto, almost verbatim the same at Joppa and Jerusalem:

> Then he heard a voice saying, "Get up, Peter; kill and eat."
>
> But Peter said, "By no means, Lord; for I have never eaten anything that is profane or unclean."
>
> The voice said to him again, a second time, "What God has made clean, you must not call profane." (Acts 10:13–15; 11:7–9)

Also, Peter's lesson was repeated "three times" (10:16; 11:10) for emphasis. And after that *theoretical justification* comes this *practical demonstration*, also told twice, first as it as happens at Caesarea and then as described at Jerusalem.

Finally, Peter preaches the peace of Jesus Christ as Lord of all to Gentiles at Caesarea and immediately "the Holy Spirit fell upon all who heard the word" (10:44; 11:15). And, with that heavenly prompting, Peter baptized them, asking rhetorically: "Can anyone withhold the water for baptizing these people who have received the Holy Spirit just as we have?" (10:47) and "Who was I that I could hinder God?" (11:17).

The forward-looking connection from Luke's omission of the Gentile mission's theory and practice in Mark 7–8 to their initial appearance in Acts 10–11 is the *fourth of seven* such major indications that Luke-Acts was originally planned, written, and published as a conceptually unified two-volume book.

———

The second step looks not at an omission in Mark, Luke's primary source, but at an insertion in the Q Gospel, Luke's secondary source. Remember, however, that we are still building toward an identification of the author's character—apart from any conclusions about that author's name.

The story of the Gentile centurion at Capernaum is extant in two independent versions: one is in John 4:46–53; and the other, from the Q Gospel, appears in Matthew 8:5–13 and Luke 7:1–10. (That other source was first recognized by German scholars and is called Q, from *Quelle*, the German word for "source." I prefer, by the way, to give Q its own dignity and integrity by calling it the Q Gospel.)

As you watch how that story develops from John, through the Q Gospel, and into Luke, you can see *how* Luke changed the received tradition with regard to this officer. And then you can ask *why* he did it that way.

John identifies the protagonist as a "royal official," presumably of Herod Antipas, although he was only a regional tetrarch rather than a royal monarch. In any case, this official's "son lay ill in Capernaum. When he heard that Jesus had come from Judea to Galilee, he went and begged him to come down and heal his son, for he was at the point of death" (John 4:46-47). Thereafter, as a symbolic prophecy of the future diaspora mission, Jesus heals this *next-generation Gentile at a distance and so without ever seeing him* (4:48–53).

The Q Gospel's protagonist is a "centurion," presumably a retired centurion from one of the Syrian legions. As with John, so with Matthew: "When Jesus entered Capernaum, a centurion came to him, appealing to him and saying, 'Lord, my servant (*pais*) is lying at home paralyzed, in terrible distress'" (Matt. 8:5–6; the Greek word *pais* can mean "child" or "servant/slave").

Both John and the Q Gospel as it appears in Matthew agree that the petitioner deals directly with Jesus. Luke, however, introduces intermediaries who petition Jesus for the absent official:

> When he [the centurion] heard about Jesus, he sent some Jewish elders to him, asking him to come and heal his slave. When they came to Jesus, they appealed to him earnestly, saying, "He is worthy of having you do this for him, for he loves our people, and it is he who built our synagogue for us." (7:3–5)

This Lukan insertion is quite deliberate, and by keeping the official at home, it creates the awkward necessity of a second "sending" of intermediaries to Jesus—as we see next.

In the Q Gospel, when Jesus tells the centurion, "I will come and cure him," the conversation continues with this magnificent declaration of absolute trust:

> The centurion answered, "Lord, I am not worthy to have you come under my roof; but only speak the word, and my servant will be healed. For I also am a man under authority, with soldiers under me; and I say to one, 'Go,' and he goes, and to another, 'Come,' and he comes, and to my slave, 'Do this,' and the slave does it." (Matt. 8:8–9)

Luke's insertion of those intermediary petitioners keeps the centurion at home and so, to retain that stunning statement, he must introduce more "sent" intermediaries like this: "Jesus went with them [the Jewish elders], but when he was not far from the house, the centurion sent friends to say to him, 'Lord, do not trouble yourself, for I am not worthy to have you come under my roof . . .'" (Luke 7:6–8).

Luke deliberately changed his Q Gospel source and re-created that Capernaum centurion petitioner as a *pro-Jewish sympathizer and synagogue supporter.* The reason for that change was so that the *Capernaum* centurion could point to and prepare readers for the *Caesarea* centurion in Acts. This latter officer is "Cornelius, a centurion of the Italian Cohort, as it was called" (Acts 10:1), who is "well spoken of by the whole Jewish nation" (10:22).

The forward-looking connection from the Capernaum centurion as a pro-Jewish Gentile sympathizer in Luke 7:3–5 to Cornelius as the same in Acts 10 is the *fifth of seven* such major indications that Luke-Acts was originally planned, written, and published as a conceptually unified two-volume book.

Still, even granted all that, how do those depictions of two *pro-Jewish* Gentile centurions reveal anything about the character of the unnamed author of Luke-Acts? The answer appears in the third of our three steps.

The third step presumes Luke's changes to the Gentile mission—from started by Jesus in Mark to started by Peter in Acts—and from that just-seen Capernaum centurion in Luke to the Caesarea centurion in Acts—to whom I now turn.

The Caesarea centurion is described as "a devout man who feared God (*phoboumenos ton theon*) with all his household; he gave alms generously to the people and prayed constantly to God" (Acts 10:2) and as "a centurion, an upright and God-fearing man (*phoboumenos ton theon*), who is well spoken of by the whole Jewish nation" (10:22). The term "God-fearer" becomes a potential option for all Gentiles because, "in every nation anyone who fears him (*phoboumenos auton*) and does what is right is acceptable to him" (10:35). Why is that particular term, "God-fearer," so important? Watch what happens as Acts continues.

On the Sabbath day in the synagogue at Pisidian Antioch—near Yalvaç in modern midwestern Turkey—Paul gives a long program- matic defense of his Jewish-Christian vision (Acts 13:14-41). At the start he addresses his audience: "You Israelites, and others who fear God (*phoboumenoi ton theon*), listen" (13:16); and, in the middle again: "My brothers, you descendants of Abraham's family, and others who fear God (*phoboumenoi ton theon*), to us the message of this salvation has been sent" (13:26).

That makes very clear distinction between, on the one hand, Jews as "Israelites" or "descendants of Abraham" and, on the other, Gentiles as "God-fearers." But both categories are present together on the Sabbath, so that Gentile God-fearers not only pray and give alms but also attend the Jewish synagogue.

Next, however, there is a somewhat startling change of terminol- ogy. In all five instances so far (10:2, 22, 35; 13:16, 26), Acts consistently uses exactly the same phrase, "God-fearers" (*phoboumenoi ton theon*). But, after those cases, the term used in the rest of Acts *is* either "ones worshiping " (*sebomenoi*; 13:43, 50; 17:4, 17; NRSV: "devout") or "ones worshiping God" (*sebomenoi ton theon*; 16:14; 18:7). "God-fearers" have become "God-worshipers."

All these final instances involve named individuals encountered by Paul as he travels from northern to southern Greece. Also, certainly in some and possibly in all cases, those named individuals sponsor Paul and/or give him hospitality in their homes.

First, at Philippi in northeastern Greece, Paul's first European con- vert is a "woman named Lydia, a worshiper of God (*sebomenē ton theon*)," who extended hospitality to Paul: "When she and her household were baptized, she urged us, saying, 'If you have judged me to be faithful to the Lord, come and stay at my home.' And she prevailed upon us" (16:14–15). That "us" indicates, as you will recall, that this is from the "we/us"-section source that we discussed earlier in this chapter.

Then, northwestward at Thessalonica, when Paul speaks in the "synagogue of the Jews . . . some of them were persuaded and joined Paul and Silas, as did a great many of the worshiping Greeks (*sebomenōn Hellēnōn*) and not a few of the leading women" (17:1, 4). Once again, Paul receives local hospitality—at the house of Justin (17:5–7).

Next, in Athens, Paul "argued in the synagogue with the Jews and the worshiping ones (*sebomenois*), and also in the marketplace every day with those who happened to be there" (17:17). After that opening, however, we hear no more about those God-worshipers.

Finally, at Corinth, Paul is again arguing with "Jews and Greeks" in the synagogue but, upon rejection by "the Jews," "he left the synagogue and went to the house of a man named Titius Justus, a worshiper of God (*sebomenou ton theon*); his house was next door to the synagogue" (18:7). Once again, Paul receives hospitality from a God-worshiper.

In summary, for Acts, "God-fearers" and "God-worshipers" are different but equivalent names for pro-Jewish Gentile sympathizers, supporters, and synagogue attendees. But "God-worshipers" is also a somewhat special term for those individual God-fearers who help or host Paul himself. In any case, these terms are used repeatedly and are unique to Acts in the entire New Testament. We do, however, know about them from outside that small library. In other words, those terms are not simply invented for use in Acts.

In his *Jewish War*, Josephus, says: "The Jewish race . . . in Syria . . . were constantly attracting to their religious ceremonies multitudes of Greeks, and these they had in some measure incorporated with themselves" (7.43, 45). Josephus's phrase "in some measure" must refer to sympathizers rather than to converts because it becomes explicit in this comment from his *Jewish Antiquities*:

> No one need wonder that there was so much wealth in our temple, for all the Jews throughout the habitable world, and worshipers of God (*theosebeis*), even those from Asia and Europe, had been contributing to it for a very long time. (14.110)

That composite word "God-worshipers" (*theosebeis*), from two Greek words, *theos* ("God") and *sebō* ("to worship"), also appears in an inscription from the Carian city of Aphrodisias, in present-day southwestern Turkey. This inscription makes a clear distinction between Jews, converts, and God-worshipers.

In 1976, excavations by New York University for the proposed site of Aphrodisias's new museum discovered a column that once formed the left-side support for the door to the city's synagogue. It was inscribed on two faces at right angles to each other—one face in front as you approached the door and the other to your left as you passed inside. Taken together, those two faces list the names of 125 donors in three separate categories: 68 names are Jews (55 percent), 3 names are "converts" (2 percent), and 54 names are "God-worshipers" (43 percent). Furthermore, the first nine names of the God-worshipers on the second and more formally inscribed face are all identified as "city councilors."

In itself, a term like "God-worshiper" could be applied—and was applied—to any human being who was normally reverent or especially pious. But within that triple distinction of Jews, converts, and God-worshipers at Aphrodisias, that final term is a quasi-technical designation for *Gentiles who did not convert fully to Judaism but who still attended and/or supported the synagogue.*

That also, by the way, raises this question: In the light of the Aphrodisias inscription as a random discovery, what percentage of

God-worshipers must we now envisage in any urban synagogue on the Sabbath across the Jewish diaspora? We have no reason to presume that Aphrodisias was unique. Maybe, instead, it was simply characteristic?

Those Gentile God-worshipers accepted Jewish monotheism in which the Supreme God combined power with justice. They valued Jewish morality, Jewish family values, and Jewish solidarity in an indifferent urban world. They probably also accepted as a bonus Jewish contacts within Mediterranean economic globalization. That is why they freely attended—and supported—their local synagogue.

This changes profoundly our understanding of the religious landscape in the early common-era centuries. In Romans, Paul makes a twofold distinction of "the Jew first and also the Greek" (1:16; 2:9, 10), and Acts writes similarly of "Jews and Greeks" (14:1; 18:4; 19:10, 17). But those "Greeks" could be anywhere on the spectrum—inimical, indifferent, or sympathetic—in relation to Judaism; they could even be closely connected to and supportive of their local synagogue as God-worshipers. And, as such, they were an *in-between category*, not converted Jewish monotheists (if male, for example, they would not be circumcised), but no longer fully Gentile polytheists.

Finally, then, why is Luke and Luke alone, among New Testament writers, so interested in those God-fearers or God-worshipers? Three proposals can be offered in cumulative response.

First, it is possible that the author of Luke-Acts was once a God-worshiper, a pro-Jewish Gentile who both attended the local Jewish synagogue and thoroughly learned the Greek translation of the Jewish scriptures. That author knows all about "the Jews" from a pro-Jewish past, but is no longer either sympathetic to or supportive of "the Jews" as the present author of Luke-Acts. Recall how he changed Paul's Damascus story to an anti-Jewish version, and watch what happens to "the Jews" in the next one and throughout the rest of this book.

Second, we can think of the term "God-lover" alongside "God-fearer" and "God-worshiper"—in Luke-Acts. As we already saw, both volumes are dedicated to one "Theophilus," a name meaning "God-lover" in Greek (Luke 1:3; Acts 1:1). This could be an individual person or a personified group. Indeed, even if it were an individual person, it is still quite a coincidence to have the precise name of another variation on "God-fearer" and "God-worshiper."

Third, while Paul changed from a Pharisaic Jew to a Messianic/Christic Jew, the author of Luke-Acts changed from a God-fearing (-worshiping, -loving) Gentile to a Messianic/Christic Gentile. Also, Luke-Acts is especially addressed to others with a similar background as its author—to lovers, fearers, or worshipers of God. In conclusion, even if we do not know the actual name of that author, we can tell the character or social identity of that person from those residual literary fingerprints and residual authorial DNA.

In the next chapter, I consider this author who lived with one foot *inside* Romanism as a Gentile and the other *outside* Judaism as an ex-God-fearer/worshiper/lover. In that chapter, we begin to discern not the Christian Judaism or Jewish Christianity of Paul's hope, but the Christian Romanism or Roman Christianity of Luke-Acts's vision. We also begin to see clearly, if we look back from the start of the fourth to the start of the second century, the road that would lead from Christ to Constantine and Nazareth to Nicaea.

8

THE VISION
OF ROMAN
CHRISTIANITY

B Y THE EARLY DECADES OF THE SECOND CENTURY, AS SEEN
already, the teachings of the "Christians" were described by ruling
Roman aristocrats like Tacitus, Pliny the Younger, and Suetonius as
a pernicious, depraved, excessive, contagious, new, and evil superstition. The Roman Empire also operated, of course, on local, regional,
and provincial levels, which could judge "Christians" less for religious
superstition on a theoretical level than for social turmoil or urban disturbance on a practical level.

Granted a century of contact between Roman power and Christian
faith, Luke-Acts had to control that narrative on certain crucial points,
and had to create a counternarrative that insisted on these four inter-
active themes:

First, the Christian community is peaceful, because it is led by
unified and harmonious leaders. That leadership has no internal
disagreements, disputes, or factions, but works through open
discussion and general consensus.

Second, it is true that urban turmoil or social discord often occurs around Christians, but that is not their fault. Such civic *strife is not caused by them but perpetrated against them by riotously greedy Gentiles.*

Third, such local *strife is also caused by murderously jealous Jews.* Here Luke-Acts has to move very cautiously between depicting Christianity as old and Jewish or as new and non-Jewish—and either way would create problems within the contemporary Roman Empire.

Finally, and above all else, local and provincial *Roman authorities*, who know those preceding two points very well, *are just and impartial* and repeatedly and officially insist that *Christians are completely innocent* of any crimes against Roman law and order.

In Luke's counternarrative, those just and impartial Roman officials close the circle with the unified and harmonious Christian leaders. Together they frame Luke's counternarrative as an *apologia pro vita Christiana* that opened up the future as not Jewish but *Roman* Christianity. We turn now to those four themes in the above sequence but with full detail.

In the first theme of its counternarrative to the Roman one of Christian origins, Luke-Acts insists that the *leadership of the Christian community operated together in idyllic harmony and complete agreement.* Such *internal* accord, therefore, could never create *external* discord, public turmoil, social strife, or political conflict. But here, once again, we can compare how Luke-Acts retells a tale that we know very differently from elsewhere.

The basic historical question was whether the future would entail a *Jewish Christianity*, a *Gentile Christianity*, or a *Jewish-Gentile Christianity*—with whatever adaptations were possible, whatever changes were necessary, and whatever names were acceptable. In this particular and typical human clash between past and future, tradition and vision, and old and new, two specific questions arose requiring leadership decision: first, whether Gentile male converts had to *accept circumcision* to become full members of the Messianic/Christic community; and second, whether Gentile converts had to *observe kosher* rules during common meals or Eucharists for both Jews and Gentiles in the Messianic/Christic community.

The most revealing comparison is between Paul's description of *acrimonious* leadership clashes in Galatians 2:1–14 and Luke-Acts's retelling of those same events as *amicable* leadership discussions in Acts 15:1–35. And, by the way, since Paul is defending his version of events, he does so under oath: "In what I am writing to you, before God, I do not lie!" (Gal. 1:20).

First, according to Paul, the question of circumcision for Gentile male converts arose at Jerusalem from "false brothers secretly brought in, who slipped in to spy on the freedom we have in Christ Jesus, so that they might enslave us" (Gal. 2:4). Traditionalists are nastily named "false brothers."

Second, Paul continues his pejorative language for "those who were supposed to be acknowledged leaders (what they actually were makes no difference to me; God shows no partiality)" (Gal. 2:6), even though he admits that those "leaders" ultimately agreed with him on no-circumcision for Gentile male converts.

Third, Paul records that agreement three times, but also admits that it entailed a separation between a *mission to Jews* under Peter and a *mission to Gentiles* under him:

> When they [those "acknowledged leaders"] saw that I had been entrusted with the gospel for the *uncircumcised*, just as Peter had been entrusted with the gospel for the *circumcised* (for he who worked through Peter making him an apostle to the *circumcised* also worked through me in sending me to the *Gentiles*), and

when James and Cephas and John, who were acknowledged pillars, recognized the grace that had been given to me, they gave to Barnabas and me the right hand of fellowship, agreeing that we should go to the *Gentiles* and they to the *circumcised*. (Gal. 2:7–9)

Granted such a mission split on the theoretical level, an attempt was made to hold those divergent communities together on the practical level: "They asked only one thing, that we remember the poor, which was actually what I was eager to do" (Gal. 2:10).

That promise, by the way, did not involve charitable alms for the street poor in Jerusalem, but financial support given by the Gentile mission to the Jewish mission and specifically to the share community in Jerusalem under James, "the Lord's brother" (Gal. 1:19). Known as "the Poor," James's common-propertied community was to be a unifying focus for the separated Petrine and Pauline missions of the Christian community. (Acts, by the way, makes use of traditions about that ideal small community of "the Poor," but applies its lifestyle to the entire Jerusalem community—despite some inevitable contradictions in Acts 2:44–45; 4:32–35; 5:4.)

Finally, at Antioch, capital of the Roman province of Syria, the second question, about kosher rules, arose. In common meals for Jewish and Gentile Christians, who should adapt to whom? Should those meals be kosher for none or kosher for all?

When Cephas came to Antioch, I opposed him to his face, because he stood self-condemned; for until certain people came from James, he used to eat with the Gentiles. But after they came, he drew back and kept himself separate for fear of the circumcision faction. And the other Jews joined him in this *hypocrisy*, so that even Barnabas was led astray by their *hypocrisy*. (Gal. 2:11–13)

This time the increased bitterness of Paul's language—"hypocricy"—indicates the depth of the discord within the leadership itself, discord that resulted in a split between Paul and the other three, James, Peter, and Barnabas—*even* Barnabas!

Next, compare how Luke-Acts tells that same story—it emphasizes harmonious discussion over bitter confrontation and omits any mention of separated missions or any need for their practical financial reconciliation. First, Acts agrees with Paul that the question concerned circumcision for Gentile male converts, but it starts at Antioch not Jerusalem:

> Certain individuals came down from Judea [to Antioch]
> and were teaching the brothers, "Unless you are *circumcised*
> according to the custom of Moses, you cannot be saved." . . .
> Some believers who belonged to the sect of the Pharisees stood
> up and said, "It is necessary for them to be *circumcised and*
> *ordered to keep the law of Moses.*" (Acts 15:1, 5)

Notice that the challenge is mentioned twice, but, although only circumcision is mentioned the first time, the repetition includes both circumcision and keeping the "law of Moses." In other words, Luke-Acts's repetition poses *both* questions—circumcision and kosher rules—at the start and therefore at Antioch.

Second, at Jerusalem, all is harmonious as "the apostles and the elders met together to consider this matter" and "after there had been much debate, Peter stood up" and reminded them how "God made a choice among you, that I should be the one through whom the Gentiles would hear the message of the good news and become believers" (15:6–7). Recall from Acts 10–11 that *Peter, not Paul, is the God-appointed apostle to the Gentiles*—for Luke-Acts.

Next, "the whole assembly kept silence, and listened to Barnabas and Paul"—note the order—"as they told of all the signs and wonders that God had done through them among the Gentiles" (15:12). That is one brief sentence sandwiched swiftly between the quoted speeches of Peter and James.

Third, Luke-Acts, having collapsed circumcision and kosher into a single problem (15:5), solves both with the same unanimously accepted decree, which is then sent by letter from Jerusalem to Antioch. James, whose authority was already recognized but not explained in Acts (but is in Galatians 1:19 as Jesus's brother) refers back to Peter's speech and announces: "I have reached the decision that we should not trouble those Gentiles who are turning to God, but we should write to them to abstain only from things polluted by idols and from fornication and from whatever has been strangled and from blood" (Acts 15:19–20). Those were the same four conditions for Israelites and "resident aliens" to live together in Leviticus 17–18.

James's decision is then repeated in an official letter from "the apostles and the elders, with the consent of the whole church" (15:22) that is sent north to Syria and Cilicia, carried by "unanimously" chosen representatives along with "Barnabas and Paul, who have risked their lives for the sake of [the] Lord Jesus Christ" (15:25–26). At Antioch, "they gathered the congregation together [and] delivered the letter. When its members read it, they rejoiced at the exhortation" (15:30–31).

Fourth, granted that serenely harmonious discussion and the unanimous acceptance of its rather authoritative conclusions, there is not even the slightest hint in Acts 15 about any separation between Peter's mission to Jews and Paul's mission to Gentiles. Neither, of course, is there any mention of a Gentile collection for "the Poor," for James's model share community in Jerusalem. For Luke-Acts, there is no disunity among the leadership, and therefore no need for even symbols of unification.

Even after a comparison of those four points in Paul and Luke, you might conclude that Acts 15:1–35 is simply Luke's more irenic version of Galatians 2:1–14 and that he is not deliberately obfuscating leadership strife on those two problems arising from an inaugural Jewish/Gentile Messianic/Christic community.

What makes that benign explanation untenable is that Luke goes far beyond obscuring the *actuality* of those leadership conflicts by positively negating even their *possibility*, since Paul was not *sent* independently *by* God and Christ as were the Twelve—including especially Peter (Luke 6:13; Acts 1:26; 2:14, 37). Instead, for Luke, Paul is a supremely important but completely subordinate missionary *sent by* and subordinate to the communities of Jerusalem and Antioch (Acts 13:1–3; 14:4, 6, 14). Compare, for example, the depictions by Paul and by Acts of his relationship to the twelve apostles and especially to Peter as their leader.

For Paul, his vocation and mission, his identity, authority, and integrity come from being an *apostle*: "God, who had set me apart before I was born and called me through his grace, was pleased to reveal his Son to me, so that I might proclaim him among the Gentiles" (Gal. 1:15–16). He was, indeed, "apostle to the Gentiles" (Gal. 2:8; Rom. 11:13).

An *apostle* is a person sent by some person or group to do something elsewhere—from Greek *apostellein*, "to send forth." For Luke-Acts, the Twelve had *seen* the earthly Jesus and were apostles *sent* by him as official witnesses of his resurrection (Luke 6:13; Acts 1:21–22). But Paul insists that he *saw* and was *sent* by the heavenly Jesus, and that gave him exactly the same apostolic status: "Am I not an apostle? Have I not seen Jesus our Lord?" Later, he answers that question: "Last of all, as to one untimely born, he appeared also to me" (1 Cor. 9:1; 15:8; "appeared" is *ōphthē* in Greek, meaning "was seen").

Paul, therefore, places himself among the "apostles of Christ" (1 Thess. 2:7) and speaks of "those who were already apostles before [him]" (Gal. 1:17). He is one among "us apostles" (1 Cor. 4:9), one like "other apostles" (1 Cor. 9:5), but admits: "I am the least of the apostles, unfit to be called an apostle, because I persecuted the church of God" (1 Cor. 15:9). But the least and latest apostle is still an apostle!

Also, in the formal opening address of several letters, Paul identifies himself immediately as "Paul, called to be an apostle of Christ Jesus" (1 Cor. 1:1); "Paul, an apostle of Christ Jesus" (2 Cor. 1:1); "Paul, a servant of Jesus Christ, called to be an apostle" (Rom. 1:1); and, defensively and pugnaciously, "Paul an apostle—sent neither by human commission nor from human authorities, but through Jesus Christ and God the Father, who raised him from the dead" (Gal. 1:1).

For Luke-Acts, however, Paul was not and, in fact, never could have been an apostle on the same level and with the same status as the twelve apostles or their leader Peter—for two reasons. First, an apostle had to be "one of the men who have accompanied us during all the time that the Lord Jesus went in and out among us, beginning from the baptism of John until the day when he was taken up from us" (Acts 1:21–22). Paul could never be considered an apostle under that protocol.

Second, even granted a heavenly call from Christ, Paul had never actually *seen* the risen Lord, unlike the Twelve, who had *seen* both the earthly and the risen Lord. This was the unkindest cut of all. Luke tells the full story of Paul's Christ-given vocation three times, and each time Paul hears the *voice* of Christ but never *sees* his face. In fact, he could not have seen his face, as he was blinded by heavenly light in each of the three accounts (Acts 9:3–4, 8; 22:6–7, 9; 26:13–14).

Acts could, of course, accept Paul as an "apostle" as long as he was *sent* not by God and Christ from heaven, but by Jerusalem and Antioch on earth. As long as Barnabas and Paul are *sent* to Anatolia by the community of Antioch and "the Holy Spirit," Acts can readily call them both "apostles" (13:1–4; 14:4–5, 14). Also, for Acts, Paul travels from Ephesus to Jerusalem to Antioch and back to Ephesus in five verses simply to assert that subordinate status (18:19–23).

Furthermore, Simon/Peter dominates the first half of Acts (1:13–15:14) as Saul/Paul does the second half (9:1–30; 13:1–28:25). When they overlap in the middle, we are first told of Paul's election by God "to bring [God's] name before Gentiles and kings and before the people of

Israel" (9:15); but that is then countered by Peter's election by God to be the apostle to the Gentiles (15:7, 14).

Finally, in Acts, events repeatedly happen to Peter *before* they happen to Paul. For example, an angel twice frees Peter from prison by unfastening chains and opening doors (5:19; 12:7, 10) and an earthquake does the same for Paul once (16:26). For Luke, such parallels do not indicate the equality of Peter and Paul, but the ascendancy of Peter over Paul.

In summary, even though Luke tells three times the full story of Paul's vocation and even though Paul takes up over half of Acts, there could never be any leadership discord with Paul, around Paul, or because of Paul. He is subordinate to the Twelve—and even to James, whose authority is clear but never explained in Acts.

Still, that description of harmonious apostolic leadership in Acts 15 deliberately negated serious disagreements involving Paul; contradicted two separate missions, one with James and Peter for Jews, the other with Barnabas and Paul for Gentiles (Gal. 2:7–9); and excluded thereby the necessity of practical cohesion by "remembering" "the Poor" at Jerusalem.

In the second theme of its counternarrative to the Roman one of Christian origins, Luke-Acts insists that *Christians were not the cause of civil strife*; it was begun by *riotous and greedy Gentiles*. The first example of a public disturbance perpetrated not *by* but *against* the Christian community comes when Paul and Silas are guests of Lydia at Philippi in northern Greece. She was a Gentile adherent to Judaism, a God-fearer/worshiper who became Paul's first Christian convert in Europe.

One day at Philippi, Paul and his companions "met a slave-girl who had a spirit of divination and brought her owners a great deal of money by fortune-telling." When she repeatedly harassed the group, Paul exorcised her divining spirit. "But when her owners saw that their hope of making money was gone, they seized Paul and Silas and dragged them into the marketplace before the authorities" (Acts 16:16–19).

The accusation against them, however, says nothing about the owners' loss of profit because the slave girl had lost her divining spirit. Instead, they claim: "These men are disturbing our city; they are Jews and are advocating customs that are not lawful for us as Romans to adopt or observe" (16:20-21). That "they are Jews" is irrelevant except as prejudicial anti-Judaism—and this formulation comes from Luke-Acts! The rest is nothing but double-talk hiding the greed or monetary self-interest of the owners—despite their secondary concern for Roman law and order.

The second example is an even more serious one in which anti-Christian Gentile greed or monetary self-interest causes public conflict. This time Christians are not just bad for magical commercial business, but for official divine worship. This incident happened when Paul was at Ephesus on the mid-Aegean coast of Roman Asia Minor (modern western Turkey), where he was known for his criticism of polytheistic images:

> A man named Demetrius, a silversmith who made silver shrines of Artemis . . . said, "Men, you know that we get our wealth from this business. You also see and hear that not only in Ephesus but in almost the whole of Asia this Paul has persuaded and drawn away a considerable number of people by saying that gods made with hands are not gods. And there is danger not only that this trade of ours may come into disrepute but also that the temple of the great goddess Artemis will be scorned, and she will be deprived of her majesty that brought all Asia and the world to worship her." (Acts 19: 24–27)

(At twice the size of the Parthenon temple to Athena on the Athens acropolis, Artemis's great temple at Ephesus was one of the Seven Wonders of the Ancient World.)

Once again, however, riotous reactions come first from monetary self-interest and are touched once again with anti-Judaism, this time against Alexander, "whom the Jews had pushed forward. And Alexander motioned for silence and tried to make a defense before the people. But when they recognized that he was a Jew, for about two hours all of them shouted in unison, 'Great is Artemis of the Ephesians!'" (19:33–34).

In the third theme of its counternarrative to the Roman one of Christian origins, Luke-Acts argues that that social disturbances or even urban riots are never caused by the Christian community, but stem— apart from those greedy Gentiles—from *jealous and murderous Jews*. But Luke-Acts faced a major dilemma in handling this theme.

On the one hand, if the Christian movement was a peaceful sect within the ancient Jewish religion, that would neutralize the most dangerous adjective used for Christianity by Roman historians at the start of the second century. As we saw earlier, they accused Christianity of being a depraved, excessive, contagious, pernicious, evil, and *new* superstition. But "new" was possibly the most damning indictment of all—for conservative Romans. But if Christianity were a Jewish sect, it would not be a new religion.

On the other hand, the Christian community was part of a religion whose homeland had been devastated for revolting against Rome in 66–74 and whose diaspora had been forced to pay an annual punitive tax to the Capitoline Temple of Jupiter Optimus Maximus in Rome. But if Christianity were a *Jewish* sect, it would be part of a community seen as militarily defeated and financially penalized by Rome.

Luke-Acts needed to describe Christianity as an old rather than a new religion, but also as outside rather than inside Judaism. How did it, how could it, have both ways at once? To understand the strategy of Luke-Acts, we look at two deliberately linked examples—one about Jesus in the synagogue of Nazareth in the Jewish homeland, the other about Paul in the synagogues of the Jewish diaspora.

Watch, then, how Luke's comparison of Jesus and Paul solves his dilemma of presenting Christianity as *neither* a dangerous new religion *nor* a part of Judaism inimical to Rome.

As we have seen already, one of the best ways of grasping Luke's authorial purpose is to watch how he adopts and adapts Mark's Gospel, which, by scholarly consensus, is his major source. On Nazareth, therefore, we look first at Luke's Markan source and then at how—and why—Luke changes it both deliberately and radically.

Mark begins the public life of Jesus with a day of great success at Capernaum (1:16–34). His teaching is successful: "They were astounded at his teaching, for he taught them as one having authority, and not as the scribes" (1:22). So is his healing: "They brought to him all who were sick or possessed with demons. . . . And he cured many who were sick with various diseases, and cast out many demons; and he would not permit the demons to speak, because they knew him" (1:32, 34).

Later, Mark counterpoints this great success at Capernaum with almost complete failure at Nazareth: "On the sabbath he began to teach in the synagogue, and many who heard him . . . took offense at him. Then Jesus said to them, 'Prophets are not without honor, except in their hometown, and among their own kin, and in their own house'" (6:2–4).

Luke, on the other hand, begins its account with a fleeting bow to Mark by the summary statement that Jesus "began to teach in their synagogues and was praised by everyone" (4:15). But then, as Luke accepts Mark's specific synagogue stories, it changes them in two fundamental ways. It reverses Mark's sequence of success at Capernaum (Mark 1:16–34) followed by failure at Nazareth (Mark 6:2–6); Luke has the failure at Nazareth (Luke 4:16–30) first, followed by success at Capernaum (Luke 4:31–44). That is not just a minor change. It means

Jesus begins with success among his fellow Jews in Mark but with failure among them in Luke.

Also, in a far more serious alteration of his Markan source, Luke's inaugural day at Nazareth begets not hometown cynicism (Mark 6:2–3), but an initial acceptance followed by a lethal attack (Luke 4:28–29). After Jesus's startling claim that Israel's hopes are fulfilled "today," the audience responds like this: "All spoke well of him and were amazed at the gracious words that came from his mouth" (4:22a). That is an immediate and profoundly positive reaction from "all."

Next, Luke gives a very brief and very mild version of Nazareth's disbelief in Jesus as their hometown prophet: "They said, 'Is not this Joseph's son?'" (Luke 4:22b, from Mark 6:2–3). Not even that positive followed by negative combination, however, prepares readers for what happens next. Suddenly, inexplicably, Jesus deliberately insults his audience with a comment totally out of context:

> There were many widows in Israel in the time of Elijah,
> when the heaven was shut up three years and six months, and
> there was a severe famine over all the land; yet Elijah was sent
> to none of them except to a widow at Zarephath in Sidon.
> There were also many lepers in Israel in the time of the prophet
> Elisha, and none of them was cleansed except Naaman the
> Syrian. (4:25–27)

Those miraculous healings of two Gentiles, one by Elijah in 1 Kings 17:8–16 and the other by Elisha in 2 Kings 5:1–14, are underlined by Jesus not as God's concern for Jews *and* Gentiles, but as God's choice of Gentiles *over* Jews.

The result of that rather gratuitous insult is a murderous attack on Jesus: "When they heard this, all in the synagogue were filled with rage. They got up, drove him out of the town, and led him to the brow of the hill on which their town was built, so that they might hurl him off the cliff. But he passed through the midst of them and went on his way" (4:28–30).

That incident is not very coherent either internally or externally. Internally, why does Luke have Jesus even mention Gentiles, let alone exalt them over his Jewish audience? Externally, despite this Gentile literary interlude, Luke has Jesus go next—and successfully—among Jews at Capernaum (Luke 4:31–43, from Mark 1:16–45) and then make a one-verse visit to Jews in Judea (Luke 4:44).

Why did Luke change its Markan source on Jesus from inaugural success at Capernaum to inaugural disaster at Nazareth? Why did Luke change Mark from cynical disbelief to lethal rage at Nazareth? Why did Luke have Jesus allege God's past preference for Gentiles *over* Jews rather than cite divine concern for Gentiles *as well as* Jews? Why, in any case, have Jesus even mention Gentiles when addressing Jews?

The answer is that the *inaugural* sermon of Jesus at Nazareth in the Jewish homeland (Luke 4:16–30) was created not to describe one historical Sabbath from the mission of Jesus, but to foreshadow the *inaugural* sermon of Paul at Pisidian Antioch (southwestern Turkey) in the Jewish diaspora (Acts 13:14–52).

First, with regard to *place and time*, Jesus "came to Nazareth . . . [and] went to the synagogue on the sabbath day" (Luke 4:16), and Paul "came to Antioch in Pisidia. And on the sabbath day they went into the synagogue" (Acts 13:14).

Second, with regard to *content and message*, each address claims present scriptural fulfillment. For Jesus at Nazareth, the claim is: "Today this scripture has been fulfilled in your hearing" (Luke 4:21). Similarly, for Paul at Pisidian Antioch: "To us the message of this salvation has been sent. . . . We bring you the good news that what God promised to our ancestors, he has fulfilled for us, their children" (Acts 13:26, 32, 33).

Finally, with regard to *reaction and result*, here the action must be slowed to a frame-by-frame sequence. Recall that, after Jesus's gratuitous mention of divine preference for Gentiles over Jews at Nazareth, *enthusiastic acceptance* shifts immediately to lethal but *unsuccessful rejection* at Nazareth (Luke 4:28–30).

At Pisidian Antioch that reversal is emphasized programmatically by separating *acceptance* and *rejection* between two Sabbaths. Here is the *acceptance*:

> As Paul and Barnabas were going out, the people urged them
> to speak about these things again the next sabbath. When the
> meeting of the synagogue broke up, many Jews and devout
> converts to Judaism followed Paul and Barnabas, who spoke
> to them and urged them to continue in the grace of God.
> (Acts 13:42–43)

Then comes the shift to *rejection* and, of course, Gentiles are involved:

> The next sabbath almost the whole city gathered to hear the
> word of the Lord. But when the Jews saw the crowds, they were
> filled with jealousy; and blaspheming, they contradicted what
> was spoken by Paul. Then both Paul and Barnabas spoke out
> boldly, saying, "It was necessary that the word of God should
> be spoken first to you. Since you reject it and judge yourselves
> to be unworthy of eternal life, we are now turning to the
> Gentiles." (13:44–46)

Notice, however, the somewhat contradictory reason given for this change. Do the Jews reject Christ—out of "jealousy"—because Paul accepted Gentiles (13:45), or does Paul accept Gentiles—out of necessity—because the Jews have rejected Christ (13:46)?

At Nazareth, the result was enraged rejection (Luke 4:28), lethal attack (4:29), and escape (4:30). At Pisidian Antioch, "The Jews incited the devout women of high standing and the leading men of the city, and stirred up persecution against Paul and Barnabas, and drove them out of their region" (Acts 13:50).

In summary, this is Luke's message on "the Jews." First, their ancestral traditions had promised a "Messiah/Christ," and this ancient prophecy was fulfilled in Jesus (Luke 2:11; Acts 26:23) as a "Savior" (Luke 1:47; Acts 13:23) and bringer of "Peace" (Luke 1:79; Acts 10:36). Second, "the Jews" accepted this message gladly for themselves but rioted murderously when it was also opened to the Gentiles (Luke 4:28; Acts 13:50; 17:5).

That is Luke's solution to his original dilemma of presenting Christianity as neither new nor Jewish. Only the *peaceful* Messianic/Christic community—some of whom are, of course, Jews, but most of whom are Gentiles—are the true heirs and faithful descendants of ancient Judaism. Christians are not a *new* community, but neither are they *unpeaceful* Jews like those who rioted against Jesus and Paul (and rebelled against Rome as well). The Messianic/Christic community contains the only legitimate and peaceful Jews—for Luke-Acts.

Furthermore, the forward-looking connection from Jesus at Nazareth's synagogue on the Sabbath in Luke 4 to Paul at Pisidian Antioch's in Act 13 is the *sixth of seven* such major indications that Luke-Acts was originally planned, written, and published as a conceptually unified two-volume book.

In the fourth, final, and climactic theme of its counternarrative to the Roman one of Christian origins, Luke-Acts maintains that Christians were repeatedly deemed innocent by *just and impartial Roman authorities*. (In Revelation, Romans are always executing Christians; in Luke-Acts, they are always exculpating them.) Every time Jesus and Paul came into juridical contact with a Roman official—whether military officer, client ruler, or regional governor—they were repeatedly declared to be innocent of any wrongdoing against Roman law and order. Never in the field of judicial process have so few been declared so innocent by so many.

First, the Roman governor of the island of Cyprus. "The proconsul, Sergius Paulus, an intelligent man, . . . summoned Barnabas and Saul and wanted to hear the word of God" (Acts 13:7). Then, after Paul had temporarily blinded a magician named Elymas and "the proconsul saw what had happened, he believed, for he was astonished at the teaching about the Lord" (13:12).

Second, the Roman governor of Achaia in southern Greece. From epigraphical evidence, scholars know his full name as Lucius Junius Gallio. I quote the incident in full, as it paradigmatic for how Luke thinks Rome should always respond to "the Way":

> When Gallio was proconsul of Achaia, the Jews made a united attack on Paul and brought him before the tribunal. They said, "This man is persuading people to worship God in ways that are contrary to the law." Just as Paul was about to speak, Gallio said to the Jews, "If it were a matter of crime or serious villainy, I would be justified in accepting the complaint of you Jews; but since it is a matter of questions about words and names and your own law, see to it yourselves; I do not wish to be a judge of these matters." And he dismissed them from the tribunal. Then all of them seized Sosthenes, the official of the synagogue, and beat him in front of the tribunal. But Gallio paid no attention to any of these things. (18:12–17)

The legal and then illegal actions of "the Jews" frame the incident. Their accusation concerns "the law," and Gallio dismisses that as about Jewish law ("your own law") and not about Roman law. His verdict, "I do not wish to be a judge of these matters," is an early version of later responses from Claudius Lysias (23:29) and Porcius Festus (25:18–19). Christians are innocent before Roman law, and accusations against them from Jewish law are irrelevant to Roman authority.

Third, such exculpation of Paul is also found at lower levels of Roman authority: the astonished jailer and admonished magistrates at Philippi who bade Paul and Silas "go in peace" (16:25–39); and the town clerk at Ephesus who declared that "Gaius and Aristarchus, Macedonians who were Paul's travel companions . . . are neither temple robbers nor blasphemers of our goddess" (19:29, 37).

Finally, we have already seen as a supreme and parallel example, how Luke ends with Jesus under Roman trial, Acts ends with Paul under Roman trial, and each is declared innocent on all three levels of Roman authority, by military officer, client ruler, and territorial commander.

In the preceding chapters, we saw six *forward*-looking narrative units composed in Luke as preparation for parallels or continuities in Acts. Those are, of course, the crucial proofs that Luke-Acts was originally designed and must always be interpreted as an integrated two-volume work and never as a single stand-alone book (Luke) with an appended and backward-connected sequel (Acts).

Granted all that, here is the question for the next chapter: Are such *forward*-looking connections, parallels, and continuities the only proofs that establish the integrity of Luke-Acts as a literary unity? Is there anything else to be considered?

For example, in conceiving Luke-Acts as a unified two-volume work, the author had this immediate challenge: Jesus was certainly the obvious protagonist of the former volume (Luke), but with Jesus ascended to heaven at its end, who was available as protagonist for the latter volume (Acts)? Also, would not any protagonist(s) in that latter volume be inappropriately competing with Jesus in the former one? How would one prevent, say, Paul himself, a Peter-and-Paul duo, or a Peter-over-Paul combination in Acts from becoming a literary, historical, and theological parallel to Jesus in Luke?

Finally, then, for the next chapter: Does Luke have a single protagonist linking Luke-Acts into a unified whole? Who or what is that protagonist, and how does it operate?

9

THE WAY OF THE
HOLY SPIRIT

O NE WAY TO START A PRODUCTION IN MUSIC, FILM, OR LIT-
     erature is with an *overture*, which introduces in symbol, meta-
phor, or parable the major theme or themes organizing, controlling,
and dominating the work as a whole. Barbara Tuchman, for example,
began *The Guns of August*, her brilliant 1962 history of the early stages
of World War I, not with its *beginning* on July 28, 1914, but with an
overture focusing on May 20, 1910. On that day European royalty gathered in London to bury Edward VII, but—unknown to them—they
were also there to bury themselves as the future of European monar-
chy. Her opening chapter is therefore an overture to the whole that
follows—in both Europe's history and the book—and is appropriately
entitled "A Funeral."

   Similar parabolic overtures appear in Matthew 1–2 for the whole
of Matthew and in Luke 1–2 for the whole of Luke-Acts. There are,
therefore, no "lost years" or "missing years" between Matthew 1–2 or
Luke 1–2 and the opening scenes that follow those overtures. Luke 1–2
is not simply the *start of* the story, but the *overture to* the story of
Luke-Acts.

As parabolic overture for Luke-Acts, two megathemes are presented in the overture of Luke 1–2, and they combine together slowly but surely to become the integrating and ruling vision of Luke-Acts. Only when those two megathemes come fully and finally together do we understand Luke-Acts as an authorially designed unity and a compositionally integrated whole.

The two megathemes are the *travel journey* and the *Holy Spirit* or, more briefly, *journey* and *Spirit*. Think of them as warp and woof that weave together the integrated fabric and unified vision of Luke-Acts as the *travel journey of the Holy Spirit*. And, of course, this gives Luke-Acts its single two-volume protagonist as *God's Holy Spirit*.

The first megatheme introduced in Luke 1–2 as a major integrating topic for all of Luke-Acts is the *travel journey*.

Luke 1–2 records three four-stage journeys—*Galilee, to Judea, in Judea*, and *back to Galilee*—north to south and back again to north. Furthermore, all three journeys pivot on Jerusalem's Temple (Luke 1:5; 2:22, 27; 2:41, 46):

> First, Mary, pregnant with Jesus, journeys from Galilee to Judea to visit Elizabeth, wife of a Temple priest and herself a "descendant of Aaron" (1:5, 39)—and then returns to Galilee (1:56).

> Next, Joseph and Mary, pregnant with Jesus, journey from Galilee to Judea for the census, birth, and circumcision in the Temple (2:1–4, 21)—and then they return to Galilee (2:39).

> Finally, Mary and Joseph, with the twelve-year-old Jesus, journey for Passover from Galilee to Judea, where Jesus

teaches in the Temple (2:41–42, 46)—and then they return
to Galilee (2:51).

At this point, the four-stage *journey* theme in Luke 1–2 looks quite
traditional as an overture for what should follow in Luke 3–24 and is
also traditional for the other Gospel accounts, which end with a return
to Galilee (Mark 16:7; Matt. 28:10, 16; John 21:1).

Luke 3–24, however, makes two very significant changes over Mark
and both coalesce to confirm the originally planned unity of Luke-
Acts. The first change involves the southward *route* from Galilee to
Judea, the other involves the northward return to Galilee. Mark routes
Jesus southward to Jerusalem on the east bank of the Jordan, but Luke
changes that to the west bank—and that requires some preliminary
background.

Galileans had two major routes for southward travel from Galilee to
Judea. They could go either through Samaria, *west* of the Jordan River,
or through Perea, *east* of it—with necessary river crossings at the beginning and end of that latter journey. The route through Samaria looked
the easier one, but religio-ethnic tensions between Jews and Samaritans could mean serious trouble or even lethal danger. Galilean Jews,
if traveling in a small group, could be seen as vulnerable or, if traveling
in a large group, could be seen as provocative (recall Matt. 10:5 and
John 4:9).

In Mark, Jesus travels from Galilee to Judea on the east side of the
Jordan and thereby avoids Samaria (10:1, 32–33, 46; 11:1). Luke, however, makes a very significant and surprising change over Mark. He
reroutes Jesus's southward journey from the east side to the west side of
the Jordan, that is, through Samaria:

When the days drew near for him to be taken up, *he set his face
to go to Jerusalem.* And he sent messengers ahead of him. On
their way they entered a village of the Samaritans to make ready

for him; but they did not receive him, because *his face was set toward Jerusalem*. (Luke 9:51–53)

That double mention of "face set toward Jerusalem" frames and thereby emphasizes "village of the Samaritans." Notice, however, that it is only his messengers and not Jesus himself who enters "a village of the Samaritans."

Despite that mention of Samaria, Luke does not make use of any traditions about or locations for Jesus in Samaria, like the one John has about the well of Sychar and the Samaritan woman (John 4:3–42). All Luke presents is the Good Samaritan parable (10:25–37) and a miracle that he locates when Jesus was "on the way to Jerusalem . . . going through the region between Samaria and Galilee" (17:11). Was that miracle actually in Samaria, or was it in Galilee? Or was it simply fictional rather than factual? And, in any case, why does Luke send Jesus southward through Samaria—against Mark?

Hold on firmly to that question pending a later answer. We look next at the second major change Luke makes against Mark's sequence. This concerns the traditional *back to Galilee* conclusion.

From the overture in Luke 1–2, its Markan source, and general tradition, we would expect Jesus's southward journey to have those four stages of "Galilee, to Jerusalem, in Jerusalem, back to Galilee." But that is not what we have in Luke 3–24. Instead, we have "Galilee, to Jerusalem, in Jerusalem, stay in Jerusalem"—like this:

First, there is a Galilean period (Luke 3:1–9:50).

Next, a long, slow, and almost processional journey takes place from Galilee to Judea in which readers are constantly reminded where Jesus is headed: "his face was set toward Jerusalem . . . as he made his way to Jerusalem . . . on the way to Jerusalem . . . going up to Jerusalem . . . near Jerusalem . . . going up to Jerusalem" (9:53; 13:22; 17:11; 18:31; 19:11, 28).

Then, there is a time in Jerusalem and at the Temple, consummated by execution and resurrection (19:29b–24:53).

Finally, Jesus does not return to Galilee, but his departing injunction to his disciples is: "*Stay* here in the city *until* you have been clothed with power from on high" (24:49).

Next, in the overlap about Jesus's Ascension from Luke 24 in Acts 1, the disciples are given that same injunction about Jerusalem:

He [Jesus] ordered them not to leave Jerusalem, but to wait there for the promise of the Father. "This," he said, "is what you have heard from me. . . . You will receive power when the Holy Spirit has come upon you; and you will be my witnesses in Jerusalem, in all Judea and Samaria, and to the end [Greek singular, *eschatou*] of the earth." (Acts 1:4, 8)

That repetition makes one very important addition to Luke 24:49, and it involves new geographical directions for the megatheme of the *travel journey* in Luke-Acts. This ongoing journey in Acts picks up the last stage in Luke and continues its "in Jerusalem" outward to "Judea . . . Samaria . . . and to the end of the earth" (Acts 1:8).

We can now see why Luke had to change Jesus's journey from the east to the west side of the Jordan and thereby create a journey through Samaria to Judea—despite a lack of data about Jesus in Samaria. It was because Luke has the journey in Acts move northward "throughout the countryside of Judea and Samaria" (8:1) and has traditions for Acts located in Samaria itself (8:5–25).

The forward-looking connection from Jesus going southward through Samaria in Luke 9:51–53 to the apostles going northward through Samaria in Acts 1:8 is the *last* of *seven* such major indications that Luke-Acts was originally planned, written, and published as a conceptually unified two-volume book.

Still, at first glance, Acts 1:8 seems a giant leap from the regional (Jerusalem, Judea, Samaria) to the universal ("the end of the earth")—if that phrase is taken literally. But, by it Luke-Acts intended Rome itself, the center from which all roads led outward around the world and across the earth. That conclusion rests on the following three points.

First, when Pompey conquered Jerusalem in 63 BCE, he is described as coming from "the end of the earth," that is, from Rome (*Psalms of Solomon* 8.15).

Next, at Pentecost, Luke cites a list of peoples and regions from around the world and frames it with a double mention of them all hearing in their own native languages (2:8–11). In that given list, Luke includes "Judea," which had the same native language as the apostles, and "Rome," which is neither a people nor a region. That seems a deliberate connection between Judea and Rome at this prophetic moment of apostolic universality.

Finally, that four-stage sequence in Acts 1:8 becomes a geographical map for Acts. There the journey starts in Jerusalem (2:1–8:1a), proceeds "throughout the countryside of Judea and Samaria" (8:1b–11:18), and then continues from Syria to Cyprus and Asian Anatolia to European Greece (13:1–19:20).

At that stage, geographically adept readers know that the journey has moved steadily westward and expect Paul to continue in that direction. Maybe he will pick up the Via Egnatia westward across the Balkans to the Adriatic Sea, cross over to Brindisium, on the toe of Italy, and then pick up the Via Appia to Rome.

Instead, however, "Paul resolved in the Spirit to go through Macedonia and Achaia, and then to go on to Jerusalem. He said, 'After I have gone there, I must also see Rome'" (Acts 19:21). Acts never tells us the reason for Paul's Jerusalem visit (19:22–21:16), but it allows it to conclude with a résumé of its dominant geographical direction and theological transfer—from Jerusalem (21:17) to Rome (28:14–31). Or, as the Lord said to Paul, "Just as you have testified for me in Jerusalem, so you must bear witness also in Rome" (23:11).

In summary on this first Lukan megatheme: the *travel journey* is a four-stage southward one from Galilee to Jerusalem in Luke balanced by a four-stage westward one from Jerusalem to Rome in Acts. For Luke, Galilee is the beginning, Jerusalem is the pivot, and Rome is the conclusion.

———

Next, then, and especially after those mentions of the "Holy Spirit" or "the Spirit" in Acts 1:8 and 19:21, it is time to turn to the second major megatheme in Luke-Acts. This is the *Holy Spirit*, which drives the *travel journey* from Galilee to Jerusalem in Luke and Jerusalem to Rome in Acts. Those two themes combine to establish the *journey of the Holy Spirit* as the single overarching supertheme of Luke-Acts and, therefore, establish the Holy Spirit as the single and unifying protagonist of its two volumes.

The *Holy Spirit*, "holy" because it is the Spirit of God, is emphatically introduced in the overture of Luke 1–2, but undergoes there a very basic shift in meaning for the rest of Luke-Acts. In the overture, the megatheme of the *Holy Spirit* is introduced by a sevenfold repetition of the name "Holy Spirit" (Luke 1:15, 35, 41, 67; 2:25, 26, 27). But in six of those seven uses in Luke 1–2 this Holy Spirit is intended as the *spirit of prophecy*. In general, individuals who are "filled with the Holy Spirit" speak like "the Lord God of Israel . . . [who] spoke through the mouth of his holy prophets" in the Old Testament (1:68, 70).

In particular, John the Baptist "will be filled with the Holy Spirit . . . with the spirit and power of Elijah" and "will be called the prophet of the Most High" (1:15, 17, 76). This insists that John the Baptist belongs to the Old Testament's prophetic tradition. Or, as Luke will say later so tersely, "The law and the prophets were in effect until John" (16:16)—in which "until" signifies that John is the climactic end of the Old and not the start of the New Testament. Furthermore, both John's parents are in that same prophetic tradition: "Elizabeth was filled with the Holy

Spirit and exclaimed . . ." (1:41) and "His father Zechariah was filled with the Holy Spirit and spoke this prophecy . . ." (1:67).

Finally, at Jesus's circumcision in the Temple, there is a climactic triple mention of the Holy Spirit as the spirit of prophecy: "The Holy Spirit rested" on Simeon; "it had been revealed to him by the Holy Spirit that he would not see death before he had seen the Lord's Messiah," so that, "guided by the Spirit," he took the child in his arms and prophesized about him (2:25–27).

That leaves one final mention of the Holy Spirit in Luke 1–2, and it is strikingly different from the other six cases just discussed. The archangel Gabriel announces to Mary:

> You will conceive in your womb and bear a son, and you will name ["call," in Greek] him Jesus. He will be great, and will be called the Son of the Most High, and the Lord God will give to him the throne of his ancestor David. He will reign over the house of Jacob forever, and of his *rule* there will be no end. . . . The Holy Spirit will come upon you, and the power of the Most High will overshadow you; therefore the child to be born will be holy; he will be called Son of God. (1:31–35)

This is not the *prophetic* Spirit of promise that says, "In the future this will be," but the *creative* Spirit of fulfillment that says, "In the present let this be"—recall Genesis 1. This is the initial Spirit of the world's creation, which is also the final or eschatological Spirit of its re-creation (recall *eschaton* as Greek for "last" or "final"). This is not the Holy Spirit who makes people speak, but the Holy Spirit who makes things happen.

———————

At this point, with the *Holy Spirit* theme, as previously with the *travel journey* theme, we expect that the Spirit will guide Jesus in Galilee and then from Galilee to and in Jerusalem. Watch next, however, how and why that process starts in Luke 3–4, but then is abandoned until the overlap between Luke 24:49 and Acts 1:4, 8.

First, John the Baptist proclaimed: "'I baptize you with water; but one who is more powerful than I is coming. . . . He will baptize you with the Holy Spirit and fire" (Luke 3:16). Then, when Jesus was baptized by John at the Jordan, "the Holy Spirit descended upon him in bodily form like a dove" (3:22).

Next, "Jesus, full of the Holy Spirit, returned from the Jordan" and "Jesus, filled with the power of the Spirit returned to Galilee, and a report about him spread through all the surrounding country" (4:14). The Holy Spirit is directing operations and the next step reminds us forcibly that this is not just the *prophetic Spirit of promise* for the future but the *creative Spirit of fulfillment* in the present.

Finally, "when he came to Nazareth, where he had been brought up, he went to the synagogue on the sabbath day, as was his custom" (4:16). We already saw the crucial importance of this incident—ritual, fictional, and paradigmatic—for the lethal reactions of "the Jews" throughout Luke-Acts. Here, however, we focus not on later audience reaction but on Jesus's earlier assertion that the prophecy of Isaiah 61:1–2a is fulfilled "today":

> The Spirit of the Lord is upon me, because he has anointed me to bring good news to the poor. He has sent me to proclaim release to the captives and recovery of sight to the blind, to let the oppressed go free, to proclaim the year of the Lord's favor. (4:18–19)

If the Holy Spirit is God in action, that quotation gives us the content of that divine action here and now.

Five hundred years earlier, a Spirit-filled Isaiah had announced release and liberation to the Jewish exiles held in Babylonian captivity since the conquest of Judea in the 590s–580s BCE (61:1-2). Luke now has a Spirit-filled Jesus announce the same liberation for Jews and Gentiles alike—for the poor, the blind, the imprisoned, and the oppressed.

In other words, for Luke-Acts, *the power of the Holy Spirit is power for liberation of the oppressed.* This is programmatic for Luke's understanding of Jesus, and it is repeated later in answer to John's question from prison: "Go and tell John what you have seen and heard: the blind receive their sight, the lame walk, the lepers are cleansed, the deaf hear, the dead are raised, the poor have good news brought to them" (Luke 7:22). The Holy Spirit is the present power of healing and liberation.

Finally, however, once Luke 3–4 establishes the inaugural advent and official presence of the Holy Spirit on Jesus, the rest of Luke makes no attempt to have the Holy Spirit explicitly directing major or minor steps in the life of Jesus (10:21; 11:13; 12:10, 12). The reason might be that it would be religiously risky or transcendentally tacky to have God's Spirit overcontrolling God's Son! In any case, as we see next, the theme of the Spirit as protagonist for all of Luke-Acts is picked up and expanded exponentially in Acts.

Luke establishes an explicit connection and a powerful parallel between Jesus's baptism by the Holy Spirit at the start of Luke and the apostles' baptism by the Holy Spirit at the start of Acts. He thereby picks up and then continues the double megatheme of the *travel journey of the Holy Spirit*, last seen together for Jesus in Luke 3–4.

At the start of Luke, when Jesus is baptized in the Jordan, "The Holy Spirit descended upon him in bodily form like a dove" (3:22). Then, at the start of Acts, Jesus promises his apostles: "You will be baptized with the Holy Spirit not many days from now" and "You will receive power when the Holy Spirit has come upon you" (1:5, 8). That, of course, is fulfilled when on "the day of Pentecost . . . all of them were filled with the Holy Spirit and began to speak in other languages, as the Spirit gave them ability" (2:1, 4).

Next, as seen above, after the Holy Spirit descended on and "filled" Jesus (Luke 3:22; 4:1), he proclaimed in the synagogue at Nazareth: "The Spirit of the Lord is upon me," as foretold by Isaiah 61:1–2, and, climactically: "Today this scripture has been fulfilled in your hearing" (Luke 4:18, 21).

In continued parallelism, after the apostles "were filled with the Holy Spirit" (Acts 2:4), Peter proclaimed in the Temple at Jerusalem:

> This is what was spoken through the prophet Joel: "In the last (*eschatais*) days it will be, God declares, that I will pour out my Spirit upon all flesh, and your sons and your daughters shall prophesy, and your young men shall see visions, and your old men shall dream dreams. Even upon my slaves, both men and women, in those days I will pour out my Spirit; and they shall prophesy." (Acts 2:16–18, from Joel 2:28–32)

This Holy Spirit of fulfilled prophecy comes not only on the individual Jesus, as in Luke 3:22, or only on the twelve apostles, as in Acts 2:4, but on "all flesh . . . sons and daughters . . . young men and old men . . . slaves, both men and women" (Acts 2:16–18).

Furthermore, this Spirit transforms the world not just by divine intervention, but by divine-and-human cooperation. So, when the people ask Peter what to do, he answers them: "Repent, and be baptized every one of you in the name of Jesus Christ so that your sins may be forgiven; and you will receive the gift of the Holy Spirit" (2:38). The Holy Spirit is offered freely to "all flesh" but, like any *offer*, it becomes a *gift* only when received, accepted, and embodied as life.

In summary so far: Luke 3–4 narrates the Spirit baptism of Jesus at the Jordan, his Spirit-empowered proclamation at Nazareth, and his claim that Isaiah 61:2 is here and now fulfilled. In calculated parallelism, Acts 2 narrates the Spirit baptism of the Twelve in Jerusalem, Peter's Spirit-empowered proclamation there, and his claim that Joel 2:28–32 was now fulfilled. Granted all that, what happens next to the *Holy Spirit* as a theme in Acts?

The *Holy Spirit* appears repeatedly in Acts: for the disciples in general (2:4; 4:31) and for certain individuals in particular—Peter (4:8), Stephen (7:55), Barnabas (11:24), and Paul (9:17; 13:9). More significantly, the Holy Spirit dominates Acts by intervening directly and explicitly to control crucial moments of the *geographical expansion* of earliest Christianity. Here are four very specific and important examples.

First, as seen already, Jesus promised the apostles: "You will receive power when the Holy Spirit has come upon you; and you will be my witnesses in Jerusalem, in all Judea and Samaria, and to the ends of the earth" (1:8). The *Holy Spirit* empowers the *travel journey* as Luke's twin megathemes come powerfully together in Acts.

Next, the story moves north along the Levantine coast between Joppa and the provincial government seat at Caesarea. Notice, in the following quotation, that it is the Holy Spirit and not Peter who dictates that male Gentiles may convert to Christianity without prior circumcision:

> While Peter was still speaking, the *Holy Spirit* fell upon all who heard the word. The circumcised believers who had come with Peter were astounded that the gift of the *Holy Spirit* had been poured out even on the Gentiles. . . . Then Peter said, "Can anyone withhold the water for baptizing these people who have received the *Holy Spirit* just as we have?" . . .

"As I [Peter] began to speak, the *Holy Spirit* fell upon them just as it had upon us at the beginning. And I remembered the word of the Lord, how he had said, 'John baptized with water, but you will be baptized with the *Holy Spirit*.'" (10:44–47; 11:15–16)

Peter talks, but the Holy Spirit acts in fivefold repetition. The Holy Spirit does not await Peter's decision on the inclusion of uncircumcised male Gentiles, but takes the physical lead and *falls* on them immediately—even before baptism or, better, as baptism!

Later, when debate arises about that decision, a letter is sent from Jerusalem farther up the Levantine coast to Antioch, capital of Roman Syria, stating: "It has seemed good to the Holy Spirit and to us to impose on you no further burden" (15:28) concerning male Gentile circumcision.

Furthermore, also at Antioch, the Holy Spirit dictates the next geographical expansion westward through Cyprus (13:5–12) and north onto the Anatolian plateau (13:13–14:25):

In the church at Antioch . . . [while] they were worshiping the Lord and fasting, the Holy Spirit said, "Set apart for me Barnabas and Saul for the work to which I have called them." Then after fasting and praying they laid their hands on them and *sent* them off. So, being *sent out* by the Holy Spirit, they went down to Seleucia; and from there they sailed to Cyprus. (13:1–4)

Notice that double sending: the community "sent them," but they were "sent out by the Holy Spirit."

Finally, the next major stage of geographical expansion is again westward, but this time across the upper Aegean Sea and so, for the first time, into Europe. Here, the Holy Spirit's geographical control is more explicit than ever before:

They went through the region of Phrygia and Galatia, having been forbidden by the *Holy Spirit* to speak the word in Asia. When they had come opposite Mysia, they attempted to go into Bithynia, but the *Spirit of Jesus* did not allow them; so, passing by Mysia, they went down to Troas. (16:6–8)

From the northern "region of Phrygia and Galatia" on the Anatolian plateau (modern Turkey), they could have gone *south* to Ephesus, capital of Roman Asia, but were "forbidden" by the *Holy Spirit*. Or they could have gone *north* to the Roman province of Bithynia-Pontus, but the *Spirit of Jesus*—a unique term in Luke-Acts—"did not allow them." Short of going back, the only open route approved by the Holy Spirit was westward from Troas to Neapolis, that is, from Asia to Europe (modern Turkey to modern Greece).

As we saw with the *travel journey* above, Paul now reverses direction and instead of continuing westward to Rome, goes first to Jerusalem and plans to reach Rome from there. But this *detour through Jerusalem* is also directed by the Holy Spirit, as Luke mentions four times on that journey. At Ephesus, "Paul resolved in the Spirit to go . . . to Jerusalem. He said, 'After I have gone there, I must also see Rome'" (Acts 19:21). The Spirit begins and controls Paul's detour to Jerusalem before Rome.

At Miletus on the eastern Aegean coast, Paul tells the Ephesian elders: "Now, as a captive to the Spirit, I am on my way to Jerusalem, not knowing what will happen to me there, except that the Holy Spirit testifies to me in every city that imprisonment and persecutions are waiting for me" (20:22–23).

At Tyre, "the disciples . . . through the Spirit . . . told Paul not to go on to Jerusalem" (21:4) because of the dangers there. At Caesarea, "a prophet named Agabus came down from Judea. He came to us and took Paul's belt, bound his own feet and hands with it, and said, 'Thus says the Holy Spirit, "This is the way the Jews in Jerusalem will bind

the man who owns this belt and will hand him over to the Gentiles"'"
(21:10–11).

That warning is the final mention of the Holy Spirit as the guiding
or controlling protagonist in Acts. After that prophecy, "the Jews" and
"the Gentiles" take over the fate of Paul. But how that prophecy was
fulfilled at Jerusalem and how Paul was handed by "the Jews to the
Gentiles" is another climactic example of Luke denying any hint of
high-level leadership discord within the Messianic/Christic community. It is also a final case of deliberate divergence by Luke's Paul from
something close to the heart of Paul's Paul.

In general, as already seen, Acts avoids both the actuality *and* possibility of leadership discord by denying Paul the title of apostle, one sent
directly by God in Christ, and acclaiming Peter as, in effect, the apostle
to the Gentiles. That of course takes from Paul the very basis of his
authority, identity, and integrity.

In particular, again as already seen, Acts 15 avoids any hint of a
mission division between Jewish and Gentile wings of the Messianic/
Christic community. Then, since there was never any such missionary
division, there could never be any needed reconciliation by a financial
support from Paul's Gentile communities to "the Poor," James's share-
community at Jerusalem.

Hence, we have another divergence between Luke's Paul and Paul's
Paul on a matter of Pauline integrity, since he insists he was "eager" to
heal that missionary split by practical alms support (Gal. 2:10). In this
particular case, however, Paul tells us *why* he made that last fateful visit
to Jerusalem while Luke tells us *what* happened there. We need both
together for a full or at least a fuller story.

First, we can authenticate Paul's claim that he was "eager" to ob-
tain the collection for "the Poor," by reading his long and detailed

instructions for gathering it in 1 Corinthians 16:1–4 and 2 Corinthians 8:1–9:15. Second, in gathering and taking that collection to Jerusalem from his Gentile churches in Galatia, Asia, Macedonia, and Achaia, Paul knew not to do so all by himself! "When I arrive," he says in 1 Corinthians, "I will send any whom you approve with letters to take your gift to Jerusalem. If it seems advisable that I should go also, they will accompany me" (16:3–4).

That was deemed advisable, because here is what Paul says about that collection visit to Jerusalem in his letter to the Romans:

> At present, however, I am going to Jerusalem in a ministry to the saints; for Macedonia and Achaia have been pleased to share their resources with the poor among the saints at Jerusalem. . . . So, when I have completed this, and have delivered to them what has been collected, I will set out by way of you to Spain. (15:25–28)

Note that correct phrase: "*the poor* among the saints at Jerusalem." Paul's plan is first Jerusalem, then Rome, and finally Spain. *For Luke, Rome was terminus; for Paul, Rome was transit.*

Third, Paul gives an explanation for never having visited Rome: "I make it my ambition to proclaim the good news, not where Christ has already been named, so that I do not build on someone else's foundation" (Rom. 15:20). In itself, therefore, Rome was of indirect rather than direct interest.

Paul had proclaimed Christ "from Jerusalem and as far around as Illyricum," that is, across the eastern Roman Empire, "but now," he says, "with no further place for me in these regions, I desire, as I have for many years, to come to you when I go to Spain. For I do hope to see you on my journey and to be *sent on by you*, once I have enjoyed your company for a little while" (15:19, 23–24). Paul is not going *to* Rome, only *through* Rome.

Rome was simply a stop from east to west, a pause on the way from the known world of Corinth or Ephesus to the unknown world of Tarragona or Cádiz. Paul's expressed desire to be "sent on" by the Roman Christians, by the way, did not mean simply a wave onboard at Ostia, but help with financial costs—and maybe Latin-speaking secretaries?

Finally, Paul knows that he himself is heading into lethal danger from outsiders and potential rejection by insiders at Jerusalem:

> I appeal to you, brothers and sisters, by our Lord Jesus Christ and by the love of the Spirit, to join me in earnest prayer to God on my behalf, that I may be rescued from the unbelievers in Judea, and that my ministry to Jerusalem may be acceptable to the saints, so that by God's will I may come to you with joy and be refreshed in your company. (Rom. 15:30–32)

Those are among the last words we have from the historical Paul, who is ready to risk his life for the unity of Christian Jews and Christian Gentiles in a single Messianic/Christic community.

For what follows, remember those *three* main points Paul made about the *delivery* of the collection to Jerusalem: he would accompany the collection delegates there; the collection might be refused by the "saints" there; his life might be in danger from "unbelievers" there.

Acts gives us the *what* but not the *why* of the journey to Jerusalem— Luke never tells us why Paul went there. *But he knows all about it and describes the process without ever mentioning the product.* He knows all about it because that travel diary from Paul's unidentified Philippian ship companion only makes sense if we add in the collection. Watch how that works.

First, Paul said he might accompany the delegates who carried the collection from his various provincial communities (1 Cor. 16:3). Here is how Luke describes Paul's departure for Jerusalem:

> He was accompanied by Sopater son of Pyrrhus from Beroea, by Aristarchus and Secundus from Thessalonica, by Gaius from Derbe, and by Timothy, as well as by Tychicus and Trophimus from Asia. They went ahead and were waiting for us in Troas; but we sailed from Philippi after the days of Unleavened Bread, and in five days we joined them in Troas, where we stayed for seven days. (Acts 20:4–6)

In tallying up Paul's Roman provinces, his seven companions involve Macedonia (Sopater, Aristarchus, Secundus), Galatia (Gaius and Timothy), and Asia (Tychicus and Trophimus). Only the Corinthians of Achaia are missing—did they ultimately refuse to participate in the collection?

Second, Paul knew that the "saints" in Jerusalem might not find the collection "acceptable" (Rom. 15:31). It is presented, of course, to James, for his share-community known as the Poor, but James first reminds Paul:

> How many thousands of believers there are among the Jews, and they are all zealous for the law. They have been told about you that you teach all the Jews living among the Gentiles to forsake Moses, and that you tell them not to circumcise their children or observe the customs. (Acts 21:20–21).

We know from Josephus's *Jewish Antiquities* that strict, law-abiding, non-Christian Jews defended James, "the brother of the Jesus who was called the Christ," strongly enough to unseat a high priest in 62

(20:197–203). Therefore, however James might have formulated his objection, some form of condition would have been expected in his situation. Here is that condition:

> We have four men who are under a vow. Join these men, go through the rite of purification with them, and *pay* for the shaving of their heads. Thus all will know that there is nothing in what they have been told about you, but that you yourself observe and guard the law. (Acts 21:23–24)

According to Acts, Paul agreed and so, presumably, what remained of the collection was "acceptable" to James. It is quite possible that Paul would not agree to that condition and James refused the collection—as Paul had feared he would (Rom. 15:31b).

Third, Paul also knew that his life was in danger from non-Messianic/Christic Jews in Jerusalem (Rom. 15:31a). Acts says that "the Jews from Asia, who had seen *him* in the temple, stirred up the whole crowd" and accused Paul of having "brought Greeks into the temple and . . . defiled this holy place" (21:27–28). Yet, as Acts admits, nobody had actually seen Greeks with Paul in the "Jews-only" section of the Temple: "They had previously seen Trophimus the Ephesian with him in the *city*, and they supposed that Paul had brought him into the temple" (21:29).

Be that as it may, Paul is attacked by those "unbelievers," is saved by the Romans, and, according to Acts, appeals to the imperial court. For the record, I do not think Paul was a Roman citizen but, in any case, if an accused had important and belligerent factions for and against him, local authorities often handed off the case to Rome, where lethal verdicts were distant in both time and place. Paul begins the long journey from Jerusalem to Rome and martyrdom—in chains.

Luke describes Paul's arrival at Rome, and notice how the same phrase frames his account: "So we *came to Rome.* The believers from there, when they heard of us, came as far as the Forum of Appius and Three Taverns to meet us. On seeing them, Paul thanked God and took courage. When we *came into Rome . . .*" (28:14–16).

Paul is traveling northward from Naples to Rome on the Via Appia and those two places are way stations at, respectively, the 43rd and 33rd milestones south from the city. Christians "come out to meet" (*eis apantēsin*). Acts, like the Paul we saw in 1 Thessalonians, uses the formal term for citizens welcoming an imperial visitor to their city. Luke slows down the journey, as it were, for Paul's dramatic and climactic entrance into Rome.

What happens next with Paul at Rome sums up the overall vision—apologetic, polemical, and theological—of Luke-Acts. Recall how their fellow Jews reacted to Jesus at Nazareth in Luke 4 and Paul at Pisidian Antioch in Acts 13. The conclusion of Acts recapitulates those events, but without lethal danger because Paul is now under Roman guard!

First, since Paul is "allowed to live by himself, with the soldier who was guarding him," he is able to call together "the local leaders of the Jews" and tell them:

> "Though I had done nothing against our people or the customs of our ancestors, yet I was arrested in Jerusalem and handed over to *the Romans.* When they had examined me, *the Romans* wanted to release me, because there was no reason for the death penalty in my case. But when the Jews objected, I was compelled to appeal to the emperor—even though I had no charge to bring against my nation." (Acts 28:16–19)

Paul is innocent, it is "the Jews" who cause trouble, and it is "the Romans" who recognize his innocence and want to free him.

Next, as expected, Paul delivers a Messianic/Christic sermon "testifying to the *rule of God* and trying to convince them about Jesus both from the law of Moses and from the prophets" (28:23). Although the Jewish leaders respond with disagreement among themselves rather than rejection of Paul, he responds by citing a sweeping indictment of them from Isaiah 6:9–10, introducing it with the words: "The Holy Spirit was right in saying to your ancestors through the prophet Isaiah . . ." (28:25). That, of course, is Luke's last mention of the *Holy Spirit*, and he does it in Rome.

Then, Luke concludes his interaction with the Roman Jewish leaders by proclaiming to them solemnly: "Let it be known to you then that this salvation of God has been sent to the Gentiles; they will listen" (28:28). For Luke, Israel has rejected its heritage, but the Gentiles have accepted it as an old-but-new Messianic/Christic community.

Finally, Luke-Acts concludes by saying that Paul "lived there two whole years at his own expense and welcomed all who came to him, proclaiming the *rule of God* and teaching about the Lord Jesus Christ with all boldness and without hindrance" (28:30–31). As we saw in Chapter 6, "without hindrance" (*akōlytōs*), the final word of Luke-Acts, is Luke's single-word claim from Rome, manifesto to Rome, and description of how Rome should handle Christianity—*unhindered*.

There is, of course, this obvious question. Even granted that Acts 28:16–31 is an appropriate ending for Luke-Acts on Christians, Jews, Gentiles, and Romans, why not tell what happened to Paul? Because Luke does not want to suggest that his second volume (Acts), about Paul from Jerusalem to Rome and imperial execution, exactly parallels his first volume (Luke), about Jesus from Galilee to Jerusalem and imperial execution. Luke is very careful not to suggest or allow such a misunderstanding of his purpose by ending with Paul's martyrdom at Rome—about which, writing fifty years later, he surely knew.

Luke-Acts is about the *travel journey of the Holy Spirit* from Galilee to Jerusalem in Luke and from Jerusalem to Rome in Acts. It is about the future not as Jewish Christianity, but as Roman Christianity. It is about the *journey of the Spirit* to change God's holy city from Jerusalem to Rome, to establish Rome as the new Jerusalem. It ends, therefore, how it should, when it should, and where it should—at Rome—for Luke-Acts.

One final point about Luke-Acts: If its author had named that two-volume book, how might it have been entitled? Possibly the "Acts of the Holy Spirit"? Possibly "The Travel Journey of the Holy Spirit"? Or maybe "The Way of the Holy Spirit"? The last title might be best of all, because, first, both Greek *hodos* and English "way" can mean "message," "manner," "route," or "path," and because, second, although others speak of "Christians" (Acts 11:26; 26:28), Acts's own preferred term for Christianity is "the Way."

The first use of the term occurs when the pre-Christian Paul persecutes in "the synagogues at Damascus . . . any he found who belonged to the Way, men or women" (Acts 9:2). Later, Luke's Paul refers to himself as having "persecuted this Way" (22:4).

Next, at Ephesus "a Jew named Apollos, a native of Alexandria . . . had been instructed in the Way of the Lord . . . but when Priscilla and Aquila heard him, they took him aside and explained the Way of God to him more accurately" (18:24–26). Furthermore, at Ephesus, some Jews "spoke evil of the Way before the congregation," and among Gentiles "no little disturbance broke out concerning the Way" (19:9, 23).

Finally, at coastal Caesarea, Paul appears before the governor Felix, "who was rather well informed about the Way" (24:22). Paul is accused of being "a pestilent fellow, an agitator among all the Jews throughout the world, and a ringleader of the sect (*haireseōs*) of the Nazarenes" (24:5; see also 28:22).

But Paul begins his autobiographical defense by stating: "I admit to you, that according to the Way (*tēn hodon*), which they call a sect (*hairesin*), I worship the God of our ancestors, believing everything laid down according to the law or written in the prophets" (24:14). Christianity is "the Way," not simply a "sect."

Granted that, among all the New Testament authors, Luke-Acts alone glimpsed the future correctly as Roman Christianity (or Christian Romanism) rather than Jewish Christianity (or Christian Judaism); granted that Luke-Acts proclaimed that paradigm shift not as present and future hope but as past and present history; and granted that the *Holy Spirit's Way* from Jerusalem to Rome was already accomplished, there is one final and fateful question.

In this new hybrid called *Roman Christianity*, what compromises would be necessary and how much acculturation would be demanded from *each* side? Hence, two questions for the next and final chapter of Part Two.

First, according to Luke-Acts, what structural changes must Christian faith make for a credible future as Roman *Christianity*? Second, according to Luke-Acts, what structural changes must Romanism make for a credible future as *Roman* Christianity? The next chapter, therefore, asks about the acculturation required for each side in the establishment of Roman Christianity as proposed by the visionary imagination of Luke-Acts.

10

THE COST OF
ACCULTURATION

I N LUKE, JOHN ALONE BAPTIZES. HE IS "*THE BAPTIST*," AND his purification of Israel by water, by having the people pass through the Jordan, facilitated a renewed *return from exile* that was the necessary preparation for God's advent and its promised world transformation. In Acts, however, *Spirit* baptism dominates *water* baptism both *for* the disciples at Pentecost (1:5; 11:16; 19:3–4) and *by* the disciples thereafter. Acts mentions baptism by the apostles (2:41), by Philip (8:12–13, 36–38), by Peter (10:47–48), and especially by Paul—at Philippi (16:15, 33), Corinth (18:8), and Ephesus (19:3–5).

Hence this question—which continues our discussion of Luke's deradicalization of Paul's status as an apostle: What, in theory and practice, did baptism mean for Paul's Paul in his original letters? What, in theory and practice, did baptism mean for Luke's Paul in Acts? But before starting to answer that twofold question, one preliminary observation is needed.

Across the millennia of human delusion, certain differences become hierarchies, certain dichotomies become hegemonies, and certain contrasts become prejudices. Those processes create systemic levels and structural layers of "us over them" that are usually based on might over right and victor over vanquished.

Take, for example, three such prejudicially created hierarchies from Aristotle's *Politics* in 350 BCE:

> First, *Greeks over Barbarians*: "Barbarians have no class of natural rulers. . . . Hence the saying of the poets, "Tis meet that Greeks should rule barbarians.'"

> Second, *free over slaves*: "He is by nature a slave who is capable of belonging to another (and that is why he does so belong), and who participates in reason so far as to apprehend it but not to possess it."

> Third, *men over women*: "Between the sexes, the male is by nature superior and the female inferior, the male ruler and the female subject." (1.1252b, 1254b)

With that as matrix, we turn now to that double question about what baptism meant first for Paul's Paul and then for the Luke's Paul, but within this chapter's overall assessment of the cost of acculturation to *Roman* Christianity.

First, what was baptism for the historical Paul? In two separate letters Paul refers to a *pre*-Pauline baptismal ceremony and quotes the formulaic declaration of intentional life commitment required from the baptizand. I cite the texts woodenly, close to the original Greek, use italics for parallel frames, and line them out to show structural emphasis:

> In *one Spirit* we *all* into one body were baptized (*ebaptisthēmen*), either Jews or Greeks,

either slaves or free,
and *all one Spirit* were given to drink (*epotisthēmen*).
  (I Cor. 12:13)

For you are all sons of God through faith *in Christ Jesus*.
As many of you as were baptized into Christ have clothed
  yourselves with Christ.
there is no Jew or Greek,
there is no slave or free,
there is no male and female.
For you are all one *in Christ Jesus*. (Gal. 3:26–28)

The word "all" frames both versions, "one spirit" frames the first, and "in Christ Jesus" the second formula. That baptismal declaration is about the many becoming a single community by rejecting Aristotle's three fundamental hierarchies. No more Greek over Jew in religio-ethnic superiority, no more free over slave in politico-economic supremacy, and no more male over female in gender ascendancy.

Those creeds are programmatic confessions of faith. They represent public commitment to a religious *lifestyle* that Rome could correctly call high treason—not because it was militarily violent, but because it was socially, economically, and politically subversive. Baptizands are not just born again, but created anew. Baptism is about radical re-creation and not just about liberal rebirth. Baptism is, in a medical analogy, a Spirit transplant or, in a technological analogy, a new operating system.

Next, does the historical Paul practice that theory, live out that baptismal commitment, or simply proclaim it as an eschatological dream or utopian idyll?

First, what does Paul say about "no Jew or Greek"? Paul was permanently proud of his own Jewish heritage: "circumcised on the eighth day, a member of the people of Israel, of the tribe of Benjamin, a Hebrew born of Hebrews; as to the law, a Pharisee" (Phil. 3:5). But, as a Messianic/Christic Jew and apostle to the Gentiles, Paul knew that all had not gone as expected with that promised unity of Greek and Jew in the one Spirit of Christ Jesus. And it sears his soul to see it: "I have great sorrow and unceasing anguish in my heart. For I could wish that I myself were accursed and cut off from Christ for the sake of my own people, my kindred according to the flesh" (Rom. 9:2–3).

Still, even if many or most of his fellow Jews are opposing such unity, Paul says: "I want you to understand this mystery: a hardening has come upon part of Israel, until the full number of the Gentiles has come in" (Rom. 11:25). For Paul, "no Jew or Greek" is a divine mystery with an open future "until" . . .

Second, what about Paul on the topic of "no slave or free"? For this we have a practical example. A slave named Onesimus, in danger of severe punishment or even death for some domestic offense, flees to Paul for intercession with his master, Philemon. Paul converts Onesimus to Christianity, and that creates a perfect individual baptismal test case: Can Onesimus and Philemon be unequal and at the same time equal—in Christ Jesus? Can Onesimus and Philemon be physically unequal and yet spiritually equal—in the same Spirit? Can a *Christian* master own a *Christian* slave?

In writing to Philemon, Paul alternates expressions of praise and affection with quite clear expectations that Philemon *must* free Onesimus:

> Though I am bold enough in Christ to command you to do your duty, yet I would rather appeal to you on the basis of love. . . .
>
> Perhaps this is the reason he was separated from you for a while, so that you might have him back forever, no longer as a slave but more than a slave, a beloved brother—especially to me but how much more to you, both in the flesh and in the Lord. . . .
>
> Confident of your obedience, I am writing to you, knowing that you will do even more than I say. (Philem. 8–9, 15–16, 21)

Philemon's "duty" is mandated by baptism, and Onesimus must be freed "both in the flesh and in the Lord," both spiritually before Christ and physically before Rome. Baptism is present reality, not future fantasy.

Third, what about Paul on "no male and female"? Paul accepts that radical baptismal equality in *marriage, ministry,* and *apostolate.*

In speaking about *marriage,* Paul is very careful to balance male and female: "The wife does not have authority over her own body, but the husband does; likewise the husband does not have authority over his own body, but the wife does" (1 Cor. 7:4). On divorce, he advises believing and unbelieving spouses to stay together if possible because one may save the other: "Wife, for all you know, you might save your husband. Husband, for all you know, you might save your wife" (7:16). On celibacy, he balances fairly and parallels fully his advice to unmarried and to married males with that to unmarried and to married females (7:32–34).

In ministry, both men and women "pray and prophesy" in the Corinthian communities. But, as I interpret the problem that arose there, certain *wives* wanted to practice celibacy, as Paul did (7:7), but the husbands disagreed with one-sided marital celibacy and sought practical alternatives.

Furthermore, those female celibates announced their new status as *virginal wives* by displaying the unveiled hair of a virgin rather than the veiled hair of a matron (11:2–16). Paul's reaction was to demand matronly veils for wives, but not to forbid experiments with *marital celibacy* under these conditions: "Do not deprive one another except perhaps by agreement for a set time, to devote yourselves to prayer, and then come together again, so that Satan may not tempt you because of your lack of self-control" (7:5)

In the apostolate, among those greeted at Rome, only four named persons, all women—Mary, Tryphaena, Tryphosa, and Persis—get the same accolade for dedication to Christ (Rom. 16:6, 12) that Paul gives himself (1 Cor. 15:10; Gal. 4:11). The verb behind "worked hard" in Greek is *kopiaō*, which carries the sense of lifetime dedication.

The case of Andronicus and Junia is even more explicit for the *apostolate*: "Greet Andronicus and Junia, my relatives [fellow Jews] who were in prison with me; they are prominent among the apostles, and they were in Christ before I was" (Rom. 16:7). Presumably a married couple, both husband Andronicus and wife Junia are prominent apostles and therefore women can be apostles as well as men—despite Acts's exclusive term "men/males" for apostles (1:21).

The historical Paul put into practice the radical baptismal commitment to be born again, or created anew, thereby moving beyond the normalcy of basic Roman culture. What does the historical author of Luke-Acts say about each of those three hierarchies?

———————

First, what does Luke-Acts say about "no Jew or Greek"? The terms "jealous" and "jealousy" describe the Jewish reaction to Gentile admittance in both Paul's letters (Rom. 10:19; 11:11, 14) and Luke-Acts (although Luke reports particularly violent results; Acts 5:17; 13:45; 17:5). Further, although both authors admit to that ideal's failure: for Paul as a Messianic/Christic Jew it is a divine mystery to be mourned, but for the author of Luke-Acts as an ex-God-fearer it is a human failure to be accepted or even celebrated.

Second, what about Luke-Acts on the topic of "no slave or free"? On economic inequality, it gives no evidence of a radical negation of *slavery*, only a liberal criticism of *poverty*. And "no rich or poor" is to be solved by individual distributive almsgiving rather than by systemic distributive justice. Here are some examples.

In Luke alone, "Blessed are you who are poor" receives the concomitant curse, "Woe to you who are rich" (6:20, 24). But what Luke intends is, "Woe to you who are rich *and do not give alms to the poor*." In Luke alone, Jesus tells the parables of the Rich Fool (12:16–21), the

Dishonest Manager (16:1–7), and the Rich Man and Lazarus (16:19–25), where rich over poor in this world is simply reversed to poor over rich in the next. He also adds "the poor" to the parable of the Great Dinner (14:13, 21). In Luke alone, we have the admonition to "sell your possessions, and give alms" (Luke 12:33; cf. Matt. 6:19).

In Luke alone, there is the story of Zacchaeus at Jericho, who "was a chief tax collector and was rich," but who promises Jesus to give half of his possessions to the poor and make very generous restitution for any fraud: "If I have defrauded anyone of anything, I will pay back four times as much" (19:1–8). And Zacchaeus in Luke links with Tabitha in Acts. Tabitha "was full of good works and of alms which she did" (Acts 9:36), and Peter raises her from the dead.

Luke moves the focus from rejecting *slavery* to redeeming *poverty*, but the Christian baptismal commitment did not say "there is no poor or rich," but "there is no slave or free." Whether almsgiving is an adequate response to poverty, redeeming poverty is not the same as rejecting slavery. Distributive charity for poverty is not distributive justice for slavery.

Third, what about Luke on "no male and female"? Surely, here at last, Luke is in agreement with Paul and the baptismal program of gender equality, since commentators regularly note the strong emphasis on women throughout Luke-Acts.

Start, for example, by comparing Luke 1–2 with Matthew 1–2. Both are infancy narratives serving, respectively, as parabolic overtures to Luke-Acts and Matthew. But, while Matthew focuses on Joseph, to whom the angel announces Jesus's birth (1:20–21), Luke focuses on Mary, who receives the birth annunciation (1:28–35).

Next, when the shepherds report the heavenly message of transcendental peace at the Nativity, "Mary treasured all these words and pondered them in her heart" (Luke 2:19). Mary also gets a special prophecy from Simeon in the Temple (2:34–35), and it is she who questions Jesus there in the last event of the overture (2:48).

Also, apart from the choice of female *over* male parent to receive the annunciation, Luke 1–2 also balances female *and* male protagonists in other sections of his overture. A female speaker and male speaker offer parallel canticles at the start, Mary (1:46–55) followed by Zechariah (1:68–79), and parallel prophecies at the end, Simeon (2:25–35) followed by Anna (2:36–38).

Furthermore, female and male parallelism reappears frequently throughout Luke-Acts: the parable of the Widow and the Unjust Judge (Luke 18:1–8) is followed by the parable of the Pharisee and the Tax Collector (18:9–14); the parable of the Lost Sheep (Luke 15:3–7) is followed by the parable of the Lost Coin (15:8–10); the healing of the centurion's servant (Luke 7:1–10) is followed by the raising of the widow's son (7:11–17); the story of Ananias (Acts 5:1–6) is followed by the similar fate of his wife, Sapphira (5:7–10); and the healing of Aeneas (Acts 9:32–35) is followed by the raising of Tabitha (9:36–43).

Finally, the phrase "men and women" is used eight times and "men or women" once in the New Testament, but seven of those uses are in Luke-Acts. Maybe, therefore, "no male and female" is just as operational for Luke-Acts as it is for Paul? In reply, we look more deeply at how Luke describes the roles and functions of women in two key locations.

A first location is the well-known story of Mary and Martha, a tale told only in Luke. Note, by the way, that "Mary and Martha" is the usual sequence of names despite their appearance as first Martha and then Mary:

> Jesus entered a certain village, where a woman named Martha welcomed him into her home. She had a sister named Mary, who sat at the Lord's feet and listened to what he was saying. But Martha was distracted by her many tasks (*diakonian*); so she came to him and asked, "Lord, do you not care that my sister has left me to do all the work (*diakonein*) by myself? Tell her then to help me." But the Lord answered her, "Martha,

Martha, you are worried and distracted by many things; there is need of only one thing. Mary has chosen the better part, which will not be taken away from her." (10:38–42)

That story involves two sisters, each representing a different relationship with "the Lord," and Luke's point is that one is preferable to the other. But which is better—and why?

Martha is immediately given a certain priority in the opening phrase—but watch carefully to see if Luke-Acts approves of such a priority as the story unfolds. Rather than saying that Jesus "entered a certain village where two sisters welcomed him into their home," Luke immediately announces that "a woman named Martha welcomed him into her home (*hypedexato auton*)." Martha represents the householder's authority; *she* invites Jesus into the home. That is the same domestic authority exercised for Jesus by Zacchaeus at Jericho in Luke 19:6 when "he hurried down and was happy to welcome him (*hypedexato auton*)." Also, for Paul and Silas by Jason at Thessalonica (Acts 17:7) when he "entertained them as guests" (*hypodedektai*).

Those last two examples, however, were male householders, for whom that language of household authority was standard. When a female, like Lydia at Philippi, invited Jesus and that unidentified travel diarist into her home, Luke records it like this: "When she and her house were baptized, she urged us, saying, 'If you have judged me to be faithful to the Lord, *entering the house, stay.*' And she prevailed upon us" (Acts 16:15, in a literal translation from the Greek). Where is her authoritative invitation?

Next, having given Martha alone the (male) authority to make the invitation, Luke says that "she had a sister named Mary, who sat at the Lord's feet and listened to what he was saying." That is the learning posture of student or disciple—for a man with Jesus (Luke 8:35), for Paul with Gamaliel (Acts 22:3), or for Mary with Jesus here.

Martha then complains that Mary is not helping her, but the term used for "tasks" and "work" is *diakonia*, which denotes not submissive service but authoritative ministry. Matthias, for example, was selected by lot "to take the place in this ministry (*diakonias*) and apostleship from which Judas turned aside" (Acts 1:25) and to thereby fill out the twelve apostles. Martha is again functioning in a role usually reserved for males.

Finally, Luke contrasts the two roles, Martha's *receiving into the home and performing ministry* and Mary's *sitting at the feet and listening*. Jesus's reply to Martha leaves no doubt about which role is the right one for women: "Mary has chosen the better part."

Luke-Acts's preference for Mary over Martha is not simply a preference for spirituality over hospitality, contemplation over action, prayer over meal, or focus over "distraction." It is, *for females*, a downgrading from leadership to discipleship, from active governance to submissive acceptance, from *receiving* to *sitting*, and from *ministering* to *listening*. It is about authority—for men but not for women—especially in the ministry of a house-church where "the Lord" is present.

For Paul, baptism's "no male and female" meant equality in marriage, ministry, and apostolicity. But, for Luke-Acts, it meant women and men *sit and listen* equally—and women are approved for doing so—but men rather than women *receive and minister* authoritatively—and women, like Martha, are disapproved for acting authoritatively.

A second location continues and even specifies that distinction for female disciples—they do indeed have a *ministry*, but it is one of support, not command. Watch, once again, how Luke changes his Markan source.

Mark mentions "women . . . who used to follow Jesus and provided (*diekonoun*) for *him* when he was in Galilee; and there were many other women who had come up with him to Jerusalem" (15:40–41). Three women are named: Mary Magdalene, another Mary, and Salome. Luke abbreviates Mark to a mention of "the women who had followed him from Galilee" (23:49), because earlier he has given a different version about them with different names for two of the three women:

The twelve were with him, as well as some women who
had been cured of evil spirits and infirmities: Mary, called
Magdalene, from whom seven demons had gone out, and
Joanna, the wife of Herod's steward Chuza, and Susanna, and
many others, who provided (*diekonoun*) for *them* out of their
resources." (Luke 8:1–3)

Is "cured of evil spirits and infirmities" for the female but not the
male disciples a gratuitous slur on their femaleness—in Luke itself?

Further, Mary Magdalene is the only person common to both Markan and Lukan lists. Are her "seven demons" equally gratuitous—in
Luke itself? Finally, Mark had those women minister only to Jesus
("him"), but Luke has them minister to Jesus and the Twelve ("them").

Yes, women are certainly very important for Luke, but he emphasizes their service rather than their power, their importance for men
rather than their equality with men. From those two model locations,
we learn that women can listen but not lead, they can support but not
command. That is Luke-Acts, but it is not Paul—and that brings up
the following questions.

Luke-Acts—and its Paul—are already deradicalizing and re-
Romanizing the baptismal commitment seen in the letters of the historical Paul—on all three of its basic anticultural commitments. But is
Luke-Acts early or late in that ultimate rejection? Is it the start or the
end of that process? Is it a process already accomplished before it and
taken utterly for granted by it?

———

First, the general scholarly consensus is that, of the thirteen letters
attributed to Paul in the New Testament, seven are *certainly* Pauline
(1 Thessalonians, Philemon, Philippians, 1–2 Corinthians, Galatians,
Romans), three are *probably* post-Pauline (2 Thessalonians, Colossians,

Ephesians), and three are *certainly* post-Pauline (1–2 Timothy, Titus). Also neutral terms like "post-Pauline" and "pseudo-Pauline" should be replaced by "anti-Pauline"—at least with regard to the radical baptismal vision of Paul himself.

Second, we have already read about Christianity's inaugural rejection of slavery and patriarchy—in the authentic letters written earlier by Paul himself. But his creedal affirmation and baptismal commitment are flatly negated in the post-, pseudo-, and anti-Pauline letters written later in his name. Watch that process—in two stages.

The first stage is evident in pseudo-Paul's letter to the Colossians, which offers a striking contrast to that triple negation seen in Paul's letter to the Galatians 3:26–28. Here, as there, the context is baptism: "You have stripped off the old self with its practices and have clothed yourselves with the new self . . . according to the image of its creator" (Col. 3:9–10). Then follows this formulaic summary of what is involved in that new creation—similar in format but different in content from Galatians 3:26–28: "In that renewal there is no longer Greek and Jew; circumcised and uncircumcised, barbarian, Scythian, slave and free; but Christ is all and in all!" (Col. 3:11).

You notice, however, that Paul's first Galatian element, "no longer Jew or Greek," is doubled here. Paul's second Galatian element, "no longer slave or free," lacks any such contrast (in Greek) and is lost within a fourfold list here. Paul's third Galatian element, "no longer male and female," is not even present here.

Those differences, however, are only a very slight preparation for what follows as that baptismal theory is clarified in actual practice in Colossians 3:18–4:1:

> *Wives*, be subject to your husbands, as is fitting in the Lord.
> *Husbands*, love your wives and never treat them harshly.
> *Children*, obey your parents in everything . . . in the Lord.
> *Fathers*, do not provoke your children, or they may lose heart.

> *Slaves*, obey your earthly masters . . . wholeheartedly, fearing
> the Lord. . . .
>
> *Masters*, treat your slaves justly and fairly . . . you also have a
> Master in heaven.

The passage above is an example of what is known in New Testament scholarship as a household code. Household codes accept both slavery and patriarchy, with wives, children, and slaves obedient to husbands, fathers, and masters (*kyrioi*) in similarly formatted commands. This is the household of the Roman Christian paterfamilias, but now with children old enough to be disobedient. By the way, lest you think those household rules are peculiar or idiosyncratic to the pseudo-Pauline Letter to Colossians, the same sets reappear in the pseudo-Pauline Letter to Ephesians: wives and husbands (5:22–33), children and fathers (6:1–4), slaves and masters (6:5–9).

On the one hand, pseudo-Paul's serene acceptance of slavery and patriarchy despite and against Paul's own commitment to baptismal radicalism is the cost of acculturation to Roman Christianity. On the other, those two household codes might have been too liberal for a strictly conservative Roman paterfamilias. After all, pseudo-Paul addressed all groups *directly* and at least commanded responsibilities from *both* sides of each pair. A Roman father might have said: "Do not dare to address my dependents directly. If you must, address me and I will address them!" Hence, this next stage—moving from the *probably* pseudo-Pauline to the *certainly* pseudo-Pauline letters.

The second stage is not so much conservative as reactionary—there are no more direct addresses or mutual responsibilities for both sides on slavery or patriarchy. Instead, pseudo-Paul orders Timothy and Titus directly with regard to slaves:

> Let all who are under the yoke of slavery regard their masters as
> worthy of all honor, so that the name of God and the teaching

may not be blasphemed. Those who have believing masters must not be disrespectful to them on the ground that they are members of the church; rather they must serve them all the more, since those who benefit by their service are believers and beloved. Teach and urge these duties. (1 Tim. 6:1–2)

Tell slaves to be submissive to their masters and to give satisfaction in every respect; they are not to talk back, not to pilfer, but to show complete and perfect fidelity, so that in everything they may be an ornament to the doctrine of God our Savior. (Titus 2:9–10)

As with slavery, so with patriarchy. Pseudo-Paul does not address wives directly and does not mention husbands:

Let a woman learn in silence with full submission. I permit no woman to teach or to have authority over a man; she is to keep silent. (1 Tim. 2:11–12)

Encourage the young women to love their husbands . . . being submissive to their husbands. (Titus 2:4–5)

The stream of Pauline tradition on the baptismal commitment against slavery and patriarchy moves from radical acceptance in the *certainly* Pauline letters, through conservative avoidance in the *probably not* Pauline letters, to reactionary annulment in the *certainly not* Pauline letters. But where in that letter tradition from Paul to anti-Paul do we locate the Paul of Luke-Acts? Is it before the start or after the end of that process?

We already saw how the historical Paul emphasizes that he is not only a divinely appointed apostle, but the apostle for the Gentiles. The pseudo-Pauline letters acknowledge that status and had to do so to validate their negations *of the apostolic Paul by the apostolic Paul:*

Paul, an apostle of Christ Jesus by the will of God. (Col. 1:1; Eph. 1:1)

Paul, an apostle of Christ Jesus by the command of God our Savior and of Christ Jesus our hope. . . . For this I was appointed a herald and an apostle (I am telling the truth, I am not lying), a teacher of the Gentiles in faith and truth. (1 Tim. 1:1; 2:7)

Paul, an apostle of Christ Jesus by the will of God, for the sake of the promise of life that is in Christ Jesus. For this gospel I was appointed a herald and an apostle and a teacher . . . so that through me the message might be fully proclaimed and all the Gentiles might hear it. (2 Tim. 1:1, 11; 4:17)

Paul, a servant of God and an apostle of Jesus Christ. (Titus 1:1)

Although Paul takes up more than half of Acts and his vocation gets three full versions there, Luke denies his status far more radically than do those pseudo-Pauline letters. They deny his *radical baptismal vision*, but Acts denies him his *radical apostolic status*. In summary, therefore, Luke deradicalizes and Romanizes Paul as the end rather than the start of that process in the New Testament. That is the ultimate *Pauline* cost of Luke's *Roman* Christianity.

———

Finally, there is one very powerful objection to this chapter and, indeed, to this book's entire understanding of Luke's vision of *Roman* Christianity. That objection is that Luke's Messianic/Christic theology is an absolute rejection of Roman imperial theology. In other words, Luke-Acts is a more basic opposition to Rome than anything seen so far; it is a more fundamental conflict with Rome than even rejection of slavery and patriarchy. Does that not contradict the suggestion that

Luke represents a further rejection of Paul than that present in the pseudo-Pauline letters?

We begin, once again, with the overture in Luke 1–2 because of its introductory importance for all of Luke-Acts. First, even before Jesus's conception, the archangel Gabriel announces his status and destiny to Mary:

> "He will be great, and will be called the Son of the Most High, and the Lord God will give to him the throne of his ancestor David. He will reign over the house of Jacob forever, and of his *rule* there will be no end." Mary said to the angel, "How can this be, since I am a virgin?" The angel said to her, "The Holy Spirit will come upon you, and the power of the Most High will overshadow you; therefore the child to be born will be holy; he will be called *Son of God*." (Luke 1:32–35)

Then, after Jesus's birth, an angel tells the shepherds: "To you is born this day in the city of David a *Savior*, who is the Messiah, the *Lord*" (2:11).

But "Savior," "Lord," and "Son of God" are three foundational titles of Caesar Augustus, who is mentioned by name in between those two angelic announcements (2:1). Also, with regard to place, Augustus's *rule* was over "all the world" (2:1), but, with regard to time, Jesus's *rule* was "forever" and without "end" (1:33).

That puts Augustus and Jesus in transcendental confrontation. Indeed, following the biblical tradition in, for example, Daniel 7, the Messianic/Christic theology in Luke 1–2 reads like a programmatic rejection of Roman imperial theology. Granted that confrontation in Luke-Acts, then, how can it even imagine the future as Roman Christianity?

Second, with its legions providing a protected periphery around the empire, Rome boasted rightly of the Pax Romana within the military's *cordon sanitaire*. But, with imperial Roman peace already established for around thirty years, how could an angel proclaim "good news of great joy for all the people" and, backed up with "a multitude of the heavenly host," announce "on earth peace among those whom God favors!" (Luke 2:10–14)?

If the Pax Romana already ruled, how could there be a Pax Messianica/Christiana? Since there is only one world, two visions of global peace must be adversarial. Once again, is a choice between *either* Rome *or* Christianity rather than the acculturation of Roman Christianity the insistent message of Luke 1–2 as overture to all of Luke-Acts?

In response to those questions from the overture, we come back one final time to Caesarea and "Cornelius, a centurion of the Italian Cohort" (Acts 10:1). As a character, this is Luke-Acts's image of the perfect Roman Christian, the visionary personification of his Roman Christianity. This is also where we see most clearly how—for Luke-Acts—Rome must adapt to Christianity and Christianity must adapt to Rome in the acculturation envisioned as *Roman Christianity*.

On the one hand, three points in the Cornelius story implicitly reject the divinity of the Roman emperor and thereby negate the transcendental basis of Roman imperial theology. A first point is Peter's refusal to be worshiped: "On Peter's arrival Cornelius met him, and falling at his feet, worshiped him. But Peter made him get up, saying, 'Stand up; I am only a mortal'" (Acts 10:25–26). Is that not a rebuke against calling divine the emperor, who was "only a mortal (*anthrōpos*)"?

A second point is that Peter's sermon proclaims to Cornelius and his fellow Gentiles "the message God sent to the people of Israel, preaching peace by Jesus Christ" (10:36). But peace—as the Pax Romana—was the basic proclamation of Rome itself, since the emperor Augustus was *natus ad pacem*, "born for peace." Does that not reject Rome's imperial program of *peace through victory* in favor of Christ's biblical one of *peace through justice*?

A third point is Peter's confession of faith, which proclaims that

"Jesus Christ—he is Lord of all" (10:36). Does that not remove the title
of universal "Lord," *kyrios*, from Caesar and give it instead to Christ?
That would be especially true for Luke-Acts, since it uses "Lord"—
especially as "the Lord"—about a hundred times in each volume. That
is about twice as often as "Christ" is used as the title for Jesus.

Furthermore, if that data seems too implicit or oblique as a rejection of Rome, its indirect style could be justified from both ancient and modern rhetorical theory. Quintilian, Rome's most famous
teacher of rhetoric, published his twelve-volume treatise *The Orator's Education* (*Institutio Oratoria*) under the authoritarian emperor
Domitian in 95 CE. He cites three cases when the orator should use
"a hidden meaning which is left to the hearer to discern . . . first, if it
is unsafe to speak openly; second, if it is unseemly to speak openly;
thirdly . . . novelty and variety" (9.2.65–66). Maybe, therefore, Luke-
Acts rejected Rome, but without speaking openly because that was
too unsafe?

The contemporary equivalent to Quintilian's "hidden meaning"
is the term "hidden transcript," used in James C. Scott's 1992 book
Domination and the Arts of Resistance for covert resistance when overt
rebellion would be immediately fatal. Maybe, once again, Luke-Acts is
replete with hidden transcripts that add up to a safe but certain repu-
diation of Rome?

On the other hand, Cornelius's exemplary almsgiving is mentioned
three times in Luke's account: "He gave *alms* generously to the people
and prayed constantly to God"; "Your prayers and your *alms* have ascended as a memorial before God"; "Cornelius, your prayer has been
heard and your *alms* have been remembered before God" (Acts 10:2,
4, 31). That agrees, of course, with all we have seen about the importance of alms for the poor in Luke-Acts—mentioned nine out of the
twelve times in the New Testament.

For *Roman* Christianity to succeed, the divinity of the emperor,
Caesar Augustus, would have to cede its transcendent place to that of

Jesus the Christ—Lord to Lord, Son of God to Son of God, and God Incarnate to God Incarnate. That, for Luke-Acts, is the Roman cost of acculturation. What, then, is the corresponding Christian cost of acculturation, the price of Roman *Christianity*?

That price—then and now, past and present—is a shift from *justice* to *charity*, a move from demanding distributive justice on a structural and systemic level to offering distributive charity on a personal and individual level. It is a turn from solving the causes to salving the effects of poverty, a jump from biblical prophecy to affluent philanthropy, a swerve from Amos to alms. But how can anyone but the perversely indifferent challenge charity or almsgiving or philanthropy?

First, one example. A fascinating aspect of Jesus's life in the Gospels is how many people with "demons" to be cast out crowd around him. General listings and individual stories of his healing activity repeatedly feature people who are "demoniacs" or "possessed by demons" or "have an unclean spirit." Those three equivalent terms appear repeatedly to describe some of the sufferers who come to Jesus for healing.

In the opening three chapters of Mark, there are "a man with an unclean spirit" (1:23–27), people "possessed with demons" (1:32), a general casting out of demons (1:34, 39), and "unclean spirits" (3:11); Jesus himself is even accused of having a demon that casts out demons (3:22, 30)! And so it continues until the last added lines of Mark (16:17). Why is Galilee so demon-ridden at the start of that first century?

Some interpreters wonder if those demoniacs were people suffering from brain damage or mental disorder. I wonder about something else: Why were there so many demoniacs—however understood—in the Jewish homeland at the time of Jesus, but not in the Jewish diaspora at the time of Paul? And why were there so many in the Gospels of the

New Testament but not in the books of the Old Testament? Why then? Why there?

That is a question both asked and answered in Mark's Gospel— and I wonder if Mark himself created the story about the Gerasene demoniac in 5:1–20; the actual location is uncertain, but it was on the eastern shore of the lake in Galilee ("Sea of Galilee"). He is described as a superdemoniac:

> A man out of the *tombs* with an unclean spirit met him. He lived among the *tombs*; and no one could restrain him any more, even with a chain; for he had often been restrained with shackles and chains, but the chains he wrenched apart, and the shackles he broke in pieces; and no one had the strength to subdue him. Night and day among the *tombs* and on the mountains he was always howling and bruising himself with stones. (5:2-5)

This fearfully strong demoniac is also extremely unclean, as he lives among the tombs—mentioned three times to frame his description.

"Jesus asked him, 'What is your name?' He replied, 'My name is Legion; for we are many'" (5:9). The name is, I think, quite clear that this "unclean spirit" is both one and many at the same time. The demoniac does not just have a *personality disorder*. He personifies and exemplifies imperial possession as a *nationality disorder*—Legion!

After being ordered to leave the man, Legion "begged him earnestly not to send them out of the country" (5:10). "The country" is mentioned in case you have missed the point of "Legion." Rather than leave the country, the demonic legion asked to be transferred to a herd of (unclean) swine: "The unclean spirits begged him, 'Send us into the swine; let us enter them'" (5:12). But not even the swine would accept them: "The herd, numbering about two thousand, rushed down the steep bank into the sea, and were drowned in the sea" (5:13).

Finally, in case we miss this parabolic manifesto for "Romans, go home," the locals got it, recognized its rhetorical subversion and anti-imperial edge, and "began to beg Jesus to leave their neighborhood" (5:17).

When we look at the entire demonology in, say, Mark's Gospel, we can see the difference between *justice* and *charity*, the difference between a single systemic or structural root cause and manifold effects, results, and consequences. Charity for demoniacs is certainly good, and charitable healing is surely kind, *but* the only solution is the replacement of the injustice of *Rome's rule* by the justice of *God's rule*. Jesus practiced charity but also demanded justice—the former gets you canonized, the latter gets you crucified. Charity is not justice, and salving injustice is not solving injustice.

In the biblical tradition, therefore, distributive justice should be the norm, adequate alms should be for emergencies, and distributive alms should never replace distributive justice or enable distributive injustice.

Come back now from that biblical vision, from Torah and Prophets or Jesus and Paul, to Luke and Acts. Compare distributive justice and distributive charity by comparing two triads, one in Paul, the other in Acts.

That triad of baptismal commitments in Galatians 3:28 was about justice, about not turning diversity into hierarchy and distinction into discrimination: Greek *and* Jew, male *and* female, free *and* slave were not to mean Greek *above* Jew, male *above* female, and free *above* slave. And in that final case, eliminating hierarchy was to eliminate difference itself and thereby subvert slavery as the basis of Roman economic life.

The triad of accolades for Cornelius in Acts all concern charity: "he gave alms . . . your alms . . . your alms" (10:2, 4, 31). Cornelius represents, for Luke, the ideal personification of *Roman Christianity*. He is a still-in-office centurion, a God-fearer who became a Roman Christian. But to be such, his *Romanism* had to surrender heavenly transcendence from Caesar to Christ, and his *Christianity* had to surrender the earthly relevance of justice to charity.

Unfortunately, however, the heavenly transcendence of Jesus embodies precisely and incarnates exactly the earthly relevance of justice, because the *rule of God* is about earth, not heaven or, better, about what heaven looks like on earth and what God looks like in sandals. But, Luke-Acts is *the way of the Holy Spirit* and, from Isaiah 6:1–2a to Luke 4:18–19; 7:22, God's Holy Spirit is the spirit of justice—not the spirit of charity.

In summary, those post-, pseudo-, and anti-Pauline letters negated Paul's baptismal commitment to distributive justice, and Luke consummated that by denying Paul's apostolic identity, authority, and integrity. Such was the cost of acculturation in *Roman Christianity*, the price of preparation for Constantine, and the ongoing Christian compromise that demands heaven for Christ but concedes earth to Caesar.

Concluding Unscientific Postscript on Luke-Acts. You were historically right, Luke. You were right that Romans and Christians could acculturate to one another. You were right that one would eventually convert the other. You did not see, however, which would convert which.

After those quite contradictory answers on the acculturation of God and Caesar in Parts One and Two, we turn next to Part Three with this constitutive question: Although Jesus did not suggest how to relate or reconcile, accommodate or acculturate the separated God "things" and Caesar "things" in Mark 12:13–17, *did he do so elsewhere in the New Testament?*

That question raises a very obvious problem. Granted that dichotomy on God/Caesar acculturation within the New Testament, it does not seem *persuasive* to go back into that same New Testament and present another option for it. How is it *credible* to discover a third response by Jesus in a source that has already presented two absolutely contradictory ones?

In response, Part Three begins with a historical experiment, an attempt to locate Jesus on God/Caesar acculturation *totally from outside the New Testament*. Meet the first-century Jerusalem-born priest Josephus bar-Matthias, who became the Rome-based historian Titus Flavius Josephus.

PART THREE

CULTURE CONFRONTED AND CRITICIZED

Equality is the mother of justice. . . .
Justice is the offspring of equality.
—Philo of Alexandria, *The Special Laws* (4.231, 238)

Inequality, that cause of all evil.
—Philo of Alexandria, *On the Contemplative Life* (9.70)

11

THE INVENTION
OF NONVIOLENT
RESISTANCE

JOSEPHUS BAR-MATTHIAS, BORN IN 37 CE WITH BOTH PRIESTLY and royal ancestors, was, he claims, an intellectual prodigy at age fourteen: "The chief priests and the leading men of the city used constantly to come to me for precise information on some particular in our ordinances" (*Life* 1.9). You may recall that, according to Luke, Jesus did that at twelve (2:46–47).

Captured as a rebel commander in Galilee at the start of the 66–74 war, Josephus saved his life and secured his career by telling the Roman general Titus Flavius Vespasianus that he would become emperor, even already addressing him as "Caesar": "I come to you as a messenger . . . sent on this errand by God. . . . You will be Caesar, Vespasian, you and your son [Titus] here . . . for you, Caesar, are master not of me only, but of land and sea and the whole human race" (*Jewish War* 3.400–402).

When that prophecy proved correct, he became Titus Flavius Josephus and wrote at Rome under the salaried patronage of the new Flavian dynasty, Vespasian, Titus, and Domitian. There, Josephus wrote his *Jewish War* (*JW*) in the late 70s to defend Romans to Jews:

"It was the Jewish tyrants who drew down upon the holy temple the unwilling hands of the Romans" (*JW* 1.10). Then he wrote his *Jewish Antiquities* (*JA*) as its *prequel* in the early 90s to defend Jews to Greeks: "I have undertaken this present work in the belief that the whole Greek-speaking world will find it worthy of attention" (*JA* 1.5).

Granted those different purposes, Josephus must always be read carefully and critically within the matrix of his literary intentions and survival strategies—just as you read Revelation or Luke-Acts within theirs. In the case of Josephus we have two major helps for such critical readings. One is that we have Greek copies of the Hebrew scriptures he used for his *Jewish Antiquities*, and we can see precisely what he adopts, adapts, keeps, omits, and changes. Another is that there is a two-hundred-year overlap between the end of *Antiquities* and the start of *War*, giving us two accounts of common material from the 160s BCE to the 60s CE.

Granted all that, how would we locate Jesus on God/Caesar acculturation if we temporarily bracketed the New Testament and had only the first-century Jewish historian Josephus as our source?

In preparation for Josephus on Jesus in particular, this chapter focuses on Josephus on Israel in general. How does he see acculturation between "the things of God" and "the things of Caesar" for his first-century homeland under the challenge of its initial Romanization?

That focus involves two aspects of God/Caesar acculturation that Josephus both reveals and conceals, both reluctantly admits and tendentiously obfuscates. It is precisely those two negated aspects that are both significant—and significant together—for what he eventually tells us about Jesus on God and Caesar.

The first aspect of the God/Caesar relationship that Josephus denies is any *eschatological and/or messianic-based* first-century Jewish resistance to Romanization. The reason is that any God-controlled destiny for the earth or any God-decreed future for the world pertains not to Judaism but to Romanism. God's prophetic Pax Divina ("divine peace") actually meant Rome's imperial Pax Romana!

Instead of the biblical hope of peace through nonviolent justice, Josephus proclaims the Roman fact of peace through violent victory: "Divine assistance . . . is ranged on the side of the Romans, for, without God's help, so vast an empire could never have been built up" (*JW* 2.390); "God, who went the round of the nations, bringing to each in turn the rod of empire, now rested over Italy. . . . There was, in fact, an established law, as supreme among brutes as among men, 'Yield to the stronger' and 'The mastery is for those preeminent in arms'" (*JW* 5.367).

Also, God—named either directly as such or indirectly as Fate, Providence, or Destiny—had chosen the new Flavian dynasty to rule Rome: "Now that Fortune was everywhere furthering his wishes . . . Vespasian was led to think that divine Providence had assisted him to grasp the empire and that some just Destiny had placed the sovereignty of the world within his hands" (*JW* 4.622); and, more explicitly, "[Titus] was still at Alexandria, assisting his father [Vespasian] to establish the empire which God had recently committed to their hands" (*JW* 5.2).

Then, since "God was on the Roman side," any revolt was not just against the Romans, but against God. "You are warring not against the Romans only," as Josephus told the besieged Jerusalemites, "but also against God." That is why "the Deity has fled from the holy places and taken His stand on the side of those with whom you are now at war" (*JW* 5.368, 378, 412).

Furthermore, within God's pro-Roman and pro-Flavian judgment, the only possible eschatological agent or messianic leader is Vespasian himself:

> What more than all else incited them to the war was an ambiguous oracle . . . in their sacred scriptures . . . that at that time one from their country would become ruler of the world.

This they understood to mean someone of their own race. . . .
The oracle . . . signified Vespasian, who was proclaimed emperor
on Jewish soil. (*JW* 6.312–13)

The destined messianic ruler of this eschatological world was not
to be a Jew *from* Israel but a Roman *in* Israel—an interpretation also
celebrated in Tacitus's *Histories* (5.13) and Suetonius's *Vespasian* (4.5).
(It was probably that interpretation or perversion of Jewish messianic
expectation that inspired Josephus to prophesy Vespasian's ascendancy
after his capture in Galilee.)

Sometimes, however, despite all that negation of Jewish eschatological/
messianic motivation as mistake at best and delusion at worst, Josephus
allows it to peer through the cracks in the marble of his Roman overlay.
When Josephus records rebel leaders claiming to be "kings," that is his
code word for messianic contenders.

The first armed revolt in 4 BCE produced three such (messianic)
"kings": Judas, to the north in Galilee; Simon, to the east in Perea
beyond the Jordan; and Athronges, to the south in Judea (*JW* 2.56–64;
JA 17.271–84). The second armed revolt, in 66–74 CE, produced two
more (messianic) "kings": Menahem in 66 (*JW* 2.434–44) and Simon
bar Giora in 70 CE (*JW* 4.508, 510; 7.29).

Finally, twenty years after his Romanizing of Jewish eschatology in
his *Jewish War*, Josephus had to face the book of Daniel in his *Jewish Antiquities*. Although written in the 160s BCE, the book was fictionalized
as if written in the 500s BCE and so all its "prophecies" were infallibly
accurate (*JA* 10.188–281). But what about the parallel Jewish eschatological promises of the *rule of God* on earth in Daniel 2:44 and 7:14, 22, 27?

In Daniel 2 and 7, the imperial rules of the Babylonians, Medes,
Persians, and Greeks were to be destroyed and, along with Alexander's
successor sub-empire of the Syrian-Greeks, to be replaced by the *rule of
God* on earth. But how could Josephus record such Jewish eschatology,
especially since "in the very same manner Daniel also wrote concerning

the Roman government, and that our country should be made desolate by them" (*JA* 10.27b)?

Watch how he handles Daniel's Jewish eschatology in those two particular chapters, first with Daniel 2 and its dream vision of a Great Statue and the Great Stone:

> The head of that statue was of fine gold, its chest and arms of silver, its middle and thighs of bronze, its legs of iron, its feet partly of iron and partly of clay. As you looked on, a stone was cut out, not by human hands, and it struck the statue on its feet of iron and clay and broke them in pieces. Then the iron, the clay, the bronze, the silver, and the gold, were all broken in pieces and became like the chaff of the summer threshing floors; and the wind carried them away, so that not a trace of them could be found. But the stone that struck the statue became a great mountain and filled the whole earth. (2:32–35)

Daniel then interprets the Great Statue as the rule of Babylon (gold), of Media (silver), of Persia (bronze), of Greece (iron), and of Greco-Syria (iron/clay), which are all to be destroyed by the Great Stone as the eschatological *rule of God*: "In the days of those kings the God of heaven will set up a *rule* that shall never be destroyed, nor shall this *rule* be left to another people. It shall crush all these rules and bring them to an end, and it shall stand forever" (2:44).

In his *Jewish Antiquities*, Josephus was quite content to follow Daniel 2 up to that eschatological interpretation of the Great Stone (*JA* 10.195–207). Instead of following Daniel's Jewish vision of God's eschatological *rule* on earth, Josephus beats a strategic hermeneutical retreat by avoiding that just-cited verse:

> Daniel did also declare the meaning of the stone to the king; but I do not think proper to relate it, since I have only undertaken

to describe things past or things present, but not things that
are future: yet if anyone be so very desirous of knowing truth,
as not to waive such points of curiosity, and cannot curb his
inclination for understanding the uncertainties of futurity,
and whether they will happen or not, let him be diligent in
reading the book of Daniel, which he will find among the sacred
writings. (*JA* 10:210)

Finally, having avoided mention of Judaism's eschatological *rule of God* in Daniel 2:44, Josephus avoids it again by totally omitting all of Daniel 7. That omission is also quite obviously deliberate. Although Josephus copied the stories in Daniel 1–6 in their proper sequence (*JA* 10.188–218, 232–63), he then skipped Daniel 7 completely and picked up again with Daniel 8 (*JA* 10.269–76).

As Josephus describes the *Jewish* response to Romanization, his first negation is of any *God*-founded eschatological motivation for it or any *God*-decreed messianic expectation about it. For Josephus, Jewish eschatology was mistake at best, delusion at worst, because the climax of time, the end of history, the last or eschatological "rule of God" on earth was the rule of Rome itself. Any validity to a Jewish eschatological vision or a Jewish messianic hope was buried by Josephus in the charred wreckage of Jerusalem.

That, however, is but a first negation. A second one is equally important and, indeed, as we see next, when this second one first appears, it is almost a subset of that eschatological/messianic negation.

The second aspect of the God/Caesar relationship that Josephus denies the existence of is any philosophically based and carefully organized first-century Jewish *nonviolent* resistance to Romanization. But such resistance did exist, and it must be emphasized, immediately, that Jewish *nonviolent resistance* was not pacifism but activism, not just internal but external, not just individual and personal but large-scale and organized. It was programmatic nonviolent response to violent imperial domination.

Still, at first glance even the *idea* of Jewish nonviolent resistance to Romanization may seem counterfactual or even counterintuitive—on the basis of these two objections. One objection points out that resistance in the first two hundred years of Israel's Romanization was in fact *violent* rather than nonviolent. Four major violent revolts broke out against it—three of them in the Jewish homeland, in 4 BCE, 66–74 CE, and 132–35 CE, and one across the adjacent Jewish diaspora from North Africa to Mesopotamia in 115–17 (see Appendix B). Another objection says that claims about nonviolent resistance in the first century are simply a modern *projection* backward into an ancient world of a philosophical theory and strategic practice that nobody ever did, or imagined, at that time and place.

The evidence for first-century organized Jewish nonviolent resistance against Romanization comes, however, massively from Josephus himself—despite Josephus himself. In the lull between the violent revolts of 4 BCE and 66 CE, there were *repeated Jewish experiments with organized nonviolent resistance to Romanization* backed by a readiness for *communal martyrdom* if necessary (Appendix B). All of that is in Josephus, but told with rhetorical strategies that describe and obscure, record and obfuscate, admit completely and condemn pejoratively at the same time

We look, to begin with, at the origins of that movement of nonviolent resistance and emphasize that Josephus does not connect it with 4 BCE, but with a specific Roman provocation—and there is always one for nonviolent resistance—that occurred in 6 CE. In that year the Herodian client prince Archelaus was dismissed, and a Roman governor, Coponius, replaced him as ruler of Samaria, Judea, and Idumea; as governor, Coponius was subordinate to the Syrian legate, Quirinius. Such *direct* Roman rule required an "assessment of property" (*JA* 18.1-3)—not a census of population (Luke 2:1–2; Acts 5:37)—for taxation purposes. That began, of course, the *direct* Roman tribute represented by the coin from Mark 12:13–17 in this book's Overture.

Josephus records the Jewish response to this taxation twice, once in his earlier pro-Roman *War* and again in his later pro-Jewish *Antiquities*, and there are striking differences between the two accounts. The instigator is one Judas the Galilean. Here is the first version:

> Under Coponius's administration a Galilean named Judas
> incited his countrymen to revolt, upbraiding them as cowards
> for consenting to pay tribute to the Romans and tolerating
> mortal masters, after having God for their lord. This man was
> a sophist who founded a sect of his own, having nothing in
> common with the others. (*JW* 2.117–18; see also 2.433)

Judas the Galilean is dismissed as a "sophist"—a teacher more rhetorically clever than philosophically learned—whose "sect" had "nothing in common with the others." What others?

Josephus immediately answers that question by saying that "Jewish philosophy, in fact, takes three forms . . . Pharisees . . . Sadducees . . . Essenes," which he then differentiates in great detail (*JW* 2.119–66). In other words, Judas's "sophistic sect" is securely quarantined from the three—*and only three*—ancient Jewish "philosophical schools."

Then, in his pro-Jewish *Antiquities*, Josephus explains what happened in 6 CE much more fully and accurately. He even names what is in actuality the *theory and practice of nonviolent resistance* as a "fourth philosophy." Watch how he admits and obscures at the same time.

First, longer and *double* space is given to Judas the Galilean (*JA* 18.4–10 and 18.23–25). Those twin accounts now *frame* and dominate the shorter account of the "three philosophies from the most ancient times" recorded between them (*JA* 18:11–22).

Second, Judas's activism is now given special designation and reluctant admission as "a fourth philosophy" that is "intrusive" into the other three "most ancient ones":

> Judas and Saddok started among us an intrusive fourth school of philosophy . . . (*JA* 18.9)

> The Jews, from the most ancient times, had three philosophies . . . (*JA* 18:11)

> As for the fourth of the philosophies, Judas . . . set himself up as leader of it . . . (*JA* 18.23)

This fourth philosophy represents "an innovation and reform in ancestral traditions" (*JA* 18.9), and that is why the reaction in 6 CE is not just a repetition of the violent reaction of 4 BCE. Instead, 6 CE adds *nonviolent resisters*—disguised behind the prophylactic title "fourth philosophy"—to the three philosophies of Pharisees, Sadducees, and Essenes. All four are admitted as "pertaining to their [Jewish] traditions" (*JA* 18.11).

Third, with a fourth philosophy rather than a mere sophistic sect, Judas the Galilean is now described as, "Judas, a Gaulanite from a city named Gamala, [who] had enlisted the aid of Saddok a Pharisee." And, further, Judas's "school agrees in all other respects with the opinions of the Pharisees, except that . . . they are convinced that God alone is their leader and master" (*JA* 18.4, 23).

Fourth, in the first account of Judas's school, Josephus records what this fourth philosophy believes:

> In case of success, the Jews would have laid the foundation of prosperity, while if they failed . . . they would win honor and renown for their lofty aim; and that Heaven would be their

zealous helper . . . all the more if with high devotion in their hearts they stood firm and did not shrink from the bloodshed that *might* be necessary." (*JA* 18.5)

In that torturous prose, Josephus is describing the group's eschatological motivation without admitting it, except by rhetorical obfuscation with expressions like "prosperity," "honor," "renown," "lofty aim," Heaven as "zealous helper," and "high devotion." Also, he is describing nonviolent resistance, and in nonviolent resistance the "bloodshed that *might* be necessary" is not the death of opponents in a violent revolt, but the group's own death as martyrs in a nonviolent one.

A final point is that Josephus brings together there both of his major denials about Jewish resistance to show that *it contained eschatologically based nonviolent resistance*.

Then, in the second account of Judas's philosophical faction, Josephus picks up that theme of martyrdom, but once again the prose obscures as much as it clarifies:

> They think little of submitting to death in unusual forms and permitting vengeance to fall on kinsmen and friends if only they may avoid calling any man master. Inasmuch as most people have seen the steadfastness of their resolution amid such circumstances, I may forgo any further account. For I have no fear that anything reported of them will be considered incredible. Then danger is, rather, that report may minimize the indifference with which they accept the grinding misery of pain. (*JW* 18.23–24)

That is a long quotation to describe once again organized nonviolent resistance backed by a willingness to accept martyrdom—within an eschatological matrix of absolute fidelity to God as Lord and Master. It is all there, in Josephus, despite Josephus.

The invention of Judaism's "fourth philosophy" raises an immediate question—for the next chapter. On the one hand, having invented that new term for this new philosophy, Josephus never uses it again anywhere in his work. Should we think of it, then, as one special response to one special occasion, namely, the first arrival of *direct* control by a Roman governor—as distinct from *indirect* control by a Rome-appointed Jewish client ruler—of any part of the Jewish homeland?

On the other hand, the philosophical schools or political factions of the Pharisees, Sadducees, and Essenes were ongoing movements throughout the decades from 6 to 66 CE. We would, then, expect the same from Josephus's "fourth philosophy" even as an "intrusive . . . innovation and reform in ancestral traditions" (*JA* 18.9, 23).

That expectation is confirmed by this final point. Josephus claims that the fourth philosophy was responsible for all the *violence* that led from 6 CE to national disaster in 70 CE:

> These men *sowed the seed* of every kind of misery, which so afflicted the nation. . . . When wars are set afoot . . . when raids are made by great hordes of brigands and men of the highest standing are assassinated . . . civil strife . . . butchery . . . war . . . famine. . . . They *sowed the seed* from which sprang strife between factions and the slaughter of fellow citizens . . . *planting the seeds* of those troubles which subsequently overtook the body politic. (*JA* 18.6; 7.9)

That seed metaphor, used three times, accuses the fourth philosophy of all ensuing disasters "until at last the very temple of God was ravaged by the enemy's fire through this revolt" (*JA* 18.8).

Just think about that accusation for a moment: not the *violent* revolt of 4 BCE, which required suppression by the Roman legions from

Syria, but the *nonviolent* revolt of 6 CE—which did not require legionary response—was the "seed" for all the *violence* to follow (*JW* 18.8–9). That is a Josephan indictment against nonviolent resistance composed deliberately to offset the admission of its invention.

Even if that accusation is clearly and extremely unfair, it indicates that the "fourth philosophy" did not arise and flame out against direct Roman taxation in 6 CE. Josephus's splenetic indictment indicates its continued existence and continuing culpability for everything bad that happened from 6 to 66 CE.

The purpose of the next chapter is to confirm that indication by looking at two streams within the ongoing vitality of this Jewish nonviolent resistance movement. One stream, with three main examples, revolves around named leaders and, with one positive exception, Josephus describes them pejoratively and dismisses them contemptuously. The other stream, again with three main examples, has no named leaders and, with one slightly negative exception, Josephus describes them at least neutrally and maybe even positively.

As we consider those two streams of nonviolent response to initial Romanization (Chapter 12), we are preparing the necessary Josephan matrix within which to locate his account of Jesus on the relationship between "the things of God" and "the things of Caesar" (Chapter 13).

12

"WE ARE UNARMED, AS YOU SEE"

JOSEPHUS MENTIONS FOUR NAMED LEADERS CONNECTED with Jewish nonviolent resistance to Rome, and all four are mentioned in the New Testament as well: Judas the Galilean (Acts 5:37), John the Baptist (Mark, Q Gospel, Acts), Theudas (Acts 5.36), and "the Egyptian" (Acts 21:38). That serves at least to associate those named leaders with the nonviolent resistance evident from the Messianic/Christic followers of Jesus.

Having just seen the case of Judas the Galilean in Chapter 11, we turn next to the actions of those last three leaders as the first stream of nonviolent opposition to Rome narrated—and usually, with one exception, denigrated disdainfully—by Josephus.

John the Baptist (28 CE) is the only leader of the triad that Josephus describes positively and respectfully—as later he will describe Jesus (Chapter 13). I suspect the reason is authorial prudence about leaders with enough extant followers, supporters, or even memories to render neutral depiction advisable.

Be that as it may, John the Baptist appears in Josephus as a flashback to 28 CE from events in 36 CE. Herod Antipas, ruler of Galilee and Perea, having repudiated a marriage alliance with the daughter of Aretas IV, ruler of Nabatea, in the mid-20s, finally went to war with him over a Transjordanian boundary dispute in 36 CE (*JA* 18.109–15).

In the context of Antipas's total defeat, Josephus says that "to some of the Jews the destruction of Herod's army seemed to be divine vengeance, and certainly a just vengeance, for his treatment of John nicknamed (*epikaloumenos*) the Baptist" (*JA* 18.116). Then, in a flashback from 36 to 28 CE, Josephus continues to explain about John:

> Herod had put him to death, though he was a good man and had exhorted the Jews to lead righteous lives, to practice justice toward their fellows and piety toward God, and so doing to join in baptism (*baptismos*). In his view this was a necessary preliminary if baptism (*baptisis*) was to be acceptable to God. (*JA* 18.117a).

Josephus uses two different words for John's "baptism" and he never explains what that ritual involved. All he says is that it was not some magic rite but simply "a consecration of the body implying that the soul was already thoroughly cleansed by right behavior" (*JA* 18.117b).

Faced with such extremely positive behavior, Josephus is reduced to saying that what happened was due to "Herod's suspicions." Since the crowds were "aroused to the highest degree by his words," Antipas feared "some form of sedition" might occur, and so he took John "in chains to Machaerus," a fortress-palace on the northeastern side of the Dead Sea, and executed him there (*JA* 18.118–19).

That is a supreme example of Josephan obfuscation. How could a crowd aroused to righteousness, justice, and piety create suspicions of insurrection unless we accept that Antipas, who had already ruled for thirty-two years, had suddenly turned paranoid. Antipas's suspicions notwithstanding, any reader would know *something* is left out, *something* is needed to understand John's baptismal ritual.

We should suspect—even without knowing John the Baptist's movement in the New Testament—that Josephus's account of John's ritual is so vacuous because he deliberately deletes—that is, he knows—that it had eschatological overtones, purposes, and meanings. Also note, for future reference, that Antipas executes John, but does not arrest any of his closest followers or attack his crowds in any way.

Footnote from outside Josephus. We know how to supply what he omitted by adding in some Gospel data: John's ritual was to reenact the return from Babylonian exile by taking people from the eastern desert through the Jordan River—where forgiveness cleansed their souls as water cleansed their bodies—and so to enter the promised land anew as a purified people. Then of course, God would come—and imminently—in eschatological deliverance.

John's model was the return from exile and not the exodus from Egypt—which Theudas and the Egyptian used—because he programmatically cited Isaiah 40:3: "A voice cries out: 'In the wilderness prepare the way of the LORD, make straight in the desert a highway for our God'" (Mark 1:3; John 1:23).

Next we look at the case of Theudas (44 CE). At the death of Herod Agrippa I, the second and last Rome-appointed "king of the Jews," Fadus was appointed as *procurator*, governor of the whole country (44–46). Then, as with the arrival of *direct* Roman control for the south in 6 CE, so now with *direct* Roman control for the whole country in 44 CE, nonviolent resistance appeared:

> A certain imposter named Theudas persuaded the majority of the masses to take up their possessions and to follow him to the Jordan River. He stated that he was a prophet and that at his command the river would be parted and would provide them an easy passage. With this talk he deceived many. (*JA* 20.97–98a)

That recalls when, on entering the promised land after the exodus from Egypt, Joshua said to the people: "The LORD your God dried up the waters of the Jordan for you until you crossed over, as the LORD your God did to the Red Sea, which he dried up for us until we crossed over" (Josh. 4:23; Exod. 24:21–22).

Even with Theudas as a "new Moses," that symbolic repetition ended, according to Josephus, not with eschatological deliverance, as of old, but with Theudas captured and "his head brought to Jerusalem" (*JA* 20.98b–99).

Under the procurator Felix (52–60), Josephus records the story of *"the Egyptian"* (50s CE)—he is named only but significantly by that provenance. Here is his earlier account in the pro-Roman *Jewish War*:

> The Egyptian false prophet. A charlatan, who had gained for himself the reputation of a prophet, this man appeared in the country, collected a following of about forty thousand dupes, and led them by a circuitous route from the desert to the Mount called of Olives. From there he proposed to force an entrance into Jerusalem and, after overpowering the Roman garrison, to set himself up as a tyrant of the people, employing those who poured in with him as his bodyguard. (*JW* 2.261–62)

That seems like a *violent* revolt with enough followers to capture Jerusalem, but in his later pro-Jewish version in his *Jewish Antiquities*, Josephus tells the program this way:

> At this time there came to Jerusalem from Egypt, a man who declared that he was a prophet and advised the masses of the common people to go out with him to the Mount called of Olives. . . . For he asserted that . . . at his command Jerusalem's walls would fall down, through which he promised to provide them an entrance into the city. (*JA* 20.169–70; see Acts 21:38)

Even apart from its much more restrained rhetoric, that version depicts a very different scenario. We are back, as for Theudas, with a symbolic repeat of the exodus from Egypt and the entrance into the promised land as of old. At that time, on the seventh day, after seven circuits around the walls of Jericho, "the people shouted, and the trumpets were blown. As soon as the people heard the sound of the trumpets, they raised a great shout, and the wall fell down flat; so the people charged straight ahead into the city and captured it" (Josh. 6:20). So, now, with the walls of Jerusalem.

Once again, however, that action did not result in the advent of God's eschatological deliverance, but of the governor's well-armed troops. Still, that mysterious "Egyptian" was never captured; he "escaped" and "disappeared" (*JW* 2.263; *JA* 20.171–72).

Finally, what is most striking about Josephus's reaction to this first stream of *nonviolent* resistance to Rome is that he uses more negative dismissive and pejorative rhetoric on it than on *violent* resistance. Watch, for example, the following example of two back-to-back accounts, the first one of violent resistance and the second one of nonviolent resistance, in the 50s CE.

Josephus first describes the Sicarii, violent religiopolitical rebels who carried concealed daggers (Latin *sicae*) beneath their cloaks. "The festivals were their special seasons, when they could mingle with the crowd," assassinate high-profile targets, and disappear immediately, so that "the panic created was more alarming than the calamity itself" (*JW* 2.254–57; *JA* 20.164–65). That is a precise and very early description (invention?) of urban terrorism—but focused on officials rather than randomly on civilians.

Josephus then turns immediately to describe *nonviolent resisters* as "another body of villains with purer hands but more impious intentions

who no less than the assassins ruined the peace of the city" (*JW* 2.258).
As he continues to describe their program, Josephus reveals indirectly
the association those resisters made between eschatological/messianic
and nonviolent resistance:

> Deceivers and imposters, under the pretense of divine
> inspiration fostering revolutionary changes, they persuaded the
> multitude to act like madmen, and led them out on the desert
> under the belief that God would there give them tokens of
> deliverance. (*JW* 2.259; *JA* 20.167–68)

But how, one might ask Josephus, were so-called deceivers, imposters,
and false prophets able to persuade "the multitude to act like madmen"?

In any case, since all three of those named leaders attracted crowds
and were executed for their actions, even a minimal respect demands
we ask what they thought they were doing and what about them led
crowds to follow them?

In past history, God had offered two powerful deliverances to Israel
with a very obvious parallel scenario: leaving a foreign domination,
crossing a great desert, fording the Jordan from the east, and entering
the promised land. That had happened in the exodus from Egyptian
bondage and again in the return from Babylonian exile. So why not
now a third time in freedom from Roman occupation?

Would a symbolic repetition or a sacramental reenactment prepare
the way, facilitate the process, or effect the consummation of a divine
deliverance from Rome—as once from Egypt and again from Babylon?
Was there not a divine pattern for Israel's escape from empire? What
if they went back out and came back in over Jordan from the eastern
desert? If they conducted such a scenario unarmed and nonviolently
with utter faith in and dependence on God, would not God act again
as of old?

You can surely disagree with the wisdom of such apocalyptic

eschatology or even lament for the result when the troops arrived, but belated mockery is certainly not an adequate response, especially not from Josephus under imperial patronage in Rome. *Caveat lector* by reading critically from but against Josephus.

We turn next to a second stream of first-century nonviolent opposition to Romanization. Once again Josephus gives three main examples, but leaders are not named and only one of them is portrayed more negatively than the other two. Also, in these three cases, provocation and reaction, purpose and intention, strategy and tactics are described much more fully. Finally, all three provocations are closely connected with the Temple as a potential flash point between Jerusalem and Rome. The first two involve reaction against the Roman lower-level *prefect* governing southern Israel, but the third one involves reaction against the Roman emperor and the higher-level *legate* governing Syria along with his legions.

The Case of the Iconic Standards in Jerusalem (26 CE). The date was soon after Pontius Pilate (26–36 CE) arrived as the prefect or procurator of southern Israel. The provocation was that his soldiers brought into Jerusalem—presumably into the Fortress Antonia, overlooking the Temple—their standards bearing "images (*eikonas*) of Caesar" (*JW* 2.169–74; *JA* 18.55–59).

The people considered that a breach of ancestral law and previous custom: "The indignation of the townspeople stirred the countryfolk, who flocked together in crowds" from Jerusalem to Pilate's base at coastal Caesarea (*JW* 2.170). They implored Pilate to remove the offending images, he refused, and "they fell prostrate around his house and for five whole days and nights remained motionless in that position." Then, threatened by soldiers with drawn swords, "the Jews, as by concerted action . . . extended their necks, and exclaimed that they were ready rather to die than to transgress their law" (*JW* 2.171, 174). And this time, Pilate gave in and removed the iconic standards.

The Case of the Temple-funded Aqueduct (26 CE). In this second example, Pilate used money from the Temple's sacred treasury— the *corbanas* of Matthew 27:6—to build an aqueduct into Jerusalem (*JW* 2.175–77; *JA* 18.60–62). Also, this second provocation must have happened shortly after the preceding one because, this time, Pilate was prepared beforehand to handle a readiness for martyrdom.

Josephus's earlier account said only that "the populace formed a ring around the tribunal of Pilate . . . and besieged him with angry clamor" (*JW* 2.175), but that he "interspersed among the crowd a troop of his soldiers, armed but disguised in civilian dress, with orders not to use their swords, but to beat any rioters with cudgels." When they attacked, "large numbers of the Jews perished, some from the blows which they received, others trodden to death by their companions in the ensuing flight" (*JW* 2.175–77).

Josephus's later account is more detailed and nuanced: "Tens of thousands of men assembled and cried out against him. . . . Some too even hurled insults and abuse of the sort that a throng will constantly engage in" (*JA* 18.60). Pilate had disguised "a large number of soldiers in Jewish garments under which they carried clubs," but those soldiers "inflicted much harder blows than Pilate had ordered, punishing alike both those who were rioting and those who were not. But the Jews showed no faintheartedness; and so caught unarmed, as they were . . . many of them were slain on the spot, while some withdrew disabled by blows" (*JA* 18.61–62).

That can be considered another incident of unarmed resistance. Pilate's preparatory strategy tends to confirm that he was expecting it, and his plan was to infiltrate the crowd with disguised soldiers and deliberately create a rout as his solution to nonviolent resistance and a readiness for martyrdom.

It is also possible that Josephus so tells that latter incident with Pilate as to negate the success of the former one or at least qualify its programmatic validity. Be that as it may, this next case is strong enough to establish, almost all by itself, the presence of large-scale nonviolent Jewish resistance to Romanization between 6 and 66 CE.

The Case of Caligula's Statue in the Temple (40 CE). On March 18, 37 CE, with Tiberius dead, Gaius Julius Caesar became the third emperor of the Julio-Claudian dynasty. He was almost twenty-nine years old, was the last remaining son of Tiberius's brother Germanicus, and was nicknamed "Caligula" by his father's legionaries for the little military boots he wore as a child on campaign with his popular father.

We know about the present incident from both Josephus and the Jewish philosopher Philo. Both authors emphasize—with heavy novelistic details added—the divine protection that guaranteed the plan's ultimate failure. Josephus's secondary emphasis is on the goodness of the Syrian legate Petronius (*JW* 2.184–203; *JA* 18.261–309), while Philo's is on the evil of the Roman emperor Gaius/Caligula (*On the Embassy to Gaius* [henceforth *EG*] 184–346, especially 225–260).

The situation was as follows. Philo was in Rome, leading an embassy from his fellow Jews to complain about anti-Jewish actions in Alexandria and had already received a preliminary and apparently favorable hearing from Gaius/Caligula when he received this news from Israel:

> "Gaius has ordered a colossal statue to be set up within the
> inner sanctuary dedicated to himself under the name of
> Zeus." . . . He wishes to be thought a god. . . . He ordered his
> legate for the whole of Syria, Petronius, . . . to bring half his
> army for the conduct of the statue to Judea. (*EG* 188, 198, 207;
> see *JW* 2.185; *JA* 18.261)

A statue of Caligula as Jupiter in Jerusalem's Temple would have been what biblical tradition calls the supreme sacrilege or, more literally, the "abomination that desolates" (Dan. 9:27; 11:31; 12:11; Mark 13:14).

Four legions were stationed at Antioch, capital of the Roman province of Syria. Think of them as the Army of the Euphrates, whose primary function was to guard against incursions from the Parthian Empire to the east. Caligula expected—or wanted—war.

With regard to the *location*, both authors agree that Petronius took his legions from their bases near Syrian Antioch to a staging area at Ptolemais, a city on the coast of Phoenicia—now Acre on Haifa Bay—in preparation for moving into Israel. At that point he would have had about three hundred miles behind him and a hundred still to go in potentially hostile territory.

Both authors agree that the first encounter between Jewish protesters and Petronius's legions took place there. Philo simply says that it occurred in "Phoenicia where Petronius chanced to be" (*EG* 225). Josephus says: "Petronius . . . left Antioch on the march for Judea," and the army soon reached Ptolemais in coastal Phoenicia (*JW* 2.187–88; *JA* 18.262–63).

Ptolemais was the Roman staging area for legionaries and auxiliaries moving against the Jews in the two wars on either end of the time frame for the nonviolent resistance under discussion. As the assembly point for Varus in 4 BCE (*JW* 2.67; *JA* 17.286) and for Vespasian in 66 (*JW* 3.29, 110, 409), an army at Ptolemais could easily indicate a Jewish-Roman war. Hence the mistake Tacitus makes when he reports: "When Caligula ordered the Jews to set up his statue in their temple, they chose rather *to resort to arms*, but the emperor's death put an end to their uprising" (*Histories* 5.9). Here, and against Tacitus's supposition of the use of arms, is what actually happened.

With regard to the demonstration itself, Philo and Josephus agree on the large-scale opposition that met Petronius at Ptolemais of Phoenicia:

> The inhabitants of the holy city and the rest of the country . . .
> as if at a single signal . . . a vast crowd moving along . . . the
> multitude of the Jews suddenly descended like a cloud and
> occupied the whole of Phoenicia. (*EG* 225–26)

Philo even organizes that multitude as if they were choral groupings at a religious festival—coming for sacrifice (maybe their own?): "They were divided into six companies, old men, young men, boys, and . . . old women, grown women, maidens" (*EG* 227).

Josephus agrees about this confrontation at Ptolemais and, although he does not have Philo's sixfold division, he says: "The Jews assembled with their wives and children in the plain of Ptolemais and implored Petronius to have regard first for the laws of their fathers, and next for themselves . . . a vast multitude" (*JW* 2.192). And again, "Many tens of thousands of Jews came to Petronius at Ptolemais with petitions not to use force to make them transgress and violate their ancestral code" (*JA* 18.263–64).

Also, there *might* be a *hint* of apocalyptic eschatology behind this statement placed on their lips by Josephus: "In order to preserve our ancestral code, we shall patiently endure what may be in store for us, with the assurance that for those who are determined to take the risk, there is hope even of prevailing; for God will stand by us if we welcome danger for his glory" (*JA* 18.267). Would God avert beforehand or avenge afterward such unarmed slaughter?

So far, for both authors, the Jewish opposition occurs at Ptolemais on the Phoenician coast, but now, while Philo keeps it there, Josephus moves the action to Tiberias, on the lake in Galilee. Bluntly, I do not think that happened because of the *how* and *why* he gives for that change of venue.

According to Josephus, Petronius "left the statues [*sic*] and his troops at Ptolemais and advanced into Galilee, where he summoned the people, with all persons of distinction, to Tiberias" (*JW* 2.192–93), and Petronius "gathered up his friends and attendants and hastened to Tiberias for he wished to take note of the situation of the Jews there" (*JA* 18.269). That private thirty-mile relocation is simply not what a Roman legate with legionary forces on a military mission would do in a potentially hostile territory.

Why, then, did Josephus create this alleged detour to Tiberias? Most likely to elevate the appeal process from a popular demonstration to an aristocratic conference. At Tiberias, "Aristobulus, the brother of King Agrippa, together with Heleias the Elder, and other most powerful members of this house, together with the civic leaders appeared before Petronius" (*JA* 18.273). What *that* underlines, by the way, is the complete absence of official-level leadership in the demonstration and Josephus's need to rectify that situation.

In the disposition of the affair, both authors agree that this huge Jewish multitude was unarmed and that the men came with their wives and children to demonstrate programmatic nonviolence. Furthermore, even if violently attacked, they would not respond violently but would die as martyrs:

> "We are unarmed, as you see. . . . we present our bodies as an
> easy target for the missiles of those who want to kill us. We
> have brought our wives, our children and our families . . . we
> have prostrated ourselves before Gaius . . . that you and he
> may either save us from ruin or send us all to perish in utter
> destruction. . . . If we cannot prevail with you in this, we offer
> up ourselves for destruction. . . . We gladly put our throats at
> your disposal." (*EG* 229, 230, 233)

> The multitude cried out that they were ready to endure anything
> for the law . . . they offered sacrifice twice daily for Caesar
> and the Roman people, but that if he [Petronius] wishes to set
> up these statues [*sic*], he must first sacrifice the entire Jewish
> nation; and that they presented themselves, their wives and their
> children, ready for the slaughter. (*JW* 2.196–97)

> "On no account would we fight," they said, "but we will die
> sooner than violate our laws." And falling on their faces and

baring their throats, they declared that they were ready to be slain. (*JA* 18.271).

For our present concern, those three quotations are the heart of the matter and the fullest evidence for nonviolent resistance in this most fully attested case.

We have some clues as to the *timing* of the event as well. In first-century Israel, the major cereal crops of barley and wheat were planted during October-November in the fall and harvested during April-May in the following spring. On the religious calendar that went along with the seasons, the Passover festival was the start of the harvest season and, fifty days later, the Pentecost festival was its conclusion.

In Philo's account, Petronius, confronted with the demonstration at Ptolemais, wrote a letter to Caligula giving three reasons for his delay in delivering the statue:

First, the time required to make the statue (which he was getting made at Sidon and would pick up on his way south);

Second, that "the wheat crop was just ripe and so were the other cereals and he feared that the Jews in despair for their ancestral rites and in scorn for life might lay waste the arable land or set fire to the cornfields on the hills and in the plain";

Third, that on his upcoming visit to Egypt, Caligula would need provisions from the Levantine coast of Israel for his coastal passage (*EG* 249–250).

Philo, who was in Italy between interviews with Caligula, noted that the emperor muted his fury and basically replied, "Get on with it!"

Those arguments, however, give us both the year and the time for this event. Caligula visited France and Germany in 40 and planned to go to Egypt in 41 CE, so the statue's southward travel was in 40 CE and the unarmed demonstration was in Ptolemais at harvest time, that is, in April-May between Passover and Pentecost.

For Josephus, it was those alleged Herodian officials at Tiberias who persuaded Petronius to write to Caligula, because the "people . . . had left their fields to sit protesting, and . . . since the land was unsown, there would be a harvest of banditry," with no cereal harvest the following year (*JA* 18.274).

Then, with "many tens of thousands . . . so many tens of thousands . . . many tens of thousands" confronting him (*JA* 18.270, 277, 279), Petronius promises the letter to Caligula and tells the people, "Go, therefore, each to your own occupation, and labor on the land . . . to attend to agricultural matters" (*JA* 18.283–84).

Philo has the demonstration endangering the spring cereal *harvest* of 40 and creating famine that year; Josephus has it endangering the fall cereal *planting* of 40 and creating famine in 41. Once again, Philo's account is more plausible, because it explains one other problem. But, in either case, that demonstration involves—I presume quite consciously and deliberately—a sit-down agricultural strike!

Those huge crowds from the "holy city," who "as if at a single signal" sped to "Phoenicia" (*EG* 225), would be very understandable as festival crowds between Passover and Pentecost. But, be that as it may, the case of Caligula's statue centered on a single event in April-May of 40 CE at Ptolemais of Phoenicia, and it should include there what Josephus creatively but incorrectly relocated to Tiberias for the Herodian aristocracy.

In summary, debates about Philo or Josephus as the better source, Ptolemais or Tiberias as the better place, or spring harvest or fall planting as the better time should not detract from their emphatic agreement: there was massive well-organized and well-timed nonviolent resistance to an event that could have started the war of 66–74 in 40 CE. We can never know what *might* have happened if Caligula had not been assassinated by a high-level conspiracy on January 24, 41 CE (*JA* 19.105–13).

In summary and conclusion, after Revelation, in Part One, and Luke-Acts, in Part Two, flatly contradicted one another on God/Caesar acculturation from *inside* the New Testament, the historical experiment that began this Part Three in Chapters 11 and 12 was to go *outside* it on that subject from first-century Josephus alone.

Chapter 11 looked first at how Josephus himself solved the God/Christ acculturation by claiming that God had chosen the Roman Empire, the Flavian dynasty, and the messianic Vespasian to rule the world. Therefore, of course, any divine eschatology was but Jewish delusion, all opposition to Caesar was opposition to God, and acculturation was serenely complete.

But already in Chapter 11, Josephus had to admit that Judaism had invented a "fourth philosophy" in 6 CE, a theory and practice of nonviolent resistance and unarmed opposition that pitted *God against Caesar.* Then, in Chapter 12, we saw two separate streams, one with prophetic reenactments of past deliverances and the other with sit-down demonstrations from massed crowds. For each stream of nonviolent opposition, Josephus gave three good examples indicating how that theory worked in practice from the 20s to the 50s.

With that matrix from Josephus securely in place, we turn next to two successive sections in Chapter 13. The first section considers what Josephus says directly and explicitly about Jesus's position on God/Caesar acculturation. The second one considers if and how the theological Jesus of the Gospels correlates with the historical Jesus of Josephus on that same subject.

13

"JESUS CALLED CHRIST"

ONLY THREE MAJOR INDIVIDUALS FROM THE MESSIANIC/ Christic community in the New Testament reappear in Josephus: "John nicknamed the Baptist" (*JA* 18.116–19), "Jesus called Christ" (*JA* 18.63–64; 20.200), and "James, the brother of Jesus" (*JA* 20.200). The last two are fraternally connected in both Josephus and Paul (Gal. 1:19), but nothing at all connects John and Jesus in Josephus.

During the interregnum between two Roman governors in 62 CE, according to Josephus, the high priest "Ananus . . . because Festus was dead and Albinus was still on the way . . . convened the judges of the Sanhedrin, and brought before them a man named James, the brother of Jesus who was called the Christ (*Iēsou legomenou Christou*), and certain others . . . and delivered them up to be stoned"—an act for which Ananus was deposed (*JA* 20.200).

Josephus identifies James as the brother of Jesus but, since he mentions ten people named "Jesus" in his *Jewish Antiquities*, he has to identify this particular Jesus, literally, as "Jesus called Christ." That almost offhand identification fits perfectly with Josephus's obliteration of *Jewish* covenantal eschatology in favor of *Roman* imperial eschatology and Vespasian messianism.

Any non-Jewish reader would presume "Christ" was something

like Jesus's nickname, and that would not disturb Josephus's studied avoidance of Jewish eschatological messianism. Tacitus, for example, uses "Christ" rather than "Jesus" and probably thought it was simply a name—hence "Christians" as followers (*Histories* 2.8)—like Platonists for Plato or Aristotelians for Aristotle.

If we only knew the historical Jesus from *Jewish Antiquities* 20.200, we would still know that Jesus was a messianic claimant well known enough to have that claim as his titular nickname. We would also recognize that only here does a Messianic/Christic claimant break explicitly if momentarily through Josephus's careful obliteration of Jewish eschatological messianism. Quintilian, as we saw earlier, would have understood completely the wisdom of that rhetorical decision.

In summary, the phrase "Jesus called Christ" must be seen as another example of Josephus's programmatic eradication of Jewish eschatological expectations and messianic motivations, which we saw, in the last two chapters, throughout his *Jewish War* and *Jewish Antiquities*. If we only had Josephus, that is where we would have to locate Jesus. But that raises the next question: Can we tell from Josephus whether that messianic identity of Jesus involved him in *violent* resistance, as in 4 BCE and thereafter, or in *nonviolent* resistance, as in 6 CE and thereafter? The answer takes us next from Jesus in *Jewish Antiquities* 20.200 to the former and longer account of him in *Jewish Antiquities* 18.63–64.

In that account, Josephus says of Jesus's execution: "Pilate . . . hearing him accused by men of the highest standing amongst us, had condemned him to be crucified" (*JA* 18.64). What, by the way, would have been the most credible historical accusation against Jesus before a *Roman* governor? *Maybe this*: since Jesus speaks always about the present *rule of God*, he must think he is its present ruler; he is claiming that he is "ruler/king of the Jews," and that is *majestas*, or high treason.

Be that as it may, the most striking word in that sentence from Josephus is that the accusation and execution was only of "him." Josephus's preceding sentence had introduced Jesus as an activist and teacher with "many" followers, but then, for the accusation and execution, the entire focus is on "him" alone. None of those "many" followers are executed with "him." None of the most important companions are even arrested with "him." That tells us immediately how Pilate judged Jesus's program, faction, or movement: *it represented not violent, but nonviolent resistance.* That interpretation is based on Roman judicial theory and practice.

For *violent* resistance, Rome crucified the leader together with multiple supporters or followers. In 4 BCE at Jerusalem, for example, the Syrian governor captured "the authors of the insurrection . . . the most culpable, in number about two thousand, he crucified" (*JW* 2:75; *JA* 17.295).

For *nonviolent* resistance, Rome crucified only the leader on the presumption that followers would then disappear. In the early 200s, for example, the famous Roman jurist Julius Paulus, nicknamed Prudentissimus by his contemporary emperor, made a compilation of the decisions of Roman law—*opinions*, in that juridical sense—and in "Title XXII: Concerning Seditious Persons" gave this legal precedent: "The authors of sedition and tumult, or those who stir up the people, shall, according to their rank, either be crucified, thrown to wild beasts, or deported to an island" (*The Opinions of Julius Paulus Addressed to His Son* 5.22.1).

In other words, Pilate judged Jesus correctly as "an author of sedition and tumult," as someone "who stirred up the crowd," that is, as an unarmed activist and nonviolent agitator. Had Pilate judged otherwise, Jesus would have been crucified with some or all of his closest followers beside him. That conclusion is also confirmed by what follows after Josephus's statement that Jesus was "condemned to be crucified."

Since with nonviolent resistance the leader's crucifixion should disperse his following for fear of a similar fate, Josephus needed to explain why that did not happen with Jesus. He had to give some reason why "the tribe of Christians" still existed sixty years after the execution of Jesus. That is why his execution and the continuation of the movement are lumped together in a single sentence: "When Pilate, upon hearing him accused by men of the highest standing amongst us, had condemned him to be crucified, those who had in the first place come to love him did not give up their affection for him," or, more literally, for emphasis, "they did not stop, those first loving him." Josephus has to explain why the leader's execution did not finish off his movement as was expected.

Furthermore, going outside Josephus for a moment, Tacitus, writing two decades later, felt the same need to explain the continuation of "Christians" despite the execution of "Christus, the founder of the name." On the analogy of a plague, "the pernicious superstition was checked for a moment" by the execution of Jesus, but then it broke out again from Judea all the way to Rome (*Annals* 15.44). What was undying loyalty for Josephus was spreading infection for Tacitus. Still, both had to explain why the leader's' execution failed its purpose of ending his nonviolent movement.

From the preceding chapter and to this point in the present one, there are three conclusions to the experiment in reconstructing the historical Jesus from outside the New Testament and Josephus alone.

First, during Israel's initial Romanization, there were multiple experiments in *nonviolent* resistance based on eschatological or messianic motivations and backed by a readiness for martyrdom. Those happened between the *violent* revolts of 4 BCE and 66 CE (Appendix B).

Josephus describes the start of nonviolent resistance in 6 CE through a fog of obfuscation and blames it for everything violent to follow, including the destruction of the Temple. But he still concedes it the reluctant name of a "fourth philosophy," after the Pharisaic, Sadducean, and Essene philosophies. He also gives three major examples of two different streams of that *nonviolent* tradition—one of named prophets reenacting past deliverances and another of sit-down demonstrations from massive crowds.

Second, there must have been fuller—and probably differing—theological interpretations behind those multiple nonviolent revolts. Maybe a theology of immediate divine intervention to prevent communal martyrdom or a theology of eventual divine retribution to avenge it? Maybe, with the Romans now as with the Persians earlier, a theology of suffering servanthood hoped to produce a kinder, gentler empire, a more compassionate imperialism? Many maybes, but, in any case and however theologized, those organized nonviolent actions happened, are recorded, and must be emphasized.

Violent Jewish reaction to Romanization began in 4 BCE with Herod's death. Nonviolent Jewish reaction to Romanization began in 6 CE with Coponius's tax assessment. It is all in Josephus—even if he was often writing through gritted teeth.

Third, we can locate the nonviolent resistance—and resultant individual martyrdom—of both "John called (*epikaloumenou*) the Baptist" by Antipas (*JA* 18.116–19) and "Jesus called (*legomenos*) Christ" by Pilate (*JA* 18.63–64; 20.200) within that first-century Jewish matrix of nonviolent theological theory and political practice. We know both were nonviolent leader-activists, *because* both were executed without any arrest of general followers or any execution of top allegiants. Antipas and Pilate judged correctly according to Roman law.

Josephus interprets the God/Caesar acculturation as a matter of divine selection and imperial *cooperation*, but Jesus interprets it as a matter of divine challenge and human *confrontation*. For Josephus, God has ceded violent control to Caesar. For Jesus, God has decreed nonviolent resistance against Caesar.

This is emphatically not to claim that Jesus was the first to create nonviolent resistance to imperial Romanization. That strategy was *invented* by Judas the Galilean and Saddok the Pharisee in 6 CE. When he finally admitted that novel creation, Josephus *invented* a new name for it: the "fourth philosophy." With or without that name, the theory and practice of nonviolent resistance—with a readiness for martyrdom founded on eschatological faith—empowered multiple experiments from 6 to 66 CE. At that point, violent resistance took over, or as Tacitus put it: "The Jews' patience lasted until Gessius Florus [64–66] became procurator: in his time war began" (*Histories* 5.9–10).

Finally, recall the question raised in this book's Overture: granted that "the things of God" are not equated to or identified with "the things of Caesar," how are they adapted, related, or acculturated to one another?

Josephus has now given us Jesus's answer to that question: "The things of God" are acculturated with "the things of Caesar" as a confrontation between nonviolent opposition and violent domination, as a nonviolent resistance for distributive justice against the violent insistence on distributive injustice, as, in terms of programmatic slogans, *peace through unarmed justice* against *peace through armed victory*.

Presuming that view of Jesus's nonviolent resistance to Romanization *from Josephus's evidence*, we move next from Josephus's Jesus to the Gospels' Jesus. Do they correlate, and if they do, how do they correlate on that question of nonviolent resistance? Also, does the Jesus of the Gospels give any clear indication of *his* motivation for advocating that procedure against Romanization? We begin, however, not with Jesus, but with John in Josephus and the Gospels.

———

Recall that, in Josephus, John's water ritual was described innocently but never explained fully—despite that "Baptist" nickname and two other mentions of the rite as "baptism." Something major was clearly—and deliberately?—*omitted* in Josephus's account, and the Gospels supply it quite adequately.

John's program was to reenact a classical divine deliverance from the past, so that God would make it efficacious once again in the present. But, although later prophets like Theudas and "the Egyptian" chose the exodus from Egypt, John chose the return from exile as the model liberation from imperial domination to be symbolically effected here and now. Passing from the eastern desert through the Jordan with repentance cleansing their souls and water washing their bodies, participants would enter their promised land anew as a purified people and then—surely then, surely soon—divine intervention would establish *God's rule* on earth.

Isaiah had announced the return from exile with this divine chant: "A voice cries out: 'In the wilderness prepare the way of the LORD, make straight in the desert a highway for our God'" (40:3). That verse, but punctuated as in Isaiah, is the message of John proclaiming, now as of old, a return from exile facilitated by God (Mark 1:2–3; John 1:19).

That is the full story, which Josephus then truncated, and even though it was a nonviolent program, its eschatological context justified Antipas's decision to execute John—but only John. With that preamble on the Baptist's nonviolent resistance, we turn now to nonviolent resistance and the Gospel Jesus.

———

As a paradigmatic example we focus on two parabolic incidents, one in Mark and the other in John, both imagining a climactic confrontation between God and Caesar that becomes embodied and historicized as a confrontation between Jesus and Pilate. (A parable, by the way, is a story that never happened but is always true.)

The Markan Parable. Mark wrote in the early 70s and probably in the more Gentile villages around Caesarea Philippi (8:27) in the northeastern Transjordanian reaches of Israel. At that point, Jerusalem's Temple is destroyed, Jerusalem's siege is lifted, Jerusalem's slaughter is abated, and Mark writes for refugees who have lost everything—almost even faith itself (read Mark 13).

Mark takes those refugees back forty years and asks them to imagine Pilate standing between two prisoners indicted for resistance to Romanization and offering the "crowd" its choice between them in an alleged Passover amnesty. One prisoner is Jesus, the divine Bar Abba, the divine Son of the divine Father, but he is *nonviolent*, as we know, because he was arrested in the midst of his closest companions but without any of them being even detained: "They laid hands on *him* and arrested *him*" (Mark 14:46). The other prisoner is Barabbas, the human son of a human father, but he is *violent*, as we know, because "Barabbas was in prison *with* the rebels who had committed murder during the insurrection" (15:7).

In Mark's parable, the Jerusalem "crowd" chose the wrong liberator, deliverer, and savior. Jerusalem chose the violent freedom fighter over the nonviolent resister in 30, and the result was what happened to it in 70. In that reading, God versus Caesar morphs into Jesus versus Pilate, which morphs into nonviolent resistance versus violent domination.

The Johannine Parable. That Markan parable is paralleled by one that John created for his account of Jesus versus Pilate. John, by the way, does not have the tribute-coin story, but his Jesus-versus-Pilate interchange makes exactly the same point just seen in Mark.

Pilate asks Jesus, "Are you the King of the Jews?" and Jesus responds: "My *rule* is not from this world. If my *rule* were from this world, my followers would be fighting to keep me from being handed over to the Jews. But as it is, my *rule* is not from here" (John 18:33, 36).

A first point: The phrase "handed over to the Jews" is polemically tendentious rather than historically accurate. Also, the later claim that Pilate handed Jesus over to the chief priests "to be crucified" (19:15–16) is equally unhistorical. Jewish authority could accuse, but only Roman authority could crucify.

A second point: Unlike the rest of the New Testament, John mentions the *"rule of God"* only twice (3:3, 5). Here, however, in the context of John 18:33–19:21 where the official and legal Roman term "King

(*Basileus*) of the Jews" is mentioned so often, Jesus responds by using "my *rule* (*basileia*)" three times in a single short verse (18:36).

A third point: Jesus's assertion was composed by John as a form/content synergy in tribute to its climactic importance—as indicated in this more literal translation:

> My *rule* is not from this world.
> If from this world were my *rule*,
> my followers would be fighting to keep me from being
>   handed over . . .
> *Now*, however,
> my *rule* is not from *here*. (18:36)

The middle line specifies the only discriminant offered to differentiate between "my *rule*" and "this world." This is the expected "fighting" by "followers" to free their leader. But the *rule of God* will not even allow violence to save Jesus.

The Greek verb used for "fighting" (*agōnizomai*)—whence our word "agony"—indicates a spectrum of struggle from striving in a nonviolent sport to fighting in a violent battle. The former usage is always a positive metaphor in the New Testament, as, for example, Christian life as "fighting the good fight" (1 Tim. 1:18; 6:12; 2 Tim. 4:7). In the present context, "fighting" is rejected by Jesus and should be taken to mean violent attack rather than nonviolent attempt.

Furthermore, "this world" and "here" are parallel and framing words. This parable is not just about the Roman Empire by itself and to itself. That is only the "here" of "this world." The parable is about Rome as no more and no less than the contemporary manifestation or "here and now" of something far wider, broader, deeper than it, namely, "this world" as the normal violence of civilization itself.

Finally, to repeat, those two parables are very significant because, in them, "the things of God" and "the things of Caesar" are climactically invested, embodied, and incarnated in "the things of Jesus" and "the things of Pilate."

With Mark's parable, the "things of Jesus" are *nonviolent* resistance—that is why he is executed, but his closest companions are not even arrested, unlike what happens to Barabbas and his most important followers. John's parable goes much farther. It presents a flat contradiction and full confrontation between the nonviolent "things of God's *rule*" and the violent "things" not only of Caesar's rule, but of "this world's" rule.

The term "this world" raises an immediate problem. Does its pejorative usage—and it is consistently negative throughout about fifty uses in John—represent a dismissal of our present life on earth in favor of some future life in heaven?

It is not, however, a choice of future heaven over present earth, but a choice between *two* modes and meanings, two visions and programs, two theoretical images and practical plans for living together on earth. It is about living here below on earth-as-*creation* or living on earth-as-*civilization*.

On the one hand, the *world-as-creation* is the world of Genesis 1:1–2:4a (Appendix C), which the biblical God saw repeatedly as "good" (1:4, 10, 12, 18, 21, 25) and climactically as "very good" (1:31). The world-as-creation is "the world" that "God so loved" in John 3:16.

This is a world ruled by *distributive justice*, because it was started by a just divine distribution, by a free gift of a divine sharing, by a grace of "let there be" for the "the heavens and the earth" (1:1; 2:4a), and finished with God's image and likeness distributed freely to humanity as its identity and destiny (1:26–27). This world-as-creation was crowned by Sabbath, and Sabbath is not a law or command from the biblical God, but the *nature and character of the biblical God*.

On the other hand, *world-as-civilization* is "*this* world," which can be, was, and continues to be the alternative to the world-of-creation. But the "ruler of *this* world" is already judged and condemned (John 12:31; 14:30; 16:11).

This is the world of Genesis 4:1–26, where, first, farmer Cain kills herder Abel, then, next, ex-farmer Cain builds the first city, and, finally, violence escalates exponentially from Cain to Lamech and from once, to sevenfold, to seventy-sevenfold (4:8, 15, 24) within five human generations.

Notice also that no *reason* is given either for Cain's violence (did he expect to retrieve God's favor by fratricide?) or for Lamech's escalatory violence (why not just return strike for strike and blow for blow, why multiply?). The existence of violence and its tendency to escalate lie deeper than any reasons we have ever found for them. It is a challenge that threatens the evolutionary future of a species not protected from self-destruction by instinct, but only by conscience, that is, by "knowing good and evil" (Gen. 3:22).

Still, even granted that, why call "this world" the world-of-*civilization* rather than, say, the world-of-*violence*—with violence either as a means to injustice or even as an end in itself?

Genesis 4 summarizes the *consummation* of the Neolithic/Agricultural Revolution on the Mesopotamian plains between the Euphrates and Tigris Rivers (modern Iraq) about six thousand years ago. That climactic human achievement is known, with regard to time, as the "dawn of civilization" and, with regard to place, as the "cradle of civilization."

Think for a moment about how, in the story of the advent of civilization according to Genesis, it was Cain who invented the city by building the first one. In Greek, "city" is *polis*, from which we get both "politics" and "police." In Latin, "city" is *civitas*, from which we get both "citizen" and "civilization." The particular human culture known as *civilization*, that is, the world-as-civilization, is also the world of escalatory violence.

The evolutionary challenge to our species is to evolve from civilization to postcivilization, to the vision of Genesis 1:1–2:4a as the biblical overture, to the constant challenge of Jewish prophets to Jewish rulers, and to the climactic confrontation between Jewish Jesus's "things of God" and Roman Pilate's "things of Caesar."

In John's parable, therefore, the "here and now" of Romanization is the current embodiment of "this world"—in the Mediterranean as place, in the first century as time, and in the toga as dress. And "this world" is that human culture that established escalatory violence as the normalcy of civilization: from the Sumerian chariot to the Sheridan tank in thirty-five hundred years on the ground, from the battle trireme to the nuclear submarine in twenty-five hundred years on the sea, *but* from the Wright Flyer to the stealth bomber in only eighty-six years in the air.

Granted all that, the question for the next two chapters is this: Where in his preceding biblical tradition is Jesus's eschatological vision of *God's rule* on earth as nonviolent resistance to "this world" grounded and founded? Is nonviolent resistance simply human prudence or divine mandate? And if the latter, must not God act toward human evil with that same *nonviolent* resistance? But where in his preceding biblical tradition could Jesus find such a God?

In answer to those questions, we look next in Chapter 14 at two streams of biblical tradition, one I call *Sanction theology* and the other *Sabbath theology*. Then in the final chapter, 15, we consider if and how Jesus fits within one or other of those divergent theologies.

14

SANCTIONS AND
SABBATHS

YOU HAVE PROBABLY HEARD THE LIBEL, EVER ANCIENT AND
ever new, that the God of the Old Testament is a God of punishment and vengeance, but the God of the New Testament is a God of
love and mercy. That is persuasive until you read the whole Christian
Bible and recognize that its last and climactic book is the most violent
one in the entire collection and, probably, in the entire canonical liter-
ature of world religion—as we saw in Part One of this book.

Begin with the divine hatred of enemies as proclaimed in "The Battle Hymn of the Divine Warrior" toward the climactic conclusion of
the Pentateuch, the five books of the Torah:

> When I whet my flashing sword,
> and my hand takes hold on judgment;
> I will take vengeance on my enemies,
> and will repay those who hate me.
> I will make my arrows drunk with blood,
> and my sword shall devour flesh—
> with the blood of the slain and the captives,
> from the long-haired enemy.

Praise, O heavens, his people,

worship him, all you gods!

For he will avenge the blood of his children,

and take vengeance on his enemies;

he will repay those who hate him,

and cleanse the land for his people. (Deut. 32:41–43)

Then conclude by thinking of that image of God as avenger of "enemies" who "hate" God as preparation for and preface to the book of Revelation itself.

Finally, even if you leave aside those more bloodthirsty visions of God as Divine Warrior against evil, Divine Avenger of wrong, and Divine Slaughterer of enemies—from Deuteronomy to Revelation—there is still the fundamental biblical image of God as Divine Judge.

In *Sanction theology*, God as Divine Judge rewards the righteous and punishes the unrighteous rather than treating them all alike. Even if you reject that triumphant chant in Deuteronomy 32:41–43, a *Deuteronomic theology* or *Sanction theology* was already fully established in Deuteronomy 28. Watch its often verbatim balance of rewards or blessings and punishments or curses but note also that there is twice as much of the latter as the former.

First come the rewards or "blessings" (28:1–14). They open with a promise framed conditionally: *"If you will only obey the LORD your God,* by diligently observing all his commandments that I am commanding you today, the LORD your God will set you high above all the nations of the earth; all these blessings shall come upon you and overtake you, *if you obey the LORD your God"* (28:1–2). Then follows a list of blessings that emphasize fertility and prosperity, safety and security—of the land, by the land, and on the land. Also, of course, victory: "The LORD will cause your enemies who rise against you to be defeated before you; they shall come out against you one way, and flee before you seven ways" (28:7). The list of rewards is then concluded with a repetition of the opening verse's conditional promise:

"The LORD will make you the head, and not the tail; you shall be only at the top, and not at the bottom—if you obey the commandments of the LORD your God, which I am commanding you today, by diligently observing them" (28:13).

Next come the punishments or "curses" (28:15–45). They open with a conditional threat rather than a conditional promise: "If you will not obey the LORD your God by diligently observing all his commandments and decrees, which I am commanding you today, then all these curses shall come upon you and overtake you" (28:15). Then follows a list of curses corresponding to but expanding on those preceding blessings—of the land, by the land, and on the land. Victory also will be precisely reversed: "The LORD will cause you to be defeated before your enemies; you shall go out against them one way and flee before them seven ways" (28:25). Finally, the last of the curses reverses the last of the blessings, "They shall be the head and you shall be the tail," and the passage concludes: "All these curses shall come upon you, pursuing and overtaking you until you are destroyed, because you did not obey the LORD your God, by observing the commandments and the decrees that he commanded you" (28:44b-45).

Although that terminal parallelism indicates a conclusion to the curses at 28:45, they start right up again and continue to this rather ghastly conclusion: "The LORD will bring you back in ships to Egypt. . . . There you shall offer yourselves for sale to your enemies as male and female slaves, but there will be no buyer" (28:68).

Deuteronomic theology is *Sanction theology*, a transcendental theory of rewards or blessings for obedience to God and punishments or curses for disobedience. Furthermore, it is not just present only in that single chapter or that one book. It is the basic theology for understanding God in the Christian Bible, the Christian life, and the Christian afterlife—as the blessing/reward of heaven or the curse/ punishment of hell.

Sanction theology is also often read backward as well as forward: if good begets blessing and evil begets curse, then the status of blessing or curse must indicate a person as good or evil. Hence, for example, when the question was put to Jesus by his disciples, "Rabbi, who sinned, this man or his parents, that he was born blind?" you will recall that he rejected that bad theology: "Neither this man nor his parents sinned; he was born blind so that God's works might be revealed in him" (John 9:2–3).

The purpose of this chapter is not to debate the mendacity of those fateful Deuteronomic sanctions. (In his 1945 playlet *A Masque of Reason*, Robert Frost noted how, in the book of Job, God attempted "To stultify the Deuteronomist / And change the tenor of religious thought." But God failed, and Job remains but a speed bump on the Deuteronomic superhighway.) Instead, it is to ask these next questions.

Since Deuteronomy warned, for example, that God would give "rain" to the obedient and "dust" to the disobedient (28:12, 24), how could Jesus claim that God "sends rain on the righteous and on the unrighteous" alike (Matt. 5:45)? And even if Jesus disavowed Deuteronomy 28, why was his rejection credible?

Was there in his biblical tradition an equally pervasive but quite different vision of God than Sanction theology? What, for example, about *Sabbath theology*?

Earlier in this book, we looked at the two formal openings to Luke-Acts, one in Luke 1:1–4 and the other in 3:1–2a, and suggested that Luke 1–2 was added not just as a preface to Luke, but as an overture to Luke-Acts. A *preface* starts or opens a book, but an *overture* summarizes or symbolizes it—in a phrase, a paragraph, or a chapter. Remember our example of Barbara Tuchman's "A Funeral," the overture to her book *The Guns of August*, at the beginning of Chapter 9.

Keep the power of overture in mind as we turn now to the Hebrew

Bible, which begot the Greek Bible, which begot the Christian Old
Testament, which begot, *mutatis mutandis*, the Christian New—that
is, the re-New-ed—Old Testament. That Bible begins with the book of
Genesis, but how does Genesis begin—not with Genesis 2–11 but with
Genesis 1?

Genesis 2–11, for example, makes changes to the traditional Mesopotamian traditions of cosmic origins: as the primordial couple,
Adam and Eve replace Gilgamesh and Enkidu; as the players in the
fraternal farmer-herder conflict, Cain and Abel replace Enkimdu
and Dumuzi; and in the stories of the flood and ark, Noah replaces
Utnapishtim.

Then those who assembled the Hebrew Bible placed Genesis 1:1–2:4a
at the front, not just as a start but as an overture, not just as an obvious
beginning but as an enabling vision for the whole Bible. Notice, for
example, how those prebiblical traditions in Genesis 2-11 begin: "In the
day that the LORD God made the earth and the heavens . . ." (2:4b).
But before that beginning comes 1:1–2:4a as a separate unit that begins:
"In the beginning when God created the heavens and the earth" (1:1)
and ends with, "These are the generations of the heavens and the earth
when they were created" (2:4a).

You recognize some immediate differences in those two openings:
"LORD God" versus "God," "the earth and the heavens" versus "the
heavens and the earth." Those differences indicate the two sources that
scholars call the Priestly and the Yahwist traditions. But the important
point is not just that we have the two creation accounts, but that the
former one is an overture to the whole Bible and the second one is simply the start of the whole Bible. So what is so important about 1:1–2:4a
as such an overture?

One immediate hint is that it takes eight chunks of cosmic stuff,
each created and signaled by the repetitive "God said: 'Let . . . be'"
refrain, and shoehorns them rather obviously into *six days*, with one
chunk apiece on days 1, 2, 4, and 5, but two apiece on days 3 and 6 (see

Appendix C). The creation must be done in six days, so it can be climaxed and consummated by the Sabbath on day 7. (That, for example, is why day and night must be created on day 1 even if repeated on the parallel day 4.) Put bluntly, if impolitely: "It's about the Sabbath, stupid!" (We are not the crown of creation; we are the work of a late Friday afternoon—a time when best work is seldom done.)

Any intelligent reader, ancient or modern, should realize that this biblical God could simply have said "Let everything be" or "Let creation be" with one single command—and it would have come into existence. That was not done. The process was spread over six days to indicate as clearly as possible that the climax of creation is the Sabbath itself. In poetic parable or parabolic poetry, creation must take six days, because creation is for Sabbath and, as we shall see, the Sabbath is for distributive justice, so that human time beats to the rhythm of divine justice.

In this climactic section, however, there is one rather significant point—usually ignored. On day 6: "God said, 'See, I have given you every plant yielding seed that is upon the face of all the earth, and every tree with seed in its fruit; you shall have them for food. And to every beast of the earth, and to every bird of the air, and to everything that creeps on the earth, everything that has the breath of life, I have given every green plant for food'" (1:29–30). In this idyllic moment, creation is absolutely nonviolent. Humans and animals do not kill, and no blood ever stains the earth. "Vegetation" feeds animals and humans alike, and all are vegetarians.

Finally, on that same day 6, "God said, 'Let us make humankind in our image, according to our likeness,'" and then "God created humankind in his image, in the image of God he created them; male and female he created them" (1:26a, 27). But what exactly is the content of that twice-told status? What is the identity or destiny or responsibility of a humanity created in "the image and likeness" of God?

That question is answered immediately and again twice: "Let them have dominion (*katakurieusate, archetōsan*) over the fish of the sea, and over the birds of the air, and over the cattle, and over all the wild animals of the earth, and over every creeping thing that creeps upon the earth, . . . have dominion (*archete*) over the fish of the sea and over the birds of the air and over every living thing that moves upon the earth" (1:26b, 28). To be in God's image and likeness is to rule the earth responsibly—the verbs chosen for our cosmic "dominion" are, as you see, from Greek roots that give us *kyrios*, or "lord," and *archē*, or "head," "start," "beginning," as in Genesis 1:1: "in the beginning (*archē*)." But how exactly is humanity to rule the world only as God's stewards or administrators?

The answer comes next with the Sabbath, but not as one might expect. There is no: "And God said, 'Let there be the Sabbath,'" as if God *created* the Sabbath like everything else, but on its own day, day 7. Instead, we have this climax in Genesis 2:2b-3 with Shabbat, or from "seventh (day)" in Hebrew:

> God . . . rested on the seventh day from all the work that he
> had done.
> God blessed the seventh day and hallowed it,
> because on it God rested from all the work that he had done
> in creation.

The Sabbath is not a creation by God, but a state of God. It is not made by God but lived by God. *Distributive* justice is not a suggestion or command of God, but the nature or character of God. It derives from God's *distribution* of existence to everything and, especially, of God's own image and likeness to humanity.

That, of course, only raises the following questions: How and why can the Sabbath be of cosmic import? Is it not simply a house ritual for Jews on Friday to Saturday evening and a church ritual for Christians on Sunday morning? How can Genesis 1:1–2:4a and its Sabbath climax be an overture through which we see the entire Bible? What is the *biblical* purpose and *biblical* meaning of the Sabbath—especially for humans as agents acting for and with the God of the Sabbath?

Around 13.8 billion years ago, the big bang *created*—do you have another word for this?—matter and energy, time and space. And the biblical *theology of creation* describes matter and energy, time and space as regulated by the Sabbath, that is, by the fairness of distributive justice for everything that is.

Think of how *time,* for example, beats to the metronome of distributive justice and takes matter, energy, and space along with it—before clocks and calendars, and apart from cyclical seasons with plantings and harvestings.

First, as the seventh day, the *Sabbath day* established time as the linear progression of days and weeks—but notice the content of and reason for it:

> Six days you shall labor and do all your work. But the seventh
> day is a sabbath to the LORD your God; you shall not do
> any work—you, or your son or your daughter, or your male
> or female slave, or your ox or your donkey, or any of your
> livestock, or the resident alien in your towns, so that your male
> and female slave may rest as well as you. (Deut. 5:13–14; see
> also Exod. 23:12)

Mothers are not mentioned because, despite resident patriarchal delusions, the Sabbath is commanded not to fathers, but to *householders,* to the fathers and/or mothers of Israel. Also, those households are imagined as extended farm families.

The distributive justice of the Sabbath day focuses on *rest,* because those twice-mentioned "male and female slaves," for example, custom-arily received food, but not rest. The fair distribution of rest is, for the biblical tradition, the fundamental basis of distributive justice upon which all else—food, health, education, freedom—builds.

Next, as the seventh year, the *Sabbath year* continued that linear progression of days and weeks by dividing *time* into years—but, once again, notice how distributive justice covers three particular aspects of Israel's farming households: rest for the land, remittance of debt, and the freeing of slaves.

It is good agricultural practice to *rest the land*, leave land fallow to restore its fertility, but notice, as always, the content and reason for the fallowing—or, better, hallowing—of land by the Sabbath year:

> For six years you shall sow your land and gather in its yield;
> but the seventh year you shall let it rest and lie fallow, so that
> the poor of your people may eat; and what they leave the wild
> animals may eat. You shall do the same with your vineyard,
> and with your olive orchard. (Exod. 23:10–11)

> In the seventh year there shall be a sabbath of *complete rest for
> the land*. . . . You shall not sow. . . . You shall not reap . . . it
> shall be a year of *complete rest for the land*. You may eat what
> the land yields during its sabbath—you, your male and female
> slaves, your hired and your bound laborers who live with you;
> for your livestock also, and for the wild animals in your land
> all its yield shall be for food. (Lev. 25:4–7)

Leviticus twice mentions "complete rest for the land" itself, not just for the laborers on it. But here the "wild animals" also come under the protection of sabbatical or distributive justice.

The Sabbath year also required the *remittance of debt*. "Every seventh year you shall grant a remission of debts. . . . Every creditor shall remit the claim that is held against a neighbor . . . because the LORD's remission has been proclaimed" (Deut. 15:1–2). Also, loans were not be used to create such debt situations in the first place: "Since there will never cease to be some in need on the earth, I therefore command you, 'Open your hand to the poor and needy neighbor in your land'" (Deut. 15:11).

With regard to the freeing of slaves: "If a member of your community, whether a Hebrew man or a Hebrew woman, is sold to you and works for you six years, in the seventh year you shall set that person free" (Deut. 15:12).

That general command gives special considerations for the freed female slave: if she does not marry into the family, "she shall go out without debt, without payment of money" (Exod. 21:11). The freed male slave fares much—no, incredibly—better:

> When you send a male slave out from you a free person, you
> shall not send him out empty-handed. Provide liberally out
> of your flock, your threshing floor, and your wine press, thus
> giving to him some of the bounty with which the LORD your
> God has blessed you." (Deut. 15:13–14)

The Sabbath year continues the distribution of the Sabbath day's *rest* as a seventh-year rest for the land itself. But it also goes beyond the fair distribution of *rest* to a fair redistribution of freedom from debt and slavery.

Finally, as the fiftieth year after seven Sabbath years, the *Sabbath jubilee* continues the pattern of rest through days, weeks, and years into half centuries. The function of the Sabbath jubilee was to return every fifty years to the original moment of distributive justice and inaugural equity for Israel:

> You shall count off . . . seven times seven years. . . . You
> shall hallow the fiftieth year and you shall proclaim liberty

throughout the land to all its inhabitants. It shall be a jubilee
for you: you shall return, every one of you, to your property and
every one of you to your family. (Lev. 25:8–10)

The theory was that God had originally divided the land fairly and
equitably among all the tribes and families of Israel and, therefore, the
sale of ancestral lands was forbidden: "The land shall not be sold in per-
petuity, for the land is mine; with me you are but aliens and tenants"
(Lev. 25:23). Agents cannot sell the owner's land—it is theirs to admin-
ister as the owner wishes: recall Naboth's vineyard (1 Kings 21:1–3).

But even without sales, loans and foreclosures succeeded to the
point that Isaiah could upbraid those "who join house to house, who
add field to field, until there is room for no one" but them, and they
are "left to live alone in the midst of the land!" (5:8)—in other words,
the ancient Israelite 1 percent! The Sabbath jubilee was an attempt to
rectify that; it always started, appropriately, on the Day of Atonement
(Lev. 25:9).

Maybe, by the way, that was all theory and never practiced. Still, if
that could be ignored, if the heart of Torah could be bypassed, maybe
the Ten Commandments were just the Ten Suggestions . . .

There are, then, throughout the Christian Bible, on throughout Christian life, and even into the Christian afterlife—whether with heaven
and hell or R.I.P.—two massive and long-term theologies—*Sanction
theology* and *Sabbath theology*.

They both stem, powerfully, formally, and deliberately, from the five-
book Pentateuch or written Torah: Sabbath theology from the opening
of its first book, Genesis (1:1–2:4a), and Sanction theology from the
ending of its last book, Deuteronomy (28:1–45). But, Sabbath theology
is different and, more important, more significant in three ways.

First, Sabbath theology was not just a balanced bookend for Sanction theology in the Pentateuch's books. It was not simply start or beginning, preface or introduction. It was placed first but written last, to be the overture for the entire Bible.

Second, there are no sanctions in Genesis 1:1–2:4a, no warnings or threats, promises or incentives for refusing or accepting our humanity as created in the image and likeness of God to be agents for the just administration of the earth. What if, being free, we simply refused that role?

In response, think for a moment about the two terms "consequence" and "punishment" in their basic meanings. A *consequence* derives internally from an act or state: a drunk driver hits a tree and is killed by the impact. A *punishment* derives externally from an act or state: a drunk driver hits a tree and is fined by the police.

If you refuse *Sanction theology,* punishments are external, from outside, and you can only avoid them through *mercy* or *forgiveness.* If you refuse *Sabbath theology,* consequences are internal, from inside, and you can only avoid them by *time* within which to *change.*

Third, that is the answer to St. Anselm's claim that if God does not punish evil, God does not care about evil. True enough for a Divine Judge, but not for a Divine Creator. *Sabbath theology* establishes humanity's identity, so any *refusal of that destiny involves human consequences, not divine punishments.*

Granted those two great biblical traditions of Sabbath theology and Sanction theology, the major question for the next and final chapter is this: How does Jesus's program for *God's rule* on earth as nonviolent resistance to the normalcy of civilization resonate with one, the other, or both of those fundamental biblical visions? Does Jesus himself, for example, ever tell us clearly how and why he advocated unarmed resistance? Was it simply a prudential option or a transcendental challenge for himself and for others as well?

To start the next chapter's answer to those questions, consider this preparatory one: What metaphor grounded the vision of God, what model empowered the understanding of God, and what matrix furnished the interpretation of God in each of those theologies?

15

"LOVE YOUR ENEMIES"

S ANCTION THEOLOGY WAS ESTABLISHED AS A FORMAL AND legal contract in Deuteronomy 28:1–68, with its "if . . . then" series of blessings or rewards—in fourteen verses—and curses or punishments—in fifty-four verses! That is then summed up by saying: "These are the words of the *covenant* that the LORD commanded Moses to make with the Israelites in the land of Moab, in addition to the covenant that he had made with them at Horeb" (29:1). The term "covenant" is, of course, a previously known and well-worn biblical term for the relationship between God and Israel. But whence did it come and how does the Deuteronomist adapt it?

In the ancient world a covenant was a sacred contract sworn before the gods of both parties. It included past relations, present obligations, and future sanctions, and was how ancient empires regulated relations with vassal states.

In the 700s and 600s BCE, the two superpowers Assyria and Egypt confronted one another to the north and south of Israel, making that tiny country not the eye but the route of the storm. Marching south along the Levantine coast with its right wing secured by the Mediterranean Sea, Assyria needed covenants with the smaller states on its left wing—such as the two parts of a then divided Israel. And

Assyrian-style covenants—like those of Esarhaddon still extant from 672 BCE—were heavy on sanctions and, within sanctions, were even heavier on punishments.

Composed within the historical matrix of those fatal and fateful decades, Deuteronomic theology became Sanction theology, with curses predominant over blessings and punishments ascendant over rewards. The divine model for Sanction theology was *God as Covenanter* but, unfortunately, with too many "things of Assyria" as the contemporary "things of Caesar" in that model of God.

We turn now from Sanction theology's God of retributive justice to ask about Sabbath theology's God of distributive justice. Where did the biblical tradition ever get the idea that God, or any transcendental power by whatever name, had established a cosmos ruled by distributive justice?

From the very first chapter of this book, we saw that ancient Israel, despite or because of its location on the main route of imperial conquest, had prophesied an absolutely different vision not only for itself, but for the whole world. Is that not absolutely counterintuitive in any century chosen for focus?

The biblical tradition imagined a final world with weapons of warfare reforged into tools of agriculture and invoked an eschatological world where all would rest among their own vines and fig trees instead of on another's stolen properties. It promised a final world where no one would be "made afraid," a promise repeated like a hopeful refrain in: the 700s BCE in Isaiah 17:2 and Micah 4:4; in the 600s BCE in Jeremiah 30:10; 46:17 and Zephaniah 3:13; in the 500s BCE in Ezekiel 34:38; 39:26; and, finally, in the 100s BCE in 1 Maccabees 14:12.

This last, or eschatological, status of earth presumed that *God's rule* would be one of distributive justice and universal peace. Otherwise, of course, Romanized Josephus was right when he cited "an established law, as supreme among brutes as among men, 'Yield to the stronger' and 'The mastery is for those preeminent in arms'" (*JW* 5.367).

How did ancient Israel ever conceive that God had created, intended, or promised universal distributive justice, without which universal cosmic peace would be impossible? Again, whence came that God who indicts those who run the world with injustice to society's vulnerable ones, "the weak, the orphan, the lowly, the destitute, the weak, and the needy" (Ps. 82:3–4)?

And again, why did the biblical tradition not conclude, from obvious empirical evidence in any century it chose, that its one true living God had created a world where the strong took what they wanted and the weak lost what they had? What metaphor or what model gave that biblical tradition a God of "justice and righteousness" (Ps. 72:1; 89:14; 97:2; 99:4)?

Is all of that simply retrojecting modern ideas of human rights, political rights, or civil rights back onto an ancient biblical tradition that never thought of such things?

The biblical tradition was not about human, political, or civil rights, but about *household* rights. It got its vision of distributive justice from the everyday experience of the farming household among native Jews or resident aliens where lands, animals, and members got their due share of care and concern not as charity and gift, but as justice and right.

Household was an experience one had by simply growing up! Feeding one's children is distributive justice by right and entitlement rather than distributive charity by parental almsgiving or philanthropy. A family with half the children starving and the other half overfed is an obscene lack of distributive justice or rights rather than an unfortunate lack of distributive charity or alms.

Based on the human experience of the admittedly ideal householder of the farm household, God was imagined as the *Householder of the World Household*, so that all humans lived under distributive justice and rights and not under distributive charity and alms. Sabbath theology focused, therefore, on the farming *households* of Israel's native Jews and resident aliens; on their lands, animals, and members under distributive justice with an equitable share for all (even the wild animals); and on all of that established, maintained, and, if necessary, restored by Sabbath day, Sabbath year, and Sabbath jubilee.

Sanction theology's divine model is *God the Covenanter* of retributive justice. Sabbath theology's divine model gave us *God the Householder* of distributive justice.

Here, however, there is a special problem with translation, not on the linguistic but on the cultural level. And it is necessary to face it, since it leads directly into this chapter's main question about how Jesus's nonviolent resistance comports with Sanction and/or Sabbath theology.

Genesis 5:1–3 recapitulates the creation of humanity in Genesis 1:26–27 with this description of its continuation:

> God created humankind . . . in the likeness of God. Male and female God created them, and he blessed them and named them "Humankind" when they were created. . . . Adam . . . became the father of a son in his likeness, according to his image, and named him Seth.

Although that text explicitly recognizes that God's "likeness" was distributed alike to "male and female" humans, it seems that, prejudicially, "likeness . . . image" was only passed on from father Adam to son Seth. This is what I mean by a problem in cultural and not just linguistic translation.

First, in a predominantly patriarchal culture, the ungendered notion of "householder" takes on form from the surrounding culture as the gendered term "father"; then, with male primogeniture, the ungendered term "heir/s" becomes the gendered term "son/s" (as in "the firstborn son" or "the beloved son" or simply "the son").

Watch Paul, for example, struggling with those cultural prejudices as he tells the Messianic/Christic communities in Rome that they are "heirs of God and coheirs of Christ" (Rom. 8:17). We might have expected "subheirs under Christ" or, more simply, "heirs of God in Christ," but Paul's startling claim is "*co*heirs of Christ." In making that claim within a patriarchal world, in the Greek text Paul uses gendered terms like "sons (*huioi*) of God" twice (8:14, 19; cf. NRSV: "children of God"), invents the gendered term "sonship (*huiothesia*) from God" twice (8:15, 23; cf. NRSV: "adoption"), but uses ungendered "children (*tekna*) of God" thrice (8:16, 17, 21).

Think, therefore, "householder" and "householder's heirs" when you read "father" and "sons" in what follows. With that cultural baggage in mind, we turn finally to this chapter's main question.

How does Jesus ground and justify his program of nonviolent resistance against Israel's Romanization as the contemporary realization of "this world's" normalcy? The answer to that question will take three steps: first the *command*, next the *reason*, and then the *result*.

Surely the most striking *command* ever given by Jesus to his followers was "Love your enemies," from the Q Gospel in Matthew 5:44 and Luke 6:27, 35. Note that, in Greek, all parts of that terse command are plural rather than singular, making it communal rather than just individual. Also what is unique in that command is its very peremptory format—two words in Hebrew or Aramaic, three words in English, and four words in Greek—combined with its very extraordinary content in the juxtaposition of "love" and "enemies."

First, think about "*love* your enemies." Jesus could have said *help* your enemies if in trouble or even *protect* your enemies if in danger.

He could have said something along these lines: "When you come upon your enemy's ox or donkey going astray, you shall bring it back. When you see the donkey of one who hates you lying under its burden and you would hold back from setting it free, you must help to set it free" (Exod. 23:4–5).

In Leviticus, the Torah had commanded the Israelites: "Love your neighbor as yourself" and "Love the resident alien as yourself" (19:18, 34). That former command is cited in the New Testament by Jesus in Mark 12:3, by Paul in Galatians 5:14 and Romans 13:9, and by James in 2:8. But love of *enemies* went far beyond *neighbors* or even *resident aliens*.

Next, think about "love your *enemies*." Those enemies are not those who annoy, oppose, criticize, or even humiliate you. That startling command is accompanied by parallel ones that indicate "enemies" are those who persecute, hate, curse, and abuse you—and persecutors are often killers (Luke 11:49; Acts 7:52; 22:4). Those parallels concern life-threatening enmity:

Love your enemies, pray for those who persecute you.
(Matt. 5:44)

Love your enemies, do good to those who hate you, bless those who curse you, pray for those who abuse you. . . .
Love your enemies. (Luke 6:27–28, 35)

Furthermore, that peremptory command to "love your enemies" is the deliberate core and intended synthesis of those parallels, as you can see in its specific *avoidance* by two other authors who come closest to citing it. In Romans, for example, Paul commands: "Bless those who persecute you; bless and do not curse them. . . . Do not repay anyone evil for evil. . . . Do not be overcome by evil, but overcome evil with good" (12:14, 17, 21). That's almost a quotation from Jesus, but it lacks "love your enemies."

A first-century manual on Messianic/Christic living called the *Didachē*, or *Teaching*, has a similar combination: "Bless those that curse you. . . . Pray for your enemies. . . . Fast for those who persecute you. . . . Love those that hate you, and you will have no enemy" (1.3). That formulation avoids "love your enemies" by splitting it into "*love* those who hate you" and "pray for your *enemies*." Also, "you will have no enemy" sounds more like a linguistic conceit than a realistic result.

Finally, this next question is obvious after two thousand years of Christian history: Is that command to "love your enemies" as fatuous as it is famous and as vacuous in practice as it is virtuous in theory? Worse, does "love your enemies" enable violence, cooperate with violence, and at least suggest indifference to violence?

My answer is that, for Jesus, "love your enemies" was his succinct way of *advocating nonviolent resistance* (love) *as a response to violence from others* (your enemies). Love of enemies is embodied in, manifested by, and identified with nonviolent resistance to them. Roman authorities, by the way, did not execute—and their official Jewish collaborators did not accuse—leaders who advocated "love your enemies," but they did remove leaders who organized nonviolent resistance against them!

That understanding of the command helps to explain why Jesus did not simply advocate universal or unconditional love of "all" or "everyone." Why focus on "enemies" and thereby presume his followers would always have them? Why canonize love of *enemies* and nonviolent *resistance*?

Because, for Jesus, "this world's" rule or civilization's rule is presently embodied in the here and now of Rome's rule (John 18:34) and that incarnation is always inimical to *God's rule* on earth. "The things of Caesar" are already and always there as violence-based injustice to be opposed by the nonviolence-based justice of "the things of God." Therefore, the God/Caesar acculturation meant neither demonization (Part One) nor canonization (Part Two), but confrontation (Part Three).

Jesus not only gave "love your enemies" as his succinct summary of nonviolent resistance, he also gave this *reason* for it: "For God makes his sun rise on the evil (*ponērous*) and on the good" and "God is kind to the ungrateful and the evil (*ponērous*)" in Matthew 5:45 and Luke 6:35, respectively.

Sometimes, by the way, that command to "love your enemies" is so abrupt and astounding that it claims all attention, and we forget the even more astounding claim about the character of God given as the reason for its practice.

Think, for example, of how different Jesus's reason is from Paul's reason after coming so very close to quoting Jesus in the Romans passage cited above:

> Beloved, never avenge yourselves, but leave room for the wrath of God; for it is written, "Vengeance is mine, I will repay, says the Lord." No, "if your enemies are hungry, feed them; if they are thirsty, give them something to drink; for by doing this you will heap burning coals on their heads." (Rom. 12:19–20)

That is a combination of "Vengeance is mine, and recompense, for the time when their foot shall slip; because the day of their calamity is at hand, their doom comes swiftly" (Deut. 32:35) and "If your enemies are hungry, give them bread to eat; and if they are thirsty, give them water to drink; for you will heap coals of fire on their heads" (Prov. 25:21–22).

The common subject for Jesus and Paul is reaction to at least a quasi-lethal attack. They agree on the avoidance of revenge, vengeance, or retaliation, but disagree on the reason for that avoidance. For Paul, you do not respond violently now, because God will respond violently later. For Jesus, you do not respond violently ever, because God acts nonviolently always.

Divine punishment could, of course, be mitigated partially by mercy or totally by forgiveness. But, as St. Anselm, the archbishop of Canterbury, argued just over a millennium ago, "If sin is passed by unpunished, then with God there will be no difference between the guilty and the not guilty; and this is unbecoming to God" (*Cur Deus Homo* 1.12).

If the biblical God does not punish evil, does the biblical God not care about evil? How can a God of justice and righteousness treat alike the just and the unjust, the righteous and the unrighteous? How could Jesus even imagine, and even if he could do so, how could his hearers accept, that the biblical God treats good and evil, virtue and vice, the same? Is that not enabling indifference rather than empowering resistance?

The God described by Jesus as the reason for nonviolent resistance flatly contradicts Sanction theology, where God as Judge operates externally by distributing rewards and punishments to humanity. Jesus's God is, however, clearly consistent with Sabbath theology, where God as Creator operates internally by distributing identity and destiny to humanity. Since all humans have the same divine-image identity, all humans get the same sun and rain. But, of course, since we are free, we can reject that intrinsic identity and, when we do so, what happens are not divine punishments but human consequences.

Think, for example, of other free gifts of our identity as humans rather than, say, as birds. If we attempt to fly off the roof of a thirty-story building, the pavement is not a divine punishment but a human consequence. And, with respect, it was as human consequence and not as divine punishment that "every drop of blood drawn with the lash shall be paid by another drawn with the sword."

The *result* is given as: "So that you may be *Sons of your Father* in heaven. . . . Be perfect, therefore, as *your* heavenly *Father* is perfect" in Matthew 5:45, 48, and as: "You will be *Sons* of the Most High. . . . Be merciful, just as *your Father* is merciful" in Luke 6:35–36. That promised Father-Sons relationship is the *result*, but it frames the *reason* for Jesus's *command*.

What is common to both are the terms "Sons" and "your Father." That "heaven" and "heavenly" are typical Matthean additions, and "Most High" is a typical Lukan change—with seven out of the New

Testament's nine uses in Luke-Acts. (I translate literally using the titular uppercase for "Sons" as well as "Father.")

In both versions, the *result* invokes a new metaphorical promise, not
about entering into *God's rule*, as in the preceding Matthew 5:3, 9, 19,
20 and Luke 6:20, but about entering into *God's household* as *heirs* to
the Householder.

In other words, two megametaphors empower Jesus's visionary message. The primary one is that of the world as *God's household* on earth
but, under patriarchy's prejudicial protocols, with the Householder as
"Father" and the Householder's heirs as "sons."

The secondary metaphor, based on the former one and developed
from it, is that of the world under *God's rule*. Two metaphors, therefore, for our world, one familial and one regal, one domestic and one
royal, one parental and one imperial—for the same divine reality of a
transformed earth.

On the one hand, that primacy of God as Householder/Father with
heirs/sons is exactly what you would expect from Jesus's own Jewish
tradition. Recall how, at the start of the exodus from Egypt, Moses
and Aaron demanded of Pharaoh in the name of God: "Let my people
go"—demanded it repeatedly from Exodus 5:1 through 10:3. But what
is not so often remembered is that those reiterated demands are framed
with this initial one by God:

> I said to you, "Let my son go that he may worship me." But
> you refused to let him go; now I will kill your firstborn son.
> (Exod. 4:23)

and its climactic penalty for refusal:

> When Pharaoh stubbornly refused to let us go, the LORD killed
> all the firstborn in the land of Egypt, from human firstborn to
> the firstborn of animals. (13:15)

Apart from the morality of that fantasy, the cultural matrix is that Sons or firstborn Sons are heirs.

On the other hand, Jesus developed the metaphor of Householder as "Father" and heir as "son" in a very special and even unique way. Normally, as old as children get, they call their parents by names such as Dad or Mom. But however expressed, those are strictly *intrafamilial* address forms, and new spouses use them only when and if invited to do so. Jesus taught his followers that, when they entered God's household on earth or undertook *God's rule* for earth, they could and should address God, as Jesus himself did, with the Hebrew or Aramaic *intrafamilial* name "Abba" (Mark 14:36; Gal. 4:6; Rom. 8:15).

The Lord's Prayer, therefore, has the metaphor of God's household before that of *God's rule*. It starts with "Our Father in heaven" before getting to "may your *rule* come as in heaven so also on earth" (Matt. 6:9–10, in Greek word order), but it would have been much closer to Jesus's mind if it had kept the address as "Abba," which can only be used by those already within the household as children—of whatever age.

THE THINGS OF GOD AGAINST THE THINGS OF CAESAR

The seeds of American decline were sown not in the
past 15 years of war and recession but in the 1970s, when
economic inequality began to rise, a process that has only
accelerated in recent years. As the decline of the Roman
Republic shows, sharp inequality, left unaddressed, can be
catastrophic, unleashing political and social consequences
that can bring even a centuries-old republic to its end.[1]

—Mike Duncan, "This Is How Republics End"

I N THE BEGINNING ARE THE QUESTIONS. BEFORE JOHN SAID,
"In the beginning was the Word," he had to ask *what* was in the
beginning and *why* it was the Word, or *logos*, the divinely established
and humanly available intelligibility of the universe, that came first.
Also, the immediate answer to Descartes's proposal of starting from
methodic doubt is not denial but *pourquoi*? Why choose that and not
some other focus for initiation?

Finally, questions are not the same as doubts. Doubting is the inevitable price of our certainty. Questioning is the inevitable price of our humanity. So here are the questions—the constitutive or generative and not just rhetorical or fictive ones—that guided this book and, in epitome, the answers suggested for them.

The Prologue asked about the symbiotic relationship between imperial militarization abroad and domestic brutalization at home within the changing vision of America as Nova Roma. Recall that, while the Roman legions secured the distant periphery with military bases, the colossal monument of the capital city—the Colosseum— was a gigantic slaughterhouse that seated fifty thousand people—to watch slaughter.

That Prologue asked what biblical vision best empowers contemporary American Christians to confront not the triumph of Rome-like success with violence abroad, but the tragedy of Rome-like decline with violence at home. It asked what biblical tradition best inspires contemporary American Christians to choose truth over lies, courage over cowardice, and a communal republic over an individual dictator.

The Overture pondered what tribute coin Jesus saw (or Mark imagined), what "image and inscription" appeared on it, why Jesus separated absolutely "the things of God" from "the things of Caesar," and what, precisely, was each of those "things."

Furthermore, granted that *theoretical* separation of God and Caesar, how can contemporary Christians find them reconciled for *practical* life on earth? What about *acculturation* from Jesus's God to Jesus's Caesar when *acculturation* becomes—to repeat the Overture—the conscious or unconscious submission to the drag of normalcy, the lure of conformity, the curse of careerism that can—*under certain leaders, in certain circumstances, at certain times and places*—turn some of us into monsters, many of us into liars, and most of us into cowards?

When contemporary Christians turn to their New Testament for guidance on *acculturation* from God to Caesar, they find most obviously and immediately two serenely discordant and flatly contradictory responses on that subject.

On the one hand, in the book of Revelation acculturation between Caesar and God is *demonized* for contemporary Christians (Part One). John of Patmos declared Rome and Caesar so murderously evil for slaughtering Christians that God and Christ would *soon* destroy them in an equally murderous retribution. The authorial purpose of that historical lie about Rome and Caesar followed by that theological libel about God and Christ was to cauterize absolutely the already incipient accommodation—especially economic acculturation—between God and Caesar in the great cities of the eastern Aegean that were that book's main concern.

By convulsive shock therapy, through a whirling chiaroscuro of ever-changing symbols for damnation and salvation, an immediate past of Rome slaughtering Christians and an imminent future of God slaughtering Romans were made metaphorically visible and stunningly credible. How, Revelation asks, could anyone accept Rome with its past of demonic evil, its present of pornographic seduction, and its future of imminent destruction?

That is all past fantasy, present fantasy, and future fantasy. It brings heaven down to earth, but as heaven relocated rather than earth reimagined in a city not of distributive justice but of translucent jasper (Rev. 21). It moves from prophetic vision to apocalyptic delusion and from *Jewish Christianity* to *fantasy Christianity*. But those who grow up on fantasy grow old on brutality—as Yeats wrote in 1922–23: "We had fed the heart on fantasies / The heart's grown brutal from the fare." So today, if there is a killer God and a killer Christ, why not killer Christians to cooperate with them?

On the other hand, in the book of Luke-Acts, acculturation between Caesar and God is *canonized* for contemporary Christians (Part Two). The combination of Rome and Christ is not dismissed, but celebrated. Luke-Acts was imagined and composed as a single two-volume book, and its overall conceptual unity is certified by multiple units in the former volume written in preparation for units in the latter one.

The protagonist of those two volumes is the Holy Spirit of God, the divine Spirit who will "bring good news to the poor . . . proclaim release to the captives and recovery of sight to the blind, [and] let the oppressed go free" (Luke 4:18). The theme of the two volumes is the *journey* or, better, the *way of the Holy Spirit*.

On that *journey* or *way*, the Holy Spirit first takes Jesus from Galilee, through Samaria and Judea, to Jerusalem and its *Temple*, and then takes Peter and/or Paul from Jerusalem, through Judea and Samaria, to Rome and the *house*.

The Spirit's geographical *journey* is from Nazareth to Rome, and the Spirit's theological *way* is from *Jewish Christianity* to *Roman Christianity*. The Holy Spirit has moved from Jerusalem to Rome, and Rome is now God's new holy city on earth. Luke-Acts glimpsed the future correctly, but what it held were Constantine and Justinian.

We saw that Luke-Acts was an integrated whole and that its present separation negated the author's intention and destroyed the book's purpose. Is Luke-Acts's canonized acculturation from God to Caesar—sanctified, of course, by almsgiving from Caesar to God—the only alternative to Revelation's demonized acculturation for contemporary Christians?

Since Jesus himself denied acculturation between God and Caesar by separating—but without defining—the "things" (or culture or rule) of each, my final question asked if and how the historical Jesus had reconciled that separation in his own life (Part Three). But since those extremes of demonization and canonization were both proclaimed in the name of Jesus and within the New Testament, there was a rather obvious problem with attempting a third exploration under that same name and in that same place.

The solution was to consider God and Caesar in the life of the historical Jesus *from outside that New Testament*. The strategy was to start by reading about Jesus exclusively—but critically—in the first-century Jewish historian Flavius Josephus—as if the New Testament did not exist.

Only after that established a basic profile for Jesus on God and Caesar could we see where the Jesus of the Gospels coalesced with the Jesus of Josephus. That experiment on Jesus between God and Caesar from outside the New Testament indicated acculturation neither *demonized* nor *canonized*, but consciously and consistently *criticized*. We saw, in both Josephus and the Gospels, that Jesus's criticism of acculturation involved *nonviolent* resistance to the Romanization of his Jewish homeland, because he was crucified but none of his followers were even arrested.

Finally, a *caveat lector* lest we think that all of this is just past history of God against Rome or Christ against Caesar.

In the biblical tradition, Caesar was never just Caesar and Rome was never just Rome. Roman imperialism and its Mediterranean globalization were no more and no less than the normalcy of civilization at that time and in that place.

Civilization is the form of global culture, initiated about ten thousand years ago in Mesopotamia, that we entitle, in time, the birth of civilization and, in place, the cradle of civilization. But the infant celebrated in that birth was *inequality*, and the twin forces that rocked its cradle were *violence* and *injustice*, that is, violence to maintain the injustice of inequality—an unholy trinity whose parts guaranteed, protected, and supported one another on an escalatory trajectory (Gen. 4).

The biblical tradition knew intimately about imperial civilization—from the Egyptians and Assyrians, through the Medes and Persians, to the Greeks and Romans—and, granted that millennium-long experience of civilization's oppression, it imagined and invoked a vision of *postcivilization* or *eschatology*, or *God's rule* on earth (for example, Isa. 2:1–4; Mic. 4:1–4). It countered civilization's chant of peace through military victory with God's hymn of peace through distributive justice.

But what about those for whom that *civilization* is visible on the screens and in the streets, but the biblical God is no longer credible and the biblical vision no longer intelligible? Leave aside, then, for a moment God versus Caesar to focus more immediately on evolution versus civilization.

Whether we like it or not, and mostly we do not (viruses!), evolution is absolutely fair and equitable, nondiscriminatory and nonprejudicial to everything and everyone—in the physical, animal, and human world.

Hence this final question: What if, with all due and sincere respect, it is not just the arc of the *ethical* but of the *evolutionary* universe that is long but bends toward justice?

INTERCULTURAL TRANSLATION OF "KINGDOM OF GOD/HEAVENS"

T HE CORE OR HEART OF JESUS'S VISIONARY MESSAGE IS USU-
ally translated as the "kingdom of God," meaning the last, or
eschatological, kingdom on earth—from *eschaton*, Greek for "last."
God's kingdom was to be the final fulfillment of biblical dreams for a
world of distributive justice, the ideal realization of biblical hopes for
a world of cosmic nonviolence, and the climax of biblical promises
for a world of universal peace. Think of it as a programmatic vision of
peace through justice.

The term "kingdom of God" raises intercultural problems for many
modern readers, especially for all those who have politically rejected
a king or kingship in their past history. Also, of course, that term is
infused with patriarchal prejudices, as is obvious when an actual queen
rules over what is still called a kingdom.

For us, "kingdom" tends to be a static term meaning a place, space, or territory that remains unchanged in its boundaries whether one enters it, stays in it, or leaves it. But the underlying word, *malkuth* in Hebrew, *malkutha* in Aramaic, and *basileia* in Greek—all feminine nouns, by the way—has a much more dynamic sense; it emphasizes the *way*, *mode*, or *style* of ruling rather than a static territory or even a population headed by a king. Think, for example, of how we do not speak about living in the "kingdom of law," but rather about living under the "rule of law"—still, of course, a dream, a hope, and a promise.

Also, apart from the general idea itself, the specific phrase "kingdom of God" is practically nonexistent prior to Jesus's usage. So a good translation should offer some hint as to why Jesus invented it as his own favorite designation for a transformed world and a transfigured earth. Jesus invented that specific phrase, intending the *rule of God* to be in direct religiopolitical opposition to and socioeconomic confrontation with the *rule of Rome*, which was the contemporary realization of civilization's programmatic peace through victory.

What Rome claimed was not royal or imperial territory, but *imperium*—the heavenly granted, divinely supported, and eschatologically designated right to rule. You can see that in Virgil's *Aeneid*, where Rome is ordained *regere imperio populos*, that is (literally), "to rule, by right to rule, peoples."

Jesus's choice of that precise expression—rather than, say, "people of God" or "community of God"—deliberately intended his movement to be not just ethical, religious, and theological, but also social, economic, and political, a total alternative to the normalcy of civilization robed in his time and place in togas.

However we translate "God's kingdom," we must never lose, abandon, or deny the subversive edge of its religiopolitical challenge about full human life on this earth. It is about what our world would look like if the biblical God ruled it directly. It is about what our world would look like if ruled by a transcendental vision of equity, fairness, and distributive justice. It is about the dream of postcivilization.

In this book, therefore, I use the *rule of God* or *God's rule* instead of the "kingdom of God" or "God's kingdom," italicizing it to defamiliarize that phrase and remind us that it is a question about whose *rule* we live under in this world and on this earth.

Finally, although Matthew has no problem with using the word "God," he usually prefers "kingdom of the heavens" to "kingdom of God," by about thirty times to four. The meaning, however, is exactly the same, as you can see from their parallel usage in Matthew 19:23–24. Once again, the *rule of the heavens* is a better translation, as it clearly expresses what *style* of rule God designates for the earth: "as in heaven, so also on earth" (Matt. 6:9, Greek word order).

APPENDIX B

VIOLENT AND NONVIOLENT RESPONSE TO THE ROMANIZATION OF ISRAEL

(*JW*: Josephus's *Jewish War*; *JA*: Josephus's *Jewish Antiquities*; *EG*: Philo's *On the Embassy to Gaius/Caligula*; *RH*: Cassius Dio's *Roman History*)

Violent Response to the Romanization of Israel

1. *Under Augustus* (4 BCE): Separate revolts all over the country ending with two thousand crucified in Jerusalem (*JW* 2:39–79; *JA* 17.250–98).

2. *Under Nero* (66–74 CE): Centrally led revolt ending with Jerusalem devastated, the Temple destroyed, five hundred a day crucified until the trees ran out, and Masada captured (*JW* 2.277–7.455).

3. *Under Trajan* (115–17 CE): Revolt in Cyprus and North Africa—luridly rather than historically described at Rome (*RH* 68.32.1–3).

4. *Under Hadrian* (132–35 CE): Massive guerilla-style revolt provoked by Hadrian's actions in Jerusalem (*RH* 69.12.1–14:4).

Nonviolent Response to the Romanization of Israel

1. *Under Augustus* (6 CE): Against Quirinius's census for taxation—led by Judas the Galilean and Saddok the Pharisee (*JW* 2.118, 433; 7.253; *JA* 18.1–10, 23–25; 20.102).

2. *Under Tiberius* (26–36 CE): Against Pilate's iconic military standards in Jerusalem (*JW* 2.169–74; *JA* 18.55–59).

3. *Under Tiberius* (26–36 CE): Against Pilate's use of Temple funds for a Jerusalem aqueduct (*JW* 2.175–77; *JA* 18.60–62).

4. *Under Caligula* (40 CE): Against putting Caligula's divine statue in the Jerusalem Temple (*JW* 2.184–203; *JA* 18.261–309; *EG* 225–60; Tacitus, *Histories* 5.9.2).

5. *Under Claudius* (41–54 CE): Against Fadus (44–46 CE), the first Roman governor of the whole country—led by Theudas (*JA* 20.97–98; Acts 5:36).

6. *Under Nero* (54–68 CE): Against Felix (52–60 CE), the next governor, for "every kind of cruelty and lust"—led by multiple unnamed "prophets" (*JW* 2.258–60; *JA* 20.167b–68); also, and especially, one led by "the Egyptian" (*JW* 2.261–63; *JA* 20.169–71; Acts 21:38).

GENESIS 1:1–2:4A
AS OVERTURE
TO THE BIBLE

PREPARING

"the heavens and the earth" (2:1a)

Day 1 (1:3–5)

Then God said, "Let there be light" . . . And there was evening and there was morning, the first day.

Day 2 (1:6–8)

And God said, "Let there be a dome in the midst of the waters" . . . And there was evening and there was morning, the second day.

Day 3 (1:9–10, 11–13)

And God said, "Let the dry land appear."

Then God said, "Let the earth put forth vegetation" . . . And there was evening and there was morning, the third day.

PRESENTING

"all their multitude" (2:1b)

Day 4 (1:14–19)

> *And God said,* "Let there be lights in the dome of the sky" . . .
> *And there was evening and there was morning, the fourth day.*

Day 5 (1:20–23)

> *And God said,* "Let the waters bring forth . . . and let birds fly" . . .
> *And there was evening and there was morning, the fifth day.*

Day 6 (1:24–25, 26–31)

> *And God said,* "Let the earth bring forth living creatures of every kind."

> *Then God said,* "Let us make humankind in our image" . . .
> *And there was evening and there was morning, the sixth day.*

NOTES

Prologue: Triumph Too Soon, Tragedy Too Fast

1. Mike Duncan, *The Storm Before the Storm: The Beginning of the End of the Roman Republic* (New York: Hachette, 2017), xx–xxi; he omits "senatorial cowardice."

2. John Dominic Crossan, *God and Empire: Jesus Against Rome, Then and Now* (San Francisco: HarperOne, 2007), 2, 5.

Overture: The Things of Caesar and the Things of God

1. I accept with gratitude and appreciation, the identification of the tribute coin proposed in 1999–2002 by Peter E. Lewis. See "The Denarius in Mark 12:15," *Australian Numismatic Society Library*, June 29, 2012, http://the-ans.com/library/2012PeterLewis.html. See also his book *The Ending of Mark's Gospel: The Key to Understanding the Gospels and Christianity*. 2nd ed. (Australia: Zeus Publications, 1019), 88–123.

Part One: Culture Rejected and Demonized

1. Phillip Cole, *The Myth of Evil: Demonizing the Enemy* (Westport, CT: Praeger, 2006), 209.

Chapter 1: God Shall Overcome Someday

1. Ronald Wright, *A Short History of Progress* (New York: Carroll & Graf, 2004), 14.

Chapter 4: Among These Dark Satanic Hills

1. In this section, I am dependent on and grateful for two books: Elaine Pagels, *The Origin of Satan: How Christians Demonized Jews, Pagans, and Heretics* (New York: Random House, 1995), especially "The Enemy

Within," 149–76; and Phillip Cole, *The Myth of Evil: Demonizing the Enemy* (Westport, CT: Praeger, 2006), especially "The Enemy Within," 95–121.

2. Pagels, *Origin of Satan*, 49.
3. Cole, *Myth of Evil*, 27, 39.
4. Pagels, *Origin of Satan*, 150.

Chapter 5: The Longest Lie

1. William Mitchell Ramsay, *The Letters to the Seven Churches of Asia, and Their Place in the Plan of the Apocalypse* (London: Hodder & Stoughton, 1904), 91–92.

Chapter 6: Creating a Counternarrative

1. Joseph A. Fitzmyer, *The Gospel According to Luke*, 2 vols., Anchor Bible (Garden City, NY: Doubleday, 1981, 1985); *The Acts of the Apostles*, Anchor Bible (Garden City, NY: Doubleday, 1998).
2. Fitzmyer, *Gospel According to Luke*, vol. 1, vii, viii.
3. Fitzmyer, *Acts of the Apostles*, 49, 60, 55.
4. Fitzmyer, *Gospel According to Luke*, vol. 1, 40.
5. Fitzmyer, *Gospel According to Luke*, vol. 1, 9.

Epilogue: The Things of God Against the Things of Caesar

1. Mike Duncan, "This Is How Republics End: Warnings from the Fall of Rome," *Washington Post*, October 31, 2018, https://www .washingtonpost.com/outlook/2018/10/31/this-is-how-republics-end.